Reality Architecture

Get in touch - we'd like to hear from you!

Your opinion counts

If you have any comments about this book – positive or negative, long or short – please send them in. We want to refine our books according to the needs of our readers, so do tell us if there is anything you would like to see in future editions of this book. Your input could well appear in print! We genuinely appreciate it when people take the time to contact us, so every month we give away a free Prentice Hall book to the person with the most helpful comments.

Please feel free to e-mail me with your comments:

feedback@prenhall.co.uk

Or you can write to me:

Jason Dunne
Prentice Hall
Campus 400
Maylands Avenue
Hemel Hempstead
Herts
HP2 7EZ
United Kingdom

We would also like to hear your ideas for new books, whether it is just for a new book you would like to see in print, or for a book you intend writing yourself. Our guide for new authors is at the back of this book.

Thank you for choosing a Prentice Hall title.

Jason Dunne
Commissioning Editor

Reality Architecture

*Building 3D worlds with
Java and VRML*

MARTIN McCARTHY
ALLIGATOR DESCARTES

PRENTICE HALL EUROPE

New York   London   Toronto   Sydney   Tokyo   Singapore
Madrid   Mexico City   Munich   Paris

First published 1998 by
Prentice Hall Europe
Campus 400, Maylands Avenue
Hemel Hempstead
Hertfordshire, HP2 7EZ
A division of
Simon & Schuster International Group

Printed and bound in Great Britain by
Arrowhead Books Limited, Reading

Library of Congress Cataloging-in-Publication Data

Available from the publisher

British Library Cataloguing in Publication Data

A catalogue record for this book is available from
the British Library

ISBN 0-13-748625-1

1 2 3 4 5   02 01 00 99 98

Contents

Figures   x

Tables   xiv

1 Introduction   **1**

Virtual Reality For All 2

But Is It Real Virtual Reality Or Virtual Virtual Reality? 2

Virtual Reality—More Than Modelling 3

. . . And I Want This Because. . . ? 3

VRML Is The Standard, So It Must Be Good 4

Where We're Coming From 5

The Role Of This Book 5

Keeping Up With The Changes 6

Acknowledgements 6

2 Basic 3D Theory   **9**

Co-ordinate Systems 10

The Staples Of A Graphical Diet 16

     The Vertex 16

     The Polygon 17

     The Model 19

Moving Things Around 19

Drawing The World On To Your Screen 24

     The Window On To The World 24

WYSIWYG 32

     Wire-Frame Rendering 32

     Flat Shading 33

Gouraud Shading 35

Phong Shading 36

Texture-Mapped Pipeline 36

3 The Web of Wyrd   **41**

VRML2.0 Grouping Nodes 42

`Transform` 44

`Anchor` 45

`Billboard` 49

`Collision` 50

`Group` 51

Thoughts On Scene-Graph Optimization 51

Wayward Children 52

Inlining Objects And The `Inline` Node 54

Levels of Detail And The `LOD` Node 55

4 Virtual Lego   **59**

Throwing `Shapes` 59

Basic VRML Geometrical Nodes 60

`Box` 60

`Cone` 62

`Cylinder` 64

`Sphere` 67

Thoughts On Basic Primitive Optimization 69

Controlling Points and Polygons 72

`IndexedFaceSet` 72

`IndexedLineSet` 77

Some Thoughts On `Indexed{Face,Line}Set` Optimization 78

Complex VRML Geometrical Nodes 81

`ElevationGrid` 81

`Extrusion` 83

`PointSet` 97

`Text` 97

`PROTO` Nodes 98

5 The Illusion of Reality   **107**

`Appearance`s Can Be Deceptive 108

Splashing Colour Around 108

"Solid" Colouring 108

Per Vertex Colouring 110

Texturing 112

    `ImageTexture` 112

    `MovieTexture` 115

    `PixelTexture` 116

At last! Illumination! 117

    `PointLight` 118

    `DirectionalLight` 119

    `SpotLight` 119

Camera-derie And The `Viewpoint` Node 122

Atmospheric Effects 123

6 Have You Heard The One About. . .   **129**

Where's The Sense In Virtual Reality? 129

Sound In VRML 131

    Basic VRML Sound 131

    This Sound Thing Is Great. . . Isn't It? 136

    Making It More Realistic 137

Can You Hear Me, Mother? 144

    Coping With Limited Computing Power 145

    Coping With Limited Bandwidth 146

    Coping With Limited Software 147

7 Behave Yourself!   **149**

Passing the Event Horizon 150

`ROUTE`s 150

VRML Datatypes 152

Sensors 159

    `TouchSensor` 160

    `CylinderSensor` 162

    `SphereSensor` 164

    `PlaneSensor` 166

    `ProximitySensor` 167

    `VisibilitySensor` 169

    `TimeSensor` 170

Interpolators 172

    `ColorInterpolator` 174

    `CoordinateInterpolator` 175

    `NormalInterpolator` 177

OrientationInterpolator 179

PositionInterpolator 183

ScalarInterpolator 185

Collision Detection 186

8 Script Nodes   **197**

Anatomy Of A Script Node 197

The Java Scripting API 205

The vrml.* Hierarchy 205

vrml.node.Script and Basic Methods 206

Fields and Events 209

Accessing Field Information 213

Events Unravelled 216

Flying The Flag On Open Seas 217

Directly Interfacing Java and VRML 222

vrml.Browser 226

Creating VRML From Thin Air 226

Querying the Browser 230

9 Interlude   **231**

10 Virtual Reality Servers   **235**

Why More Servers? 235

11 Multi-Threading for a Java-Based Server   **239**

Why Multi-Thread? 239

Thread Class Or Runnable Interface? 241

Using the Runnable Interface 241

Scheduling Threads 247

Scheduling Threads Your Way 252

Synchronizing Threads 254

The Need For Inhibitions 257

Summary 263

12 Superstrings   **265**

String, Sellotape and Blu-Tack 266

Physical Networks 267

Logical Networks 268

Name That Machine In One! 278

Packet Roulette 282

Two Tins And A Bit Of String 284
Splatterfest 285
    Bandwidth and Saturation 286
    But Why?! 288
Summary 290

13 Conferring Favours   **291**
Providing Worlds To The World 291
Server Basics 292
Let Me In, Let Me In! 295
    A Simple Server 296
    Halt, Who Goes There? 308
    Structures For The Server To Hold Client Information 316
    Client Limits And Burying The Dead 319
Demanding The World, And Getting It 322
    Techniques For Pruning The World Tree 323
Looks Really *Are* Everything 324
World-Shaking Events 324
You Really Want To Know This. 327
See Me, Hear Me 334
Non-persons 335

14 Space: The Final Frontier   **339**
Introduction 339
Subdividing The World 340
    Mind The Gap 341
    I Can See For Miles 342
Communicating Between Sub-Servers 346
    Synchronization 349
    Improving Efficiency 358
    Time Synchronization 360
Summary 368

Appendix A The VRML Specification   **369**

Figures

2.1	One-Dimensional Space	10
2.2	Two-Dimensional Space	12
2.3	Three-Dimensional Space	13
2.4	A Right-Handed Co-ordinate System	14
2.5	A Left-Handed Co-ordinate System	15
2.6	Starbuck's Pebbles	17
2.7	A Simple Square Polygon With Four Vertices	18
2.8	A Square Polygon Wrongly Specified	19
2.9	Translation	20
2.10	The Rotation Transformation	21
2.11	The Scale Transformation	21
2.12	The Shear Transformation	22
2.13	The Twist Transformation	22
2.14	The Reflection Transformation In The yz Plane	23
2.15	A Complex Transformation	23
2.16	A World	25
2.17	A World As Seen Through The Viewport	26
2.18	A View Frustum	27
2.19	A View Frustum Seen From Above	28
2.20	Vanishing Point Perspective	29
2.21	A Simple Polygon Clip	31
2.22	A Correct Polygon Clip	31
2.23	A Wire-Frame Goblet	33
2.24	A Flat-Shaded Goblet	34
2.25	A Smooth-Shaded Goblet	35
2.26	A Phong-Shaded Goblet	37
2.27	An Affine-Mapped Polygon	38

2.28 A Perspective-Correct Polygon 39
2.29 A Perspective-Correct Polygon 40

3.1 A Scene Graph 43
3.2 Bounding Box "Stretching" 53
3.3 Asynchronous Loading of `Inline` Nodes 56
3.4 A Neolithic Pot At Various Distances 57

4.1 A `Box` Node 61
4.2 A `Cone` Node 63
4.3 A `Cylinder` Node 64
4.4 A `Cylicone` Node 66
4.5 Wrong and Right Tubes 67
4.6 A `Sphere` Node 68
4.7 Rotary Querns 70
4.8 Smooth-Shaded 16- And 32-Facet `Cones` 71
4.9 Flat-Shaded 16- and 32-Facet `Cones` 72
4.10 The `ccw` Field In Action! 74
4.11 `creaseAngle` In Action 76
4.12 An `ElevationGrid` Node 83
4.13 A Hexagonal `Extrusion` `crossSection` 84
4.14 Hexagon Extruded Along A Straight Spine 85
4.15 Hexagon Extruded Along A Twisted Spine 86
4.16 Hexagon Extruded Along A Straight Spine With Tapering . . . 87
4.17 The Lathe Concept 88
4.18 A Neolithic Pot with Lathe Values 89
4.19 A Roughly Thrown Neolithic Pot 91
4.20 A Well-Thrown Neolithic Pot 92
4.21 Hexagon Extruded Along A Straight Spine With Twisting . . . 94
4.22 A Dutch Cheese 94
4.23 A Drinking Goblet 96
4.24 A Trilithon 98
4.25 A Megalithic Setting Of Four Trilithons 103

5.1 Per Vertex Colouring Of An `IndexedFaceSet` 110
5.2 Random Per Vertex Colouring Of An `ElevationGrid` 112
5.3 Clamped and Repeating Textures 113
5.4 `PointLight` 119
5.5 An Orbiting `PointLight` 120

5.6   `DirectionalLight` 120
5.7   `PointLight` versus `DirectionalLight` 121
5.8   `SpotLight` 121
5.9   Various `Fog` Node Scenes 124
5.10 Far Clipping Plane Blending With The `Fog` Node 126

6.1   Sound From A Stone Thrown Into A Lake Radiates Equally In
      All Directions 131
6.2   VRML Undirected Sound 133
6.3   Sound From A Megaphone Radiates More Strongly In The Di-
      rection The Horn Is Pointed 134
6.4   VRML Directed Sound 135
6.5   VRML Not Very Directed Sound 136
6.6   VRML Very Directed Sound 137
6.7   Propagation Of Sound From A Stone-Carver in Skara Brae House
      7 138
6.8   Better Propagation Of Sound From A Stone-Carver in Skara
      Brae House 7 140
6.9   Final Model Of Propagation Of Sound From A Stone-Carver in
      Skara Brae House 7 141
6.10 Model Of Propagation Of Sound In A Solid-Walled Corridor . . 143
6.11 Model Of Propagation Of Sound In A Thin-Walled Corridor . . 144

7.1   Dragging A Cube 151
7.2   The `TouchSensor` Node 162
7.3   The `CylinderSensor` Node Acting On A Neolithic Pot 163
7.4   The `SphereSensor` Node Acting On A Neolithic Pot 165
7.5   The `PlaneSensor` Node Acting On A Neolithic Pot 166
7.6   The `ProximitySensor` Node 168
7.7   A `ProximitySensor` Union 169
7.8   Object-Level Bounding Boxes In A Scene 189
7.9   Grouping-Node-Level Bounding Boxes In A Scene 189
7.10 A Better Grouping Of Grouping-Node-Level Bounding Boxes . 190
7.11 Taking A Less Dense Path Through The Scene 191
7.12 Spherical Bounding Boxes 192
7.13 An Over-Enthusiastic Spherical Bounding Box 192

8.1   Flow Of The "Wave" `PROTO` 205

11.1 Multiple Threads Running On Multiple Processors 248

11.2 Multiple Threads On A Single Processor With Good Scheduling   249
11.3 Multiple Threads On A Single Processor With Poor Scheduling   251
11.4 Interference Between Threads   255

12.1 A Basic Network   266
12.2 Two Basic Networks   267
12.3 TCP/IP Architecture   269
12.4 IP Datagram Header Block   272
12.5 UDP Packet Header Block   275
12.6 TCP Packet Header Block   276
12.7 TCP/IP Architecture Overview   277
12.8 Class A Network IP Address   278
12.9 Class B Network IP Address   279
12.10 Class C Network IP Address   280
12.11 Multicast "Storm"   287
12.12 Multicast And "Time-To-Live"   289

13.1 Small Network With Two Clients Simultaneously Setting The
     Same Username   312
13.2 Rival Usernames Compete   313
13.3 One Username Wins   313
13.4 Network With Slow Links   315
13.5 Floating Users   321
13.6 What You See Depends On Where You Are   323

14.1 The Area Around Skara Brae   343
14.2 The Area Around Skara Brae With Overlapping Sub-Servers . .   344
14.3 Enclosed Areas Can Be Easily Managed With Overlapping Sub-
     Servers   345
14.4 Distributed Server: Different Archaeological Sites On Different
     Machines   346
14.5 Distributed Server: Copies Of The Same Model On Different
     Machines   347
14.6 Distributed Server: Different Archaeological Sites On Different
     Machines, Some Sites On Multiple Machines   348
14.7 Naïve Synchronization   350

Tables

2.1   Co-ordinate System Handedness   15
2.2   Co-ordinate System Handedness From the Screen's Point of View   16

3.1   Neolithic Pot At Various Distances   58

4.1   Polygon And Vertex Counts Of Cones   71

7.1   Single-Value VRML Datatypes   153
7.1   Single-Value VRML Datatypes *continued...*   154
7.1   Single-Value VRML Datatypes *continued...*   155
7.1   Single-Value VRML Datatypes *continued...*   156
7.2   Multiple-Value VRML Datatypes   157
7.2   Multiple-Value VRML Datatypes *continued...*   158

8.1   VRML And Java Datatypes   214

13.1   Simple Protocol: Commands From the Client   302
13.2   Simple Protocol: Commands From the Server   302
13.3   Useful Protocol: Client to Server   303
13.4   Connection and Disconnection Messages   303
13.5   Responses To Successful Client Commands   303
13.6   Asynchronous Responses—Not In Response To The Client . . .   304
13.7   Responses To Unsuccessful Client Commands   304

14.1   Sub-Server to Sub-Server   353
14.2   Sub-Server to Synchronization Master   353
14.3   Synchronization Master to Sub-Server   354

Chapter 1

Introduction

"It appears to me that almost any man may like the spider spin from his own inwards his own airy citadel."

John Keats

The use of computer graphics to represent real or imaginary worlds has been around for a good while, but this was always a specialised area due to the high cost of the equipment and the limitations of available computing power. The pioneers of computer graphics (if they were of a violent nature) would have killed to get their hands on a machine of the power of a standard desktop PC that is used for little more than word-processing.

In the late 1970s, Jim Blinn at the Jet Propulsion Laboratory in Pasadena made a famous computer-generated movie of the Voyager 1 fly-by of Jupiter. Given the complexity of the graphics and the available computing power, each frame of the movie was generated and then transfered to film in what would now be considered an agonisingly slow process. An animation with the quality and complexity of this movie might now be used as a screen saver for our word-processing machine.

And yet, with this abundance of processing power and graphics hardware, where is the abundance of world-building that shows originality and quality?

Virtual Reality For All

So the arrival of cheap computing power and cheap or free software to produce "quality" computer graphics has pushed back the bounds of the science and the art of creating artificial worlds... much like the many channels available for television broadcasting on cable and satellite TV have pushed back the bounds of... well... soap operas and game-shows.

"Unfair!" you cry. "It's not the same thing at all."

True. But there is a big gap between the possibility to do something, which is provided by the technology, and the ability to actually do it, which is provided by the skill, persistence and patience of the artist/craftsman/scientist. The ability to read and write doesn't turn you into another Shakespeare. The ability to create 3D models doesn't turn you into an architect of virtual reality. But it is a good place to start.

But Is It Real Virtual Reality Or Virtual Virtual Reality?

Before going any further, ask yourself: "What is virtual reality?"

Your answer might well depend on whether you have believed the hype. Any of the following *might* be considered part of (even an essential part of) virtual reality:

- 3D modelling;

- interaction with the world—that is, the ability to walk thought the world and view it from any angle;

- interaction with objects in the world—that is, the ability to pick up that vase of flowers;

- control over objects in the world—that is, the ability to smash the vase or the ability to pick flowers and arrange them, perhaps even the ability to take virtual yeast and flour and water and bake a virtual loaf of bread;

- interaction with other people in the world.

CAD (computer-aided design) gives you 3D modelling. Many people would say that this was different from virtual reality. MUDs (multi-user dungeons) are games where many people can interact to help or hinder each other— or, if they so choose, ignore each other altogether—and as a rule are purely textual environments where actions and locations and objects are "seen" only in terms of the words used to describe them. And despite this lack of pretty graphics many people would say that MUDs embody more of the essence of virtual reality than does CAD.

Virtual Reality—More Than Modelling

In this book, we take the attitude that there is much more to virtual reality than the generation of pretty pictures which look three-dimensional. To put it another way, we believe that *visual realism* and *virtual reality* are not one and the same thing. That is not to say that visual reality is not very important. It is. And a significant portion of the book is aimed at visual reality. But it is the *reality* that is most important word.

Of course, it will probably be a long time before anyone is going to mistake a virtual world for the real world. It might be better to use the word *believability* rather than *reality*. A world that is sufficiently believable that a person interacting with that world is willing to suspend disbelief and accept it as *a* world, if not *the* world, is a good goal to aim for. This striving for believability will be a recurring theme throughout the book.

...And I Want This Because...?

If you play with computer graphics and virtual reality for pleasure rather than profit then absolutely no further justification is required. Go ahead and play! More power to your elbow.

Of course, virtual reality can have practical and commercially viable uses, as well. Perhaps the easiest of these to understand for many people builds on the fun aspect. Games are big business. There's lots of money to be made in the entertainment sector.

Visualisation of the unseeable is another area where virtual reality has great potential. Not many of us are going to be able to make a trip to Mars or

Venus or the Moon in the next few days—but three-dimensional data is available for all of these bodies making it possible to travel across these remote worlds. Useful for entertainment, useful for education, and perhaps particularly useful for helping to chose a landing site for an interplanetary probe that is supposed to investigate the variety of rocks that can be found in an ancient Martian river valley.

At a different extreme of scale, the shapes of proteins, of viruses, of drug molecules (and how all of these and other objects fit together) are very important in the field of medicine. To be able to manipulate such objects as though they were something that could be held in the hand can provide insights into the ways that they interact.

Virtual reality can also overcome the temporal barrier... we can recreate structures that were built thousands of years ago and which can only be practically visualised with the computer.

From a more commercial point of view, virtual shops can provide a place for home shoppers to inspect, and even try out, their potential purchases, as well as provide technical support to distressed customers ("and this is how the stair-cleaning attachment is supposed to connect to the vacuum cleaner hose").

Virtual shopping malls can be attractive to small companies who might get little attention if they were a site by themselves but which might be well visited if their shop-front were alongside many other shops.

VRML Is The Standard, So It Must Be Good

VRML—the Virtual Reality Modelling Language—is a standard and popular way to model virtual reality worlds. However, it should be remembered that VRML is *an* answer rather than *the* answer. It was developed as a compromise between conflicting interests and as such it will not be the best way to implement a virtual world in all cases. VRML is perhaps easiest to use as a way to create a three-dimensional model which can be viewed and interacted with, but not necessarily to the extent that you require. A frequently encountered limitation becomes apparent when you consider not just your own interaction with an object *(when I push the vase I expect it to fall off the table—VRML can do that)* but an object's interaction with other objects *(when I throw this rock at the vase I expect the vase to break. . . or the rock to bounce off—here VRML doesn't perform so well)*. We will be looking at some of the limitations of VRML and how to cope with them.

Where We're Coming From

When we started working with virtual reality systems, VRML was still in its infancy and couldn't cope with what we saw as important parts of virtual reality (some of these features that we wanted are: the ability for objects within a world to have a life of their own, both in a metaphorical sense—such as the way you expect a fountain to continue to spray out water whether you are present or not—and in a more literal sense—such as the ability to populate a shop with artificial-intelligence shop assistants; the ability to distribute a virtual world over many machines within a network to give you a virtually[1] unlimited universe in which you can travel; the ability to have multiple users interacting within the same world; the ability to have a usable system which works effectively over slow communication links, such as telephone lines).

Because of the limitations of available systems, we set about designing our own complete distributed, multi-user virtual reality system.[2] Our experiences have provided much material for the sections of this book dealing with multi-user issues, behaviours of virtual objects and the distribution of worlds over networks, amongst others.

The Role Of This Book

For us, these areas which increase the believability of an artificial world are the difference between pretty computer graphics and virtual reality.

We provide a brief introduction to the theory behind (and the practice of) producing three-dimensional computer graphics. A thorough understanding of the mathematics behind the pictures is *not* necessary in order to produce quality worlds, but an understanding of how and why things work the way they do can help you make better decisions about building a world that can

---

[1]Pardon the pun!

[2]The Nexus system that was briefly distributed by Hermetica before evolving into other products.

be displayed quickly enough on modest hardware.

A description of the use of VRML—perhaps the most popular and certainly the fastest growing format for creating virtual worlds—is provided, with many examples. Here we attempt to give you much more than just an expansion of what is contained in the *VRML97 Specification* (which you will find on the CD-ROM which accompanies this book).

With this solid foundation, we then discuss techniques that can increase the believability of a virtual world... adding behaviours to virtual objects, creating systems that allow many visitors to the world to interact and allowing worlds to be infinitely extended across networks of servers.

We try to avoid the standard and clichéd examples of computer graphics texts and instead use examples which reflect our own non-computing interest in archaeology to create a reconstruction of a 5000-year-old village in the Orkney Islands called Skara Brae.

Whether you intend to create virtual worlds for pleasure or profit, we urge you to strive for originality and believability and hope that in twenty years' time your efforts will be admired as much as Jim Blinn's Voyager movie is now.

Keeping Up With The Changes

The realm of virtual reality is rapidly changing; in order to keep you up to date with new developments, and to provide you with any corrections to errors that are found in this book, the authors would urge you to take a look at the Web site dedicated to this purpose:

```
http://www.arcana.co.uk/technologia/reality/index.html
```

Acknowledgements

The authors would like to thank Dave Gilmour of Portfolio Solutions for support (and funding!) during the Nexus project. Chet Haase, Mark Halstead and John Hardy also get their name in lights for invaluable proofreading assistance. Thanks guys! Thanks also to Alison Stanford and her copy editors, without whom this book would have looked much worse. They have removed many errors. Any errors which remain are our own special friends and we love them!

Two special mentions go to: firstly, the talented community of Orcadians that constructed Skara Brae some 5000 years ago—an achievement that to this day is a testament to human craftsmanship and ingenuity; and finally, and most importantly, to Carolyn—wife of one of us and good friend of the other—for the continued support and patience whilst this book was being written.

Chapter 2

Basic 3D Theory

Many of the ideas and concepts presented in this book do not require a great understanding of the mathematics of geometrical representations. That said, to truly understand and extract all the goodness that you can from VRML, and any other three-dimensional graphics work that you might wish to undertake, being conversant with the terms, jargon and background is perhaps not such a bad thing.

One of the labels given to VRML is that it is "The Web in Three Dimensions". That is possibly so, but to charge into creating three-dimensional worlds head-first, and without a grounding in the basic concepts inherent in building these spaces is a lot more disastrous that being unaware of some of the funkier things you can do with HTML. HTML is textual, and text is well understood, which makes creating compelling Web pages somewhat easier than creating VRML. Creating compelling VRML can be a difficult endeavour, simply because we are used to using two-dimensional software (the majority of GUIs available today, and even the majority of three-dimensional modelling software is two-dimensional!) with two-dimensional hardware (the screen of your monitor is a two-dimensional output device, and the mouse is a two-dimensional input device). This situation acts as a clamp on creativity, which can only be hobbled by a lack of understanding of the basic concepts, so by all means skip this chapter for the moment and move on to the more interesting stuff, but feel free to come back later!

Co-ordinate Systems

As you may have detected from the previous paragraphs, future chapters in the current book or even other books, you will have no doubt noticed us discussing terms like two-dimensional and three-dimensional quite freely. What exactly do we mean here? And why exactly is a mouse two-dimensional, since I can pick it up, turn it around in my hands and swing it round my head?

A dimension can be thought of as a measurement in a particular direction. For convenience' sake, let's say we're in a long thin tunnel that we can't turn around in or jump up in. The tunnel compels us to walk either forward or backwards. We can't move to the left or right, nor can we jump up or down. We can say that this tunnel is one-dimensional, since we can only move in one direction whilst inside it. Or, more exactly, we can move in two directions, but they both run along the same straight line. In geometry, this straight line that we are constrained to moving along is known as an *axis*. Figure 2.1 illustrates the tunnel and axis.

-2   -1   0   1   2

Figure 2.1: One-Dimensional Space

An interesting point arises from this: how do we know where we are in the one-dimensional space? If another person is looking down into the tunnel and was directing you to a point in the tunnel, how can they tell you where that point is? Shouting "Go forward a bit" isn't particularly accurate, since your idea and their idea of how much "a bit" is probably differ somewhat. We need to specify some sort of way in which we standardize the one-dimensional space.

Fortunately, choosing the units that operate within one-dimensional space is quite simple, we just pick something meaningful and make everyone adhere to that definition. For example, if we want the units to be metres, that's fine, or light-years, or centimetres, or cubits. It really doesn't matter, provided everything in that space or referring to that space is in agreement as to which units are to be used. Now, the observer can say "Go forward 10 metres" and you'll wind up at the point that both of you expected to arrive at.

There is another necessary facet of space that arises once we start using accurate units to measure the space, and that is *co-ordinate systems*. A co-ordinate system is another construct that is used to provide a fixed reference point in space that we can refer to. For example, in our previous example, when the observer said "go forward 10 metres", both parties knew where the person in the tunnel was. This was a *relative* movement in space, *i.e.*, the person in the tunnel moved *relative* to their current position. Now, what would happen if the observer did not know where the person in the tunnel was in the tunnel, and there was a position that he wanted the betunnelled person to move to? He couldn't express it accurately, since there are no reference points in the tunnel to define *absolute* co-ordinates.

Therefore, we need a central reference point in our space, which is termed the *origin*. Now the observer can say "Move 10 metres forward from the origin", and the person in the tunnel will move to the correct place. The origin and the units define the co-ordinate system.

Two-dimensional space is an extension of one-dimensional space, in that we define another axis along which we can move. Since we can already move forwards and backwards, a sensible way to add this new axis would be at a right angle to the first, or *perpendicular*. So, let's allow you to move to the left and right as well.

Our tunnel has now turned into a large room, whose floor you stand on, and whose ceiling sits exactly on top of your head. So, now we can turn around and walk about in any direction we please, not necessarily constrained to moving along the axes themselves. Figure 2.2 shows this in action. Our co-ordinate system for one-dimensional space is equally applicable here, except we now have two axes along which we assign units to to specify a position in two-dimensional space, *e.g.*, (2, 4), is two units to the right and four units forward.

Which brings us back to monitors and mice. The display that your computer builds for displaying on the monitor is two-dimensional, in that each point on the screen can be located by using two co-ordinates, the origin for the

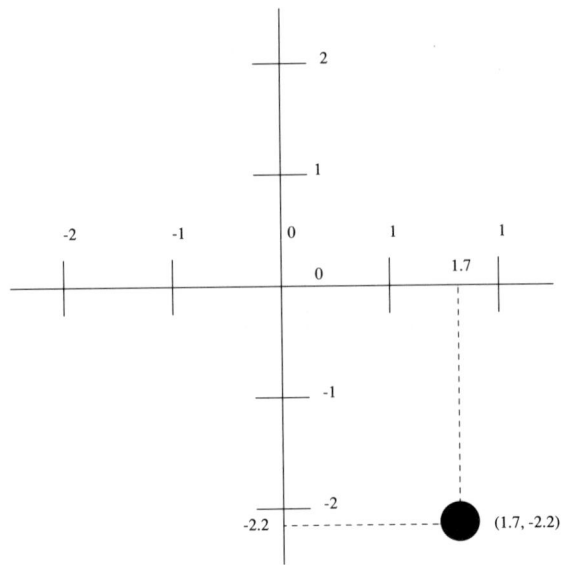

Figure 2.2: Two-Dimensional Space

screen's co-ordinate system being usually the top-left or bottom-left corner. Again, mice move left and right and forward and backward, which makes them two-dimensional input devices.

Three-dimensional space is an extension of two-dimensional space, in that we add a third axis running perpendicular to the first two axes, running directly up and down. This makes our two-dimensional room with a low ceiling into a floorless and ceilingless infinitely large box that exists in three-dimensional space. We can now tell the originally betunnelled person to move to locations in three-dimensional space, *e.g.*, "Move forward 3 units, right 1 and up 15". Three-dimensional space is the space that we operate in in the "real" world,[1] since we can move along any of three axes,

- forward and backward,

- left and right,

---

[1]Actually, we operate in four-dimensional space, but that's a matter for philosophy, not graphics.

- up and down.

We can also move in any direction that is a combination of any of these, for example, up and left, backward and down and so on. Figure 2.3 illustrates a three-dimensional space.

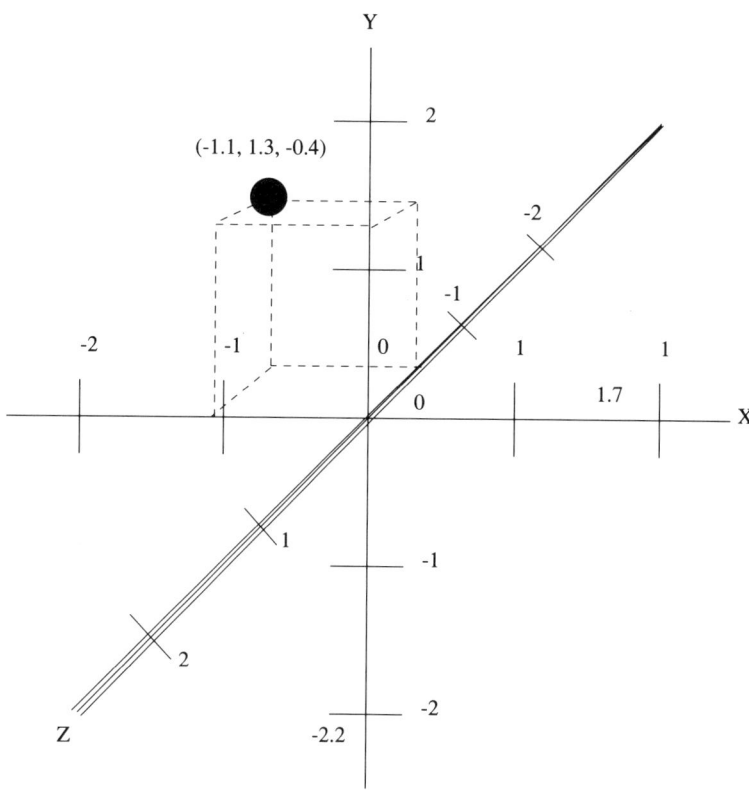

Figure 2.3: Three-Dimensional Space

The final aspect of co-ordinate systems that we must be aware of is the convention as to what is that "handedness" of our co-ordinate system.

Co-ordinate systems have two possible "handednesses", left and right.[2] The concept of "handedness" evolved by the idea of wrapping your hand around

---

[2]I bet you're really surprised by that revelation.

the Z-axis, with your thumb pointing along the Z-axis and the X-axis running back along your arm. Figure 2.4 shows a "right-handed" co-ordinate system, *e.g.*, the fingers are curled around the Z-axis axis and the X-axis runs up your right arm. Figure 2.5 illustrates a "left-handed" co-ordinate system in which the fingers of the left hand are curled around the Z-axis with the thumb pointing in a positive Z-direction, with the X-axis running back up the left arm.

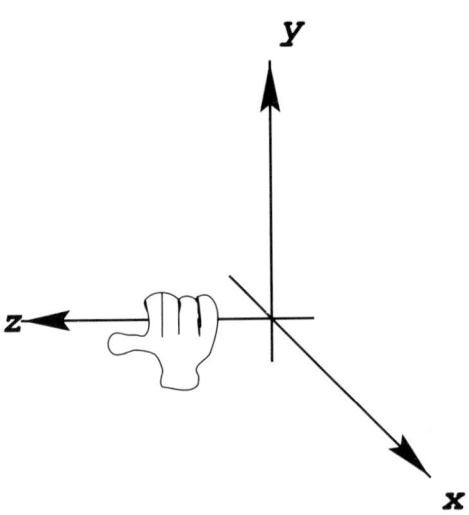

Figure 2.4: A Right-Handed Co-ordinate System

The more common co-ordinate system used in applications today is the right-handed co-ordinate system which has the corresponding direction to axis mapping as shown in Table 2.1.

And Table 2.2 is for the programmer who's looking at the screen's point of view.

So, that defines the space in which worlds that we create exist and how we can specify positions of things within that space. Now all we need to do is fill the space with something, and that is what we shall now look at.

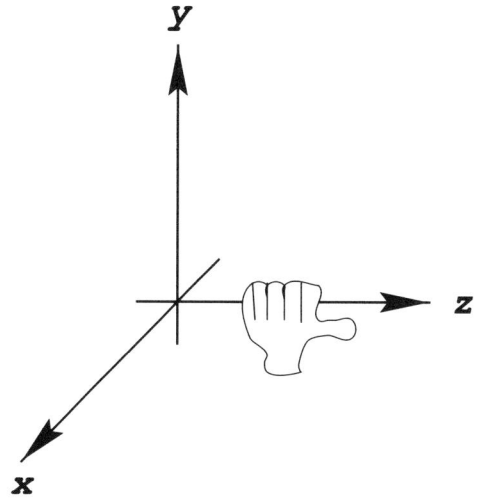

Figure 2.5: A Left-Handed Co-ordinate System

Direction	Axis
Forward	Negative Z-axis
Backward	Positive Z-axis
Left	Negative X-axis
Right	Positive X-axis
Up	Positive Y-axis
Down	Negative Y-axis

Table 2.1: Co-ordinate System Handedness

Axis	Screen Direction
Negative Z-axis	Into screen
Positive Z-axis	Out of screen
Negative X-axis	To left of screen
Positive X-axis	To right of screen
Positive Y-axis	To top of screen
Negative Y-axis	To bottom of screen

Table 2.2: Co-ordinate System Handedness From the Screen's Point of View

The Staples Of A Graphical Diet

In the following sections, we shall be discussing some mathematical constructs that allow us to build three-dimensional "objects" in our worlds. These "staples" take several forms, each of them an important part in the creation of objects, each representing a different layer within the creation process. The process as a whole is similar to the human body, in that we firstly create a skeleton, over which skin is stretched. The comparison to building object *meshes* or skeletons from vertices and then stretching the polygonal "skin" over them is a useful analogy.

The Vertex

A *vertex* is the most important part of any 3D representation. It defines a discrete point in three-dimensional space at a given location. Vertices are mathematically regarded as being infinitesimally small, which makes it somewhat difficult to understand why you'd want to use them at all in graphics, but vertices, as we mentioned before, provide the skeleton for all three-dimensional objects within a world.

Vertices have uses other than providing a skeleton for polygons, in that they are sometimes used in calculating *smooth-shading* effects, shaded colours and *texture-mapping* effects. We shall be discussing these topics later in the book.

However, a three-dimensional world rendered using vertices only might not be particularly good to look at, even if we represented a vertex with a pixel. You would get an effect known as a *point cloud*, which, although an occasionally useful effect, isn't probably what you were hoping for. Figure 2.6 illustrates a well-known problem of rendering points only. What do you see from the points? A star? Perhaps a pentagon? Perhaps something entirely different? Therein lies the rub. What we see depends entirely on who is looking at the world, which doesn't bode well for worlds that we intend to be navigated by multiple simultaneous users, or even just loaded by several people.

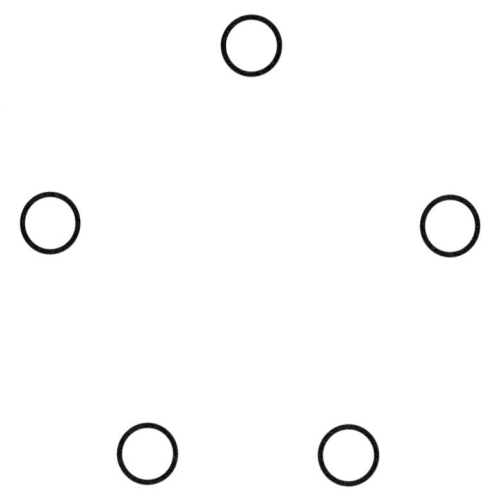

Figure 2.6: Starbuck's Pebbles

This is where we need to do some more with the vertices we have defined, we need to add in more visual cues for the brain, and the most common method that we use is to build a *polygon* from the vertices.

The Polygon

A *polygon* is a collection of vertices that represents a planar surface. A non-planar collection of vertices is generally called a *convex hull*.

To represent polygons, we need to define a rule for the way in which the vertices that comprise the polygon are interpreted. Generally, the vertex ordering can be either clockwise or anti-clockwise. It actually doesn't matter which direction the vertices are to be processed, as long as you are consistent in the way that you do it!

For example, defining a quadrilateral could be done by defining four vertices, then "stretching" the polygon between the vertices, rather like pegging a tarpaulin down. Doing this correctly would result in something like Figure 2.7. Getting the vertex order wrong, or pegging the tarpaulin down wrongly,[3] could result in a polygon like Figure 2.8, which is not quite the effect we want. We can specify the vertices in either clockwise or anti-clockwise order to form the polygon, but consistency is the key.

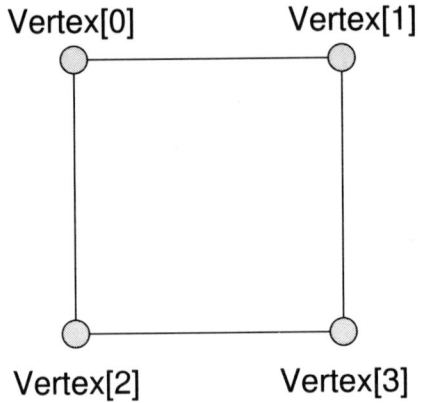

Figure 2.7: A Simple Square Polygon With Four Vertices

Of course, this is a gross simplification of things. Polygons are not always as simple as having three or four vertices, so how can we easily manage those larger ones potentially with tens or hundreds or vertices? Most modelling programs and CAD programs export models with "triangulated polygons", *i.e.*, if the polygon has more than three vertices, it will split the large polygon into separate smaller triangles. Also, most rendering engines nowadays, if fed a polygon with more than three vertices, will automatically triangulate them for you. Triangles are much faster to render, since we can make assumptions about them, such as, they are always planar, you can take the vertices in any order at all and calculation of *normals* can performed faster.

---

[3] Infrequent campers will understand this problem, especially if they have attempted to put up a tent in a force 7 gale and horizontal torrential rain whilst drunk.

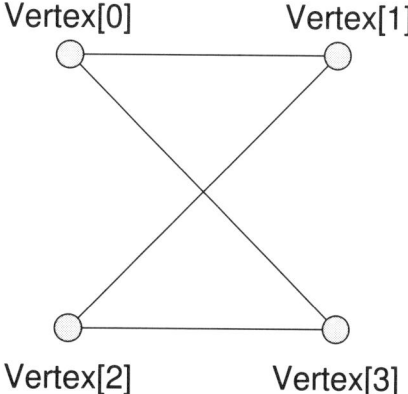

Figure 2.8: A Square Polygon Wrongly Specified

Polygons, be they formed of three vertices or many vertices, are the staple primitive in rendering, but are only a convenient construction formed from the position of vertices. This is important to remember. For example, if we rotate a polygon, we are actually rotating each of the vertices that define the polygon, not the actual polygon itself. The polygon comes into being when we actually perform the rendering stage, which we shall be discussing later.

The Model

A *model* is a high-level grouping of vertices and polygons into an "object". For example, in a cube, we have eight vertices, one at each corner, and six polygons for the faces. However, we can group these together into a logical model called a cube, which we can now manipulate instead of the individual vertices and polygons. That is not to say that the vertices and polygons are not being manipulated, just that we do not need to worry about them ourselves. This abstraction allows content creators to concern themselves with creating compelling worlds, rather than spending large amounts of time fiddling around with individual points and polygons.

Moving Things Around

After we have defined our objects within a world, the overriding desire is to place them in the correct locations, or move them about. There are all sorts of different ways that an object can be moved around within an world. We'll give a few standard definitions for these "moving around" effects, that way we'll be talking the same language and it will be easier to understand what other people, other books and other programs are talking about as they will almost certainly use these terms.

Any object can be moved around, or *transformed*, in all sorts of ways both simple and complex. These transformations can always be broken down into a sequence of simpler *primitive transformations*. These primitive transformations are *translation*, *rotation* and *scaling*—the usual, and simplest, transformations—plus *shear*, *twist* and *reflection*, which are more powerful, but less common effects.

Each of these transformations can be defined as follows:

translation the movement of an object from one position to another without a change in size or a change in the direction in which it is facing (Figure 2.9);

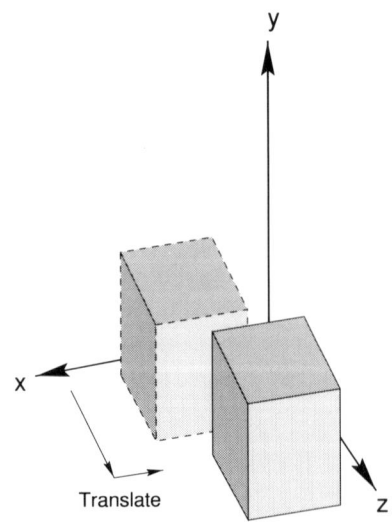

Figure 2.9: Translation

rotation the change in the direction in which an object is facing without a change in position or a change in size (Figure 2.10);

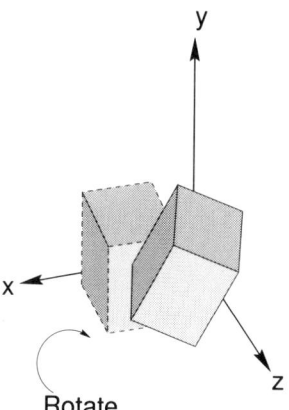

Figure 2.10: The Rotation Transformation

scaling the change in size of an object without a change in position or a change in the direction in which it is facing (Figure 2.11);

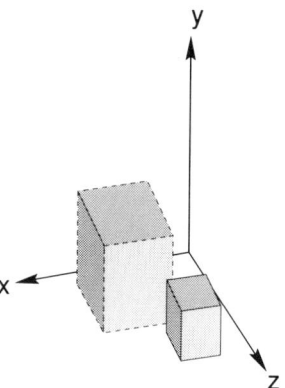

Figure 2.11: The Scale Transformation

shear (or variable translation) the change in position of each part of an object relative to a fixed point, line or plane, where the degree of change is proportional to the distance from the fixed point, line or plane (Figure 2.12);

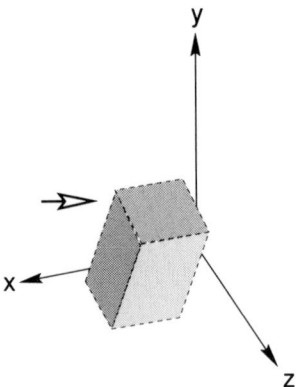

Figure 2.12: The Shear Transformation

twist (or variable rotation) the change in direction in which each part of an object is facing relative to a fixed point, line or plane, where the degree of change is proportional to the distance from the fixed point, line or plane (Figure 2.13);

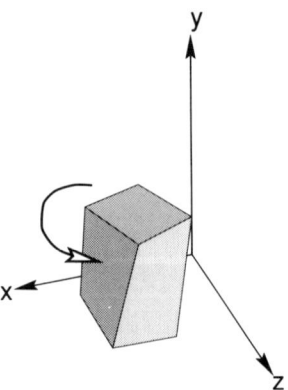

Figure 2.13: The Twist Transformation

reflection the change from an object to the mirror image of that object relative to a fixed point, line or plane (Figure 2.14).

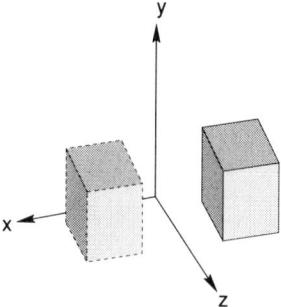

Figure 2.14: The Reflection Transformation In The yz Plane

These primitive transformations are generally combined into sequences of transformations that are applied to an object which produces a complex motion through the world. For example, we could simulate a cube being thrown through the air by translating it along a parabolic curve as shown in Figure 2.15, but that alone would not necessarily be realistic since we could expect the cube to spin when it moves. Therefore, at each point along the curve that we translate the cube to, we could also apply a rotation which would spin the cube around its centre. This is an example of a complex transformation.

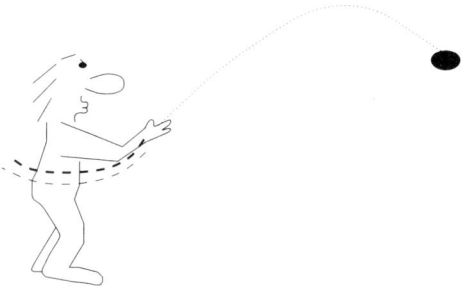

Figure 2.15: A Complex Transformation

Transformations are used quite heavily to preserve the modular notion of the model that we use. For example, in a world, we could specify the absolute co-ordinates of objects within the scene, then apply transformations to those, or we could build every model centred around the origin, for example, then use a transformation to position it within the world. This maintains the idea that each object can be reused in other worlds without needing to know where the absolute co-ordinates for the vertices within the model lie.

Drawing The World On To Your Screen

All the discussion in this chapter so far has presented some of the mathematical tools and techniques that can be used to model and manipulate virtual objects in three dimensions. However, that is only part of the story. We still have to draw the world onto your monitor for you to see.

However, as we mentioned at the beginning of this chapter, your monitor is a two-dimensional piece of equipment. It has no comprehension of displaying things three-dimensionally, so, how do we display three-dimensional worlds?

"Now, look here," you cry in alarm, "my screen-saver has a rotating cube that changes into other three-dimensional shapes and wiggles and wobbles around other three-dimensional objects! That's three-dimensional!"

All this *looks* three-dimensional, but it is no more three-dimensional than a photograph or a television picture. The trick is to take the three-dimensional representation of an object or a set of objects or a virtual world and convert them into a two-dimensional representation which *looks* like a view of that object or set of objects or world.

Of course, more than that is needed for a good impression of three-dimensional space. There is also the ability for objects within the scene to move in a realistic way with respect to other objects in the scene and there is the ability to change the viewpoint (as though you were moving your head, or as though the camera were moving). We shall discuss these aspects later.

For the moment, we shall take a closer look at the concepts that explain how three-dimensional worlds are *rendered* onto a two-dimensional monitor.

The Window On To The World

We aim to render the three-dimensional world onto our monitor, and, to do that, we need to convert the three-dimensional objects into two-dimensional ones. This is not a particularly simple problem, but to begin with, we need to establish a few concepts.

The first thing we need to do is establish what we can see in the world, *i.e.*, work out what we need to draw onto the screen, then once we have done that, actually perform the calculations to convert the objects.

So, let us define a term called the *viewport*. The viewport is simply a window onto the three-dimensional world, in that we are standing on one side of the window, and the world which we wish to render is on the other. Imagine standing inside a house and looking out of a window into the garden. The window is the viewport. Figure 2.16 illustrates this idea.

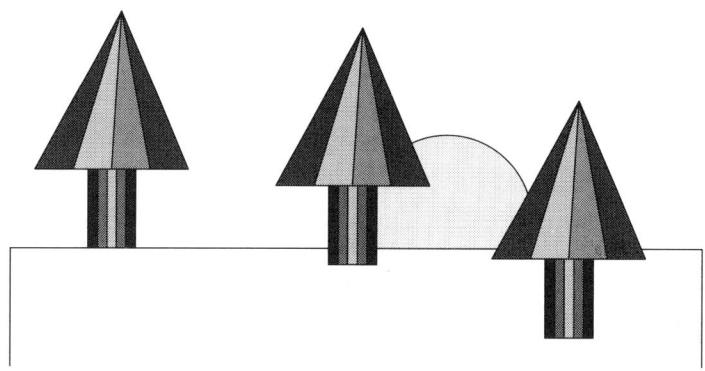

Figure 2.16: A World

The walls surrounding the window mask off parts of the world, which renders them invisible to us, *i.e.*, the objects that are to either side of us and behind us are automatically invisible, and objects outside the viewport's dimensions are also invisible. Figure 2.17 shows this masking operation in action.

Therefore, if we define a viewport, then we can start working out what objects in the three-dimensional world we need to draw, and we also know where these objects are in relation to the position from which we are viewing them.

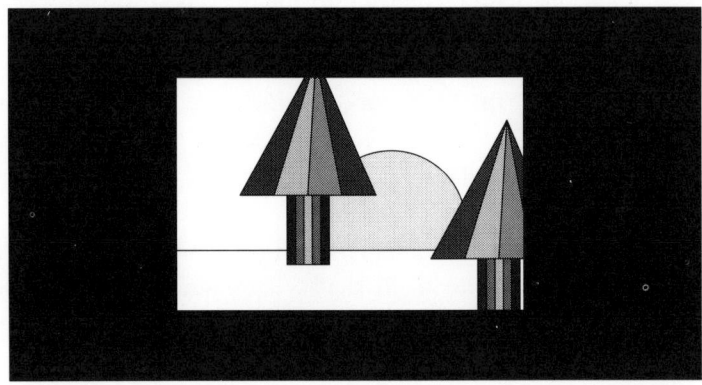

Figure 2.17: A World As Seen Through The Viewport

To help us work out what we can see, and where it is likely to appear within the viewport, we must describe a concept known as the *view frustum*. This is a volume of space which contains the visible objects for a given viewport. If we think about the window in the living room, our viewpoint, or eyes, are at one particular point in three-dimensional space. The viewport will be some distance away, therefore, the volume of space defined from the shape of the viewport and our eye position is a pyramid, the base being the window and the apex being our eyes. With a logical extension of this idea, the volume of space in the world that we can see through the window is basically a giant pyramid, and this is what a view frustum is.[4] Figure 2.18 illustrates the concept of the frustum.

If you look at Figure 2.18, you will see that we have marked the eye position, the viewport and two other viewportesque things called the *near clipping plane* and the *far clipping plane*. For the moment, we shall just say that these two planes define the nearest and furthest objects that you can see in the world. The walls of the pyramid mark the horizontal and vertical extents of the visible space, and the near and far clipping planes mark the top and base of the pyramid. Therefore, we can say that if an object is to be visible, it must lie within the main body of the pyramid.

---

[4]Some alternative names for the view frustum are *view volume* and *viewing pyramid*. They all mean roughly the same thing.

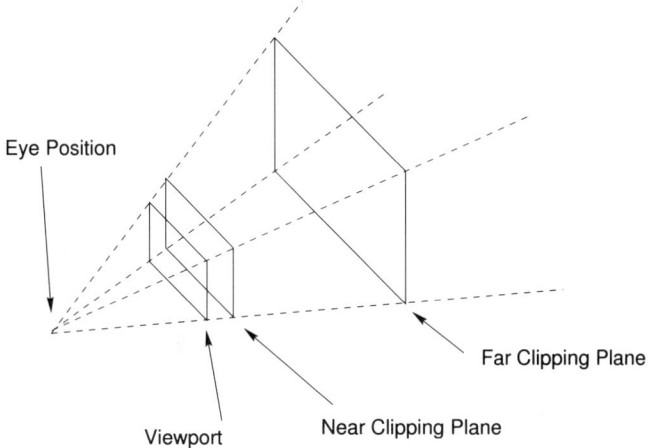

Figure 2.18: A View Frustum

To illustrate this concept further, Figure 2.19 shows the view frustum viewed from above. In this diagram, the sphere marked [0] lies completely outwith the body of the pyramid, and therefore cannot be seen if you are looking at the world through the viewport. However, the sphere marked [1] and the cube marked [2] both lie within the view frustum, and therefore are visible and should be rendered.

So that lets us calculate which objects we can see from a particular point in the world and where these objects are, but how does this help us render them onto a two-dimensional screen? The answer to that lies in a well-known optical property much beloved of artists the world over.

...Perspective.

Getting Things Into Perspective

Perspective is an optical effect that makes objects that are far away from us appear smaller than objects close to us, if the two objects being compared are identical. Therefore, we can use this difference between object sizes to judge *depth* or the *distance between* the objects. This is an extremely important principle in three-dimensional graphics and adds considerable amounts

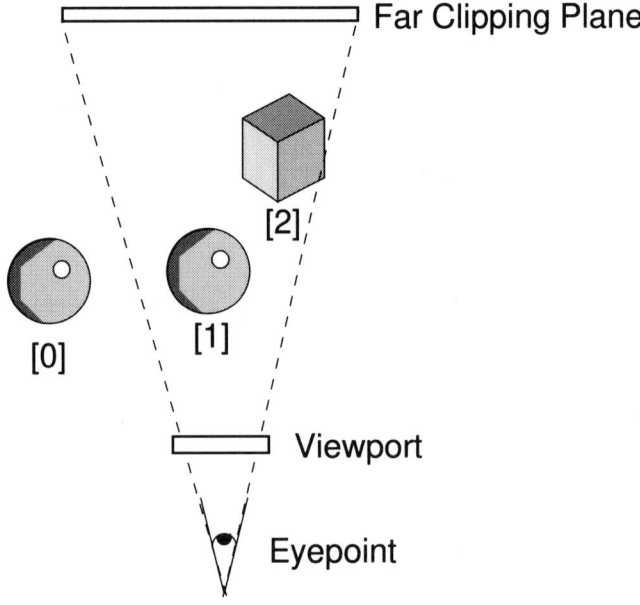

Figure 2.19: A View Frustum Seen From Above

of realism to worlds being rendered.

In an artistic and, more importantly, reality sense, we *project* objects towards a *vanishing point*, *i.e.*, a point on the horizon at which all object in the world converge. Figure 2.20 illustrates the concept and an example where we are looking down a long, straight road lined with trees. You can see the stripes narrow and bunch up as they get "further away" from the viewpoint. In addition to this, the trees, which are all the same size in the world, appear smaller.

However, this is diametrically opposite to the way that our viewing frustum appears to be designed!

Well, yes. Or rather, perhaps. In a rendering context, the viewpoint is actually the vanishing point, so, instead of our eyes projecting "rays" towards the vanishing point on the horizon that interact with any objects in their way, we are actually projecting the objects towards the vanishing point. To

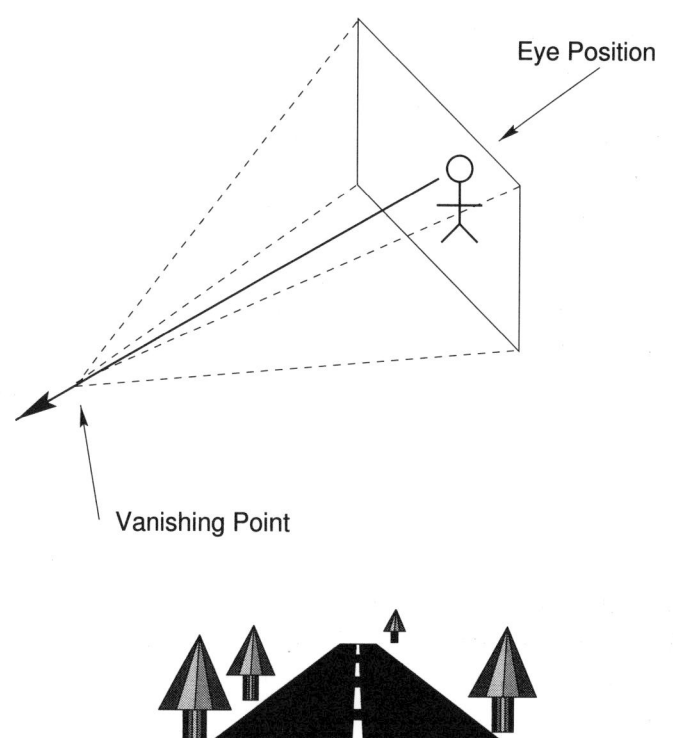

Eye Position

Vanishing Point

Figure 2.20: Vanishing Point Perspective

make this a little clearer, imagine that you are driving a car at speed along a road, and the viewport is your windscreen. In the real world, you move along the road, projecting rays towards the vanishing point, which to all intents and purposes never moves. Within a rendering context, the *objects* within the world are sucked towards your eyes instead, getting closer and closer until...*splat!*...they hit the viewport. The mush left on your viewport is the two-dimensional representation of the three-dimensional object!

OK, so what exactly happens here? Well, every vertex in the viewport is *projected* from a three-dimensional co-ordinate system to a two-dimensional co-ordinate system. The resulting two-dimensional location on the viewport of each vertex in a polygon now defines the way the polygon will appear on the screen when rendered. And that is the essence of how we render three-dimensional worlds on a two-dimensional screen.

There is one fairly obvious problem with this technique and that concerns objects that are neither completely outwith nor within the view frustum. What happens here? Do we simply discard the objects, completely render them or do something infinitely more complicated? Well, this is graphics, of course we take the complicated route, and this route is signposted *Clipping*.

Snip!

Clipping is a technique for pruning the objects within the world down to those we are interested in, and again down to the components of those we are interested in. We use the view frustum to determine whether or not the individual vertices in the world of each polygon of each object lie within or without the frustum. If a vertex lies without, it is *clipped*, or removed.

Clipping is, however, slightly more involved than removing the offending vertices. If we look at Figure 2.21 we can see the problem. If we simply remove the vertex that lies without the view volume, we end up with completely the wrong shape of polygon.

Of course, this is patently wrong. What we really want to do is not actually remove the offending vertex, but truncate the edges the polygon that *intersect* with the view frustum boundary. Figure 2.22 shows this operation in action. The truncation involves creating a new vertex along the edge at the boundary with the view volume. This preserves the shape of the polygon that lies

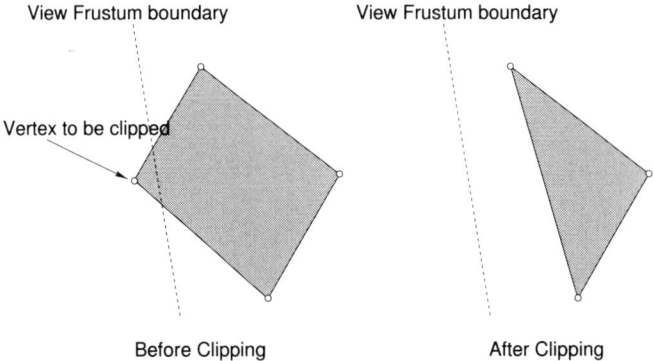

Figure 2.21: A Simple Polygon Clip

within the view volume.

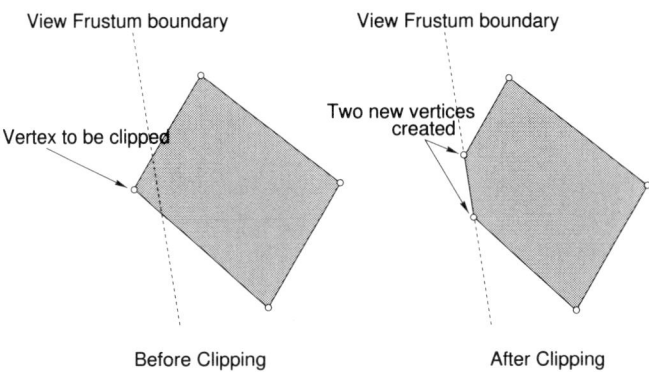

Figure 2.22: A Correct Polygon Clip

Clipping is generally not something that content creators need worry themselves about, since it is handled internally to the rendering engine, but having knowledge that clipping can drastically slow down rendering can allow the content creator to lay scenes out more carefully to minimize clipping if at all possible.

There are other methods through which we may reduce the number of polygons in a world to render, and these are generally grouped together under the notion of *culling*. We shall be discussing culling in Chapter 4.

WYSIWYG

By this point, we should have a fairly good idea of which objects we want to draw on the screen, and where those objects lie on the screen, after we have clipped the polygons and projected them onto the viewport. We now have several options open to us regarding the way in which we can render the objects depending on the effects that we wish to see.

These varying techniques are generally referred to as *rendering pipelines*,[5] and have differing properties, not to mention pros and cons.

Wire-Frame Rendering

The *wire-frame* pipeline is one which we are probably most familiar with since it has been with us for the longest period of time due to processing power constraints on computers (until very recently). This pipeline simply draws the edges of polygons on the screen as lines. This is perfectly satisfactory for representing the shapes of the objects within a world, although not particularly realistic. Figure 2.23 illustrates a goblet rendered in wire-frame. You may have problems working out which way the goblet is facing!

However, the wire-frame pipeline does have a major benefit in that it is extremely fast. This is because the major performance drags in rendering engines can sometimes occur in raw pixel throughput, which occurs when there are a lot of pixels to draw on the screen. Since we are not filling polygons in, but merely drawing their outlines, we have far fewer pixels to worry about, which speeds things up. Similarly, since all the edges are visible, we do not need to perform any visibility testing to see whether or not a polygon obscures another one, which again speeds things up.

There are some techniques available that allow you to make the output of wire-frame pipelines more comprehensible, the most common being *depth-*

---

[5]Although, in reality, the entire process, from projection to clipping and drawing is the pipeline.

Figure 2.23: A Wire-Frame Goblet

cueing, which darkens the line as it gets further away from the viewpoint. This produces a faked sense of the object dimming as it moves further away, which increases the viewer's depth perception of the scene.

However, even with advanced wire-frame techniques being used, wire-frame renderings are not particularly realistic, since the objects being rendered do not look solid. Therefore, the next step along the path is to render solid objects.

Flat Shading

A *flat-shading* pipeline generates a representation of an object using *filled polygons* instead of polygon outlines as used in wire-frame pipelines. This gives a rendered object an immediate feeling of solidity and considerably enhances the feeling of realism.

This pipeline uses a mathematical construct known as a *normal* to calculate the angle between the viewpoint and the polygon, and also between any lights and the polygon. The values from these calculations are used to choose the colour intensity that the polygon will be filled with. This produces an approximation of lighting across the object, and the lighting is uniform across each separate polygon that comprises the object. Flat-shading should produce much faster rendering than more realistic objects, but for distant objects (for example), flat-shading is more than adequate and produces excellent results. The major reason for not using flat-shading is that it tends to produce slightly "computer-generated" looking models, since the underlying polygon mesh is still clearly visible in most cases.[6] A flat-shaded goblet can be seen in Figure 2.24. However, flat-shading is extremely fast, and for fast-moving

Figure 2.24: A Flat-Shaded Goblet

objects, or objects that naturally look angular, *e.g.*, the walls of a house, it

---

[6]Cases where the underlying polygon mesh is not clearly discernible usually imply that the area of the polygons is *very* small, *i.e.*, maybe only two pixels, and there are many polygons in the model.

is definitely worthwhile to use.

Gouraud Shading

Gouraud shading is named after its developer, Henri Gouraud, who set out one of the earliest fast interpolated shading techniques. In English, this means that the intensity of the colour across each polygon varies linearly in a way that makes the polygon look "curved" instead of flat, as seen in the Gouraud-shaded goblet in Figure 2.25.

Figure 2.25: A Smooth-Shaded Goblet

Gouraud shading uses a slightly different method of filling polygons than flat-shading, in that instead of calculating a single colour value for the entire polygon, the colour values at each side of the polygon are averaged, which produces the effect of the brightnesses "blending" across the surface of the polygon, thereby producing the curved effects. This technique looks excellent in many rendering engines, and, if the objects are mobile, can be stunning.

There are, however, some caveats to Gouraud shading, in that, in cases of large polygons being shaded, the underlying polygon mesh can still be discerned. A more obvious problem is that Gouraud shading is considerably slower than flat shading, although not cripplingly slow. A reasonably powerful machine can produce Gouraud-shaded worlds with an acceptable frame rate. The major criticism that can be levelled at Gouraud shading is that objects shaded using this technique look "dulled". This is because Gouraud shading cannot handle *highlighting* objects, which gives them reflective and shiny properties. For these effects, we must look to the most complex and powerful shading model, *Phong shading*.

Phong Shading

Phong shading is a shading technique developed by Bui-Tuong Phong to rectify some of the problems in Gouraud's techniques and extend them where possible to allow more realistic lighting.

Phong shading succeeds admirably in its goals. It eliminates the underlying polygon mesh visibility except in exceptional circumstances and provides realistic highlighting that allows content creators to create objects that look plastic, shiny or reflective. Figure 2.26 shows a goblet with highlighting.

The major downside of Phong shading is that it is exponentially slower than Gouraud shading, a direct result of the more complex algorithms required to process the information. However, rendering pipelines tend to take the best of both Gouraud and Phong shading to produce a hybrid shading pipeline that allows specular highlights and complex lighting *à la* Phong, but shades non-highlit areas with the faster Gouraud pipeline. This produces models more realistic than Gouraud, but only incurs a small speed penalty.

Texture-Mapped Pipeline

Texture mapping is one of the most important, if not *the* most important aspect of any rendering engine. With the advent and mass-market acceptance of games like Doom,[7] texture mapping has been brought into the frontline of rendering engine pipelines.

---

[7]Copyright © id Software.

Figure 2.26: A Phong-Shaded Goblet

Texture mapping can be used to produce more realistic models with only minimal additional effort on top of a smooth-shading pipeline, and vastly simplified polygon meshes can be used instead of complex meshes with all the detail modelled instead of simulated. For example, if we wished to model a stone wall, we could either model each individual stone that the wall is built from, using thousands upon thousands of polygons to achieve the result, or we could texture-map an image of a stone wall onto a flat polygon. Modelling the thousands of polygons is not inherently the wrong solution to the problem, merely more time-consuming, in terms of both creating the model and rendering it. Texture mapping will be, perhaps, slightly less realistic, but much faster.

There are some problems inherent in texture mapping which have been inherited from our viewport concept, and from standard image processing. The first and most noticeable problem with texture mapping comes from the fact that the polygon onto which the texture is being mapped has been perspective projected onto the viewport, and we don't also project the texture. This is known as *affine texture mapping* or *perspective-incorrect* texture mapping and results in some horrible visual effects, as seen in Figure 2.27.

You can check whether or not the perspective is correct in the leftmost texture-mapped image. Simply try drawing a straight line from one corner of the board to the other through the diagonal corners of each square on the diagonal. You can't? Then it's not correct. The horrendous "skewing" effect that you can see in the right-hand image is due to the combination of a lack of perspective correction and rotation of the polygon. The more the polygon rotates from being face-on to the viewpoint, the worst that skewing will get.

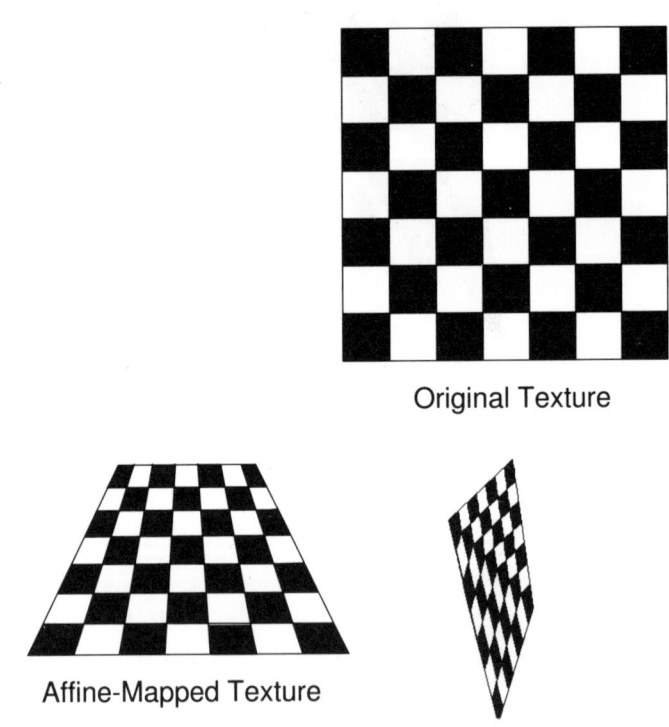

Figure 2.27: An Affine-Mapped Polygon

A further problem that can arise with texture mapping, usually in conjunction with perspective-incorrect texture mapping, is that the textures can begin to "swim" around on the polygons onto which they are mapped. This effect can be very disorientating for the viewer, as can the whole perspective-incorrection issue.

A perspective-correct texture map looks much more pleasant. Figure 2.28 shows the same polygon with perspective-correct texture mapping.

Perspective-correct
Texture-map

Figure 2.28: A Perspective-Correct Polygon

Another problem that can arise with texture mapping is that as you approach a texture-mapped polygon, it can begin to *pixelate*, rendering it impossible to work out what you're looking at. For example, if we look at the texture map that we could use to create a stone wall, and then look at the same section of that map after we move closer to the wall, there is visible pixelation of textures. This effect can be seen in Figure 2.29. That said, texture mapping is one of the most effective ways of creating realistic looking worlds, and the benefits far outweigh any of the potential trouble areas that can exist.

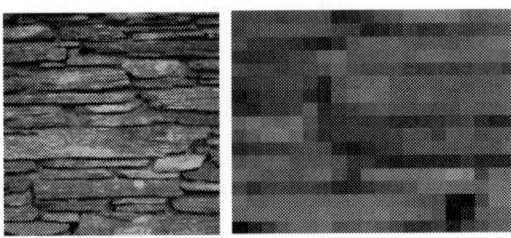

Figure 2.29: Pixelation

Chapter 3

The Web of Wyrd

"Wyrd. . . is the unfolding of the universe – a multi-dimensional cosmic web."

Christopher Hall (quoted in Brian Bates, *The Way of Wyrd*)

The design of cyberspace is quite a deceptively simple task. "It's all just sticking 3D stuff in a big box", you think. You are correct . . . it *is* all just sticking 3D stuff in a big box. Unfortunately, the big box has no top, bottom or sides that you can see, and the 3D stuff just gets more and more complicated the more you look at it.

The complexity of cyberspatial design can be quite daunting, once you make the realization that a simple object, such as a cube is actually comprised of eight distinct vertices and six distinct convex polygons. And, as we mentioned before, 3D models are more likely to become more complex before they get simpler. . .

However, to help us towards building representations of cyberspace, a plethora of *scene description languages* have sprung up, providing fairly high-level syntactic constructs which we can use to describe three-dimensional scenes and worlds. Some of the more ubiquitous of these languages are the *Neutral File Format* (NFF), *Persistence of Vision* (POV), *Open Inventor* and *Object Oriented Geometry Language* (OOGL). However, none of the scene description languages was in particularly widespread use; POV tended to be used by persons using the POV-Ray raytracer, Open Inventor by high-end Silicon Graphics' machines.

This all changed with the meteoric ascent of VRML, the Virtual Reality Modelling Language, which was originally based on a subset of Open Inventor. With the advent of VRML1.0, we could build worlds, at least in geometric form, in a generic scene description language powerful enough to be used for serious applications, and tightly integrated with the equally meteorically exploding World Wide Web.

VRML1.0 soon passed into VRML2.0, and with it came a more powerful scene description syntax, which we shall be discussing in the following chapter. Other aspects of VRML2.0, such as *3D sound* and *behaviours*, are covered in separate chapters.

Reading the following VRML chapters should be supplemented by referring to the *VRML97 Specification* that is presented on the CD-ROM which accompanies this book. We have chosen to present some discussion and possible uses of various aspects of VRML2.0 instead of slavishly reproducing material in the specification. We hope this will be of more use to the reader who wishes to become familiar with the underlying concepts of VRML2.0 and possibilities that VRML2.0 confers.

VRML2.0 Grouping Nodes

We shall begin our exploration of VRML2.0 by gaining an understanding of the overall framework in which *nodes, i.e.,* objects in a scene, exist, and how this framework can be structured to provide optimization information to the underlying rendering engine.

Since the structure of the scene is invisible, it is generally ignored in optimization strategies, but this is in fact a mistake. It is just as important to tune the framework as it is to tune the contents.

VRML2.0 uses a scene graph in the form of a tree to structure the building blocks in space, as shown in Figure 3.1. One of the keys to successful and fast VRML worlds is the understanding of the warp and weave of the scene graph. A badly designed scene graph will produce worlds that, while visually

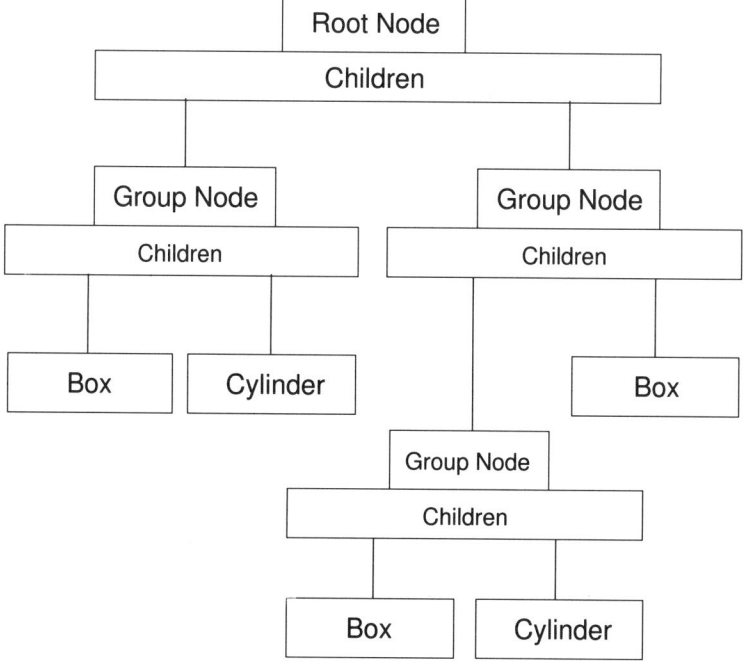

Figure 3.1: A Scene Graph

correct, will give the underlying rendering layer no help whatsoever in optimization, and therefore, possibly run more slowly. A correctly designed scene
graph will produce worlds that can be efficiently optimized by the rendering
engine.

Software renderers nowadays tend to use a low-level scene graph for optimiz-
ing rendering speed that is tree-based, which, by not a complete coincidence,
is the one which VRML uses to build its scene graph. This system is built on
the basis of *cumulative transformations* at each node; *i.e.*, at each *grouping
node* in the scene, a transformation can be applied to all *children* of that node.
This is the principle which the `Transform` node operates on, as we shall see
below.

VRML requires at least one top-level node, usually known as the *root node*
of a scene. The root node is usually a grouping node, which is a node that

contains other nodes, *i.e.*, has children.

We shall now discuss the various *grouping nodes* that VRML2.0 has to offer, starting with the most common, the `Transform` node.

Transform

The `Transform` node is a `Group` node with information regarding transformations that are to be applied to all children of the node. The types of transformation available with this node are:

- rotation

- translation

- scale

Transformations such as *shear* and *twist* are not available.

A short example illustrating the use of `Transform` node follows, in which we shall perform a rotation on the `Box` node in the previous `Group` node example above.

```
#VRML V2.0 utf8
#
# Example showing the use of the Transform node

Transform {
    rotation 0.707 0.707 0.707 0.78
    children [
        Shape {
            geometry Box {}
            appearance Appearance {
                material Material {
                    diffuseColor 1 1 1
                }
            }
        }
    ]
}
```

Since **Transform** nodes are grouping nodes, they may have many **children**, each of which is another **Transform** node. This gives us the ability to do *nested transformations*. For example, we might have a pot spinning on a potter's wheel which can be simulated with a **Transform** node. However, someone might knock the wheel over, causing both the wheel and the pot to move through space. In this case, the pot would be a child of the wheel, and any transformations applied to the wheel would also apply to the pot, in addition to any transformations applied to the pot alone.

```
#VRML V2.0 utf8
#
# Nested Transformations
#

Transform {
    rotation 1 0 0 1.57
    children [
        Transform {
            rotation 0 1 0 0.6
            translation 1 2 4
            scale 0.5 1 1.3
            ...
        }
    ]
}
```

Anchor

The **Anchor** node is a grouping node that causes a URL to be fetched when the user activates some of the geometry specified in the **children** field of this node, usually by clicking on it with a mouse. If the target URL contains valid VRML, the world which the activated **Anchor** node belongs to will be replaced with the world pointed to by the URL in question. If the target contains non-VRML data, then it is entirely up to the browser to work out what to do with the data, *e.g.*, if the target URL contains HTML, the browser may wish to pass the data to the user's default WWW browser, or if the target URL contained an image, it may pass the data to an appropriate image viewer.

To illustrate some basic **Anchor** functionality, we shall create two separate VRML scenes, one containing a blue cube, the other containing a red sphere.

We shall place each of these objects within an **Anchor** node, that, when activated, loads the other file up. The two VRML scenes are listed below:

```
#VRML V2.0 utf8
#
# Basic scene with a Blue Cube in it + Anchor to load
# scene with Red Sphere

Transform {
    children [
        Anchor {
            description "Click here to load SphereWorld!"
            url [ "anchorSphere.wrl" ]
            children [
                Shape {
                    geometry Box {}
                    appearance Appearance {
                        material Material {
                            diffuseColor 0 0 1
                        }
                    }
                }
            ]
        }
    ]
}
```

```
#VRML V2.0 utf8
#
# Basic scene with a Red Sphere in it + Anchor to load
# scene with Blue Cube

Transform {
    children [
        Anchor {
            description "Click here to load CubeWorld!"
            url [ "anchorCube.wrl" ]
            children [
                Shape {
                    geometry Sphere {}
                    appearance Appearance {
```

```
                material Material {
                    diffuseColor 1 0 0
                }
            }
        }
    ]
  }
]
}
```

The `Anchor` node offers some useful functionality, in that if the target URL ends with syntax of `#SomeViewpointName`, then, upon activation of that anchor, the viewpoint will be changed to the given `Viewpoint` in the target URL. For example:

```
#VRML V2.0 utf8
#
# The VRML file containing the Viewpoint to jump to

DEF LOOKONTO Viewpoint {
    position 0 5 5
    orientation 1 0 0 0.78
    description "Looking down onto Sphere"
}

Transform {
    children [
        Shape {
            geometry Sphere {}
            appearance Appearance {
                material Material {
                    diffuseColor 1 0 0
                }
            }
        }
    ]
}

#VRML V2.0 utf8
#
# The VRML file containing the Anchor that jumps to the above
```

```
# world

Transform {
    children [
        Anchor {
            description "Click here to load SphereWorld!"
            url [ "anchorSphere.wrl#LOOKONTO" ]
            children [
                Shape {
                    geometry Box {}
                    appearance Appearance {
                        material Material {
                            diffuseColor 0 0 1
                        }
                    }
                }
            ]
        }
    ]
}
```

We can also use this feature to provide `Viewpoint` jumping in the current world by specifying a target URL purely in the form of '#ViewpointName'. This functionality is illustrated in the following example:

```
#VRML V2.0 utf8
#
# File containing the Viewpoint to jump to

DEF DEFAULT-VIEW Viewpoint {
    position 0 0 5
    description "Default Viewpoint"
}

DEF LOOK-ONTO Viewpoint {
    position 0 5 5
    orientation 1 0 0 0.78
    description "Looking down onto"
}

Transform {
```

```
            children [
                Anchor {
                    description "Click here to load change Viewpoint!"
                    url [ "#LOOK-ONTO" ]
                    children [
                        Shape {
                            geometry Box {}
                            appearance Appearance {
                                material Material {
                                    diffuseColor 0 0 1
                                }
                            }
                        }
                    ]
                }
            ]
        }
```

Finally, the `parameter` field in the `Anchor` node can be used to specify any additional information that we may wish to pass to the VRML of the HTML browser, *e.g.*, a target "frame" that we wish to load the target URL into. For example:

```
Anchor {
    parameter [ "target=frame_to_load_Anchor_into" ]
        . . .
}
```

Billboard

The `Billboard` node is a grouping node which modifies its coordinate system so that the children of the node's Z-axes turn to point at the viewer.

This is extremely useful in certain circumstances, one most often quoted being using a single polygon with a tree image texture-mapped onto it to provide realistic trees, since no matter which way you look at the tree, it will look like a tree, because the polygon to which the tree image is texture-mapped will always turn to face you! You'll never be able to see the polygon side-on, hence the illusion will work. The `Billboard` node is also useful for building "Heads-Up Display", or *HUD*, effects, in which a three-dimensional panel is permanently displayed on the user's screen, possibly displaying orientation, speed or other world-specific characteristics.

An example scene using the `Billboard` node follows:

```
#VRML V2.0 utf8
#
# Example of a Billboard node in action

Transform {
    children [
        Billboard {
            children [
                Shape {
                    geometry Box {}
                    appearance Appearance {
                        material Material {
                            diffuseColor 1 1 1
                        }
                    }
                }
            ]
        }
    ]
}
```

There is a specified "special effect" that may be used, which is to rotate the `children` of the `Billboard` node to face the viewer on all axes, not just on one axis, as is the default behaviour. This can be accomplished by setting the `axisOfRotation` field to 0 0 0. This will cause the object to face the viewer, even if the viewer rolls, pitches or elevates their viewpoint.

Collision

The `Collision` node specifies non-default behaviour for its children with regard to collision detection. By default, all objects in the scene are collidable, but by using a `Collision` node, you may disable this, or otherwise modify any of its functionality. Without a `Collision` node parenting it, an object with default collision rules would be collided with, but no information such as the time of collision would be available.

We shall discuss the properties of the `Collision` node in much more detail in Chapter 7.

Group

A `Group` node is the simplest type of grouping node in that it merely specifies a list of its children. It is effectively a `Transform` node without the transformation information. A small example illustrating the use of the `Group` node follows:

```
#VRML V2.0 utf8
#
# Example showing the use of the Group node

Group {
    children [
        Shape {
            geometry Box {}
            appearance Appearance {
                material Material {
                    diffuseColor 1 1 1
                }
            }
        }
    ]
}
```

Thoughts On Scene-Graph Optimization

Now that we know the way that grouping nodes are used, and how they lend themselves to the process of building the scene graph, we should perhaps delve into some basic thoughts on how we can optimize our scene graph's structure to help the renderer make informed decisions about scene management.

Many renderers use a technique called "bounding box culling" which can radically reduce the number of polygons in a scene that are possibilities for rendering. This technique is in "front" of the object, polygon and vertex clipping segments of the rendering pipeline, as discussed in Chapter 1, since, if we apply bounding box culling to a scene, many objects will be discarded simply because their bounding boxes are not visible.

If we examine the grouping nodes more closely in the specification, we can see that there is a field in each node definition entitled `field SFVec3f bboxSize` which specifies the bounding box for that particular grouping node—or, to be more exact, specifies the bounding box that surrounds *all* the children of that particular grouping node. This is an important point and there are some fairly important problems that can occur:

Wayward Children

Imagine a case where one of the children of a grouping node moves around the world. If the path of this node leads it further away from the other children of the grouping node, then the bounding box will stretch in size. This is not a problem when the wayward child is fairly proximate to its siblings, but when it begins wandering further afield, the amount of space the bounding box occupies begins to seriously interfere with the renderer's ability to use bounding boxes as a useful way to trim the scene.

For example, Figure 3.2 shows a typical case in which this may happen. In phase 1, the bounding box containing the two spheres will be culled quickly and efficiently, greatly reducing processing time for the scene, since it now does not require to test and render the two spheres within the bounding box in question. The cuboid inside the bounding box within the viewing frustum will be tested and rendered as normal, but, as you can see, we've eliminated two-thirds of the scene with almost no overhead! This is where careful scene-graph structuring can give us a large performance boost.

However, in phase 2 in Figure 3.2, one of the spheres has started moving across the viewing frustum, stretching the bounding box. In this case, all the objects in the scene must now be clipped against the view frustum, which is the worst case that could hopefully happen.

In phase 3 in Figure 3.2, the mobile sphere has now passed completely across the view frustum, but the bounding box will still be tested as being visible,[1] hence, both spheres will be tested, but *neither* will actually be included in the model. At worst, every vertex in each sphere will be clipped to the view frustum, but since *neither* object will produce a single rendered pixel on the

---

[1] *Visible* in the sense that the bounding box is within the view frustrum, therefore objects within that bounding box *might* be seen from the viewpoint.

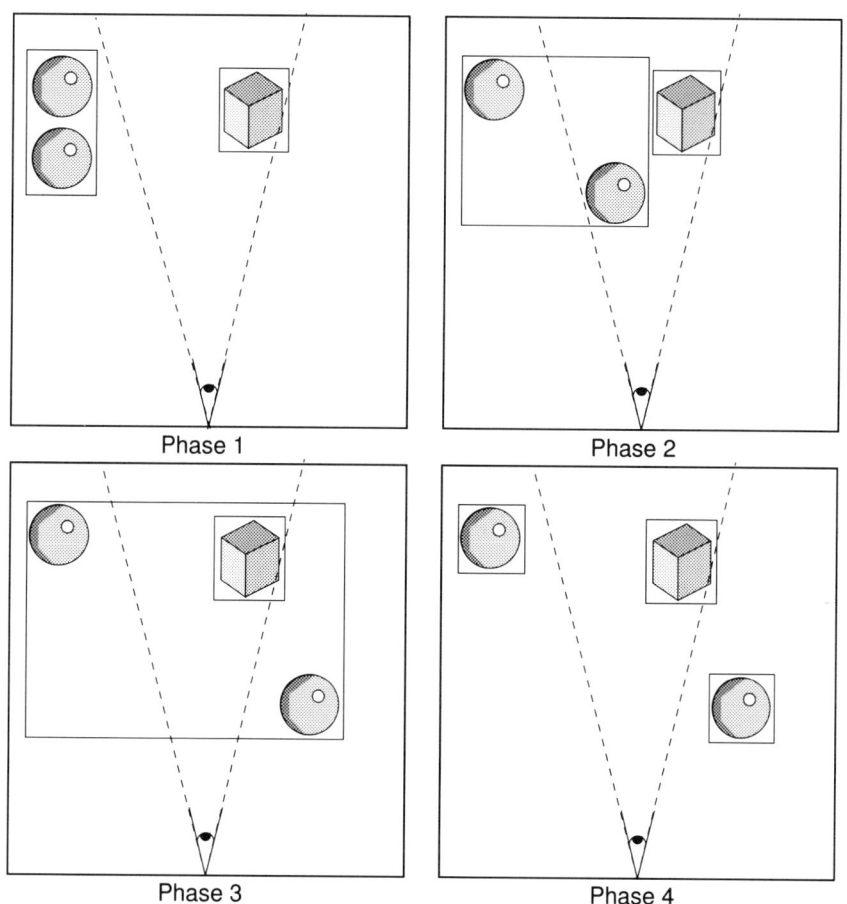

Figure 3.2: Bounding Box "Stretching"

screen, this is quite an appalling waste of resources.

A potential solution to this issue is to "reparent" objects that are causing bad deformation of bounding boxes to the bounding box that is the "parent" of the current containing bounding box. For example, if we assume that in Figure 3.2 there are three bounding boxes in total, one being the "world", one containing the two spheres and the latter containing a cuboid, then, when a certain bounding box stretch limit has been reached, the sphere causing deformation will be reparented to the "world" bounding box. This will cause the scene to look like phase 4 in Figure 3.2. As can be seen, in this case the bounding box culling would trivially reject both spheres again, thereby causing things to run considerably faster.

Inlining Objects And The `Inline` Node

The balance between lumping a large amount of objects into a single grouping node and splitting the objects down into a more hierarchical structure is a fine one.[2] Due to the hierarchical structure of the scene graph, recursion through each node in the tree is a commonplace activity, but if the scene graph is many levels deep, the tree traversal routines, combined with cumulative transformation calculations, can again lead to slow rendering speeds. If we couple this problem with the problem of wayward children, or generally badly positioned objects, the effects on rendering speeds could become relatively crippling and the world navigation could become an unpleasant experience.

Therefore, in some cases, lumping quantities of objects together into a single grouping node can have quite beneficial effects, especially if those objects are likely to always remain bunched together in a fairly tight group. This is especially true in cases of `IndexedFaceSet` and `IndexedLineSet` nodes which allow the content creator to specify actual vertex positions within the local co-ordinate system. In the case of basic nodes, such as `Box` or `Cylinder`, inlining is generally not possible, since each node requires its own `Transform` node parent to allow positioning.

---

[2]A potentially useful analogy to the programmatically minded is that of putting all your code in `main()` against splitting your code into numerous functions and procedures. The latter is more usually easier to read, although the former will most probably execute much faster due to high function-calling overhead.

This brings us nicely onto the `Inline` grouping node, which is classed as a *special grouping node* in the *VRML97 Specification*. The `Inline` node provides functionality to load the data defining the children from any arbitrary URL on the World Wide Web. This feature infuses VRML with power similar to that which makes HTML so useful, namely, the ability to build large and complex three-dimensional spaces by pulling many different datasets in from many different sources. For example, we could provide the basic geometry for Skara Brae locally, then use humanoid figures from another remote site which specializes in the humanoid modelling, not to mention Acme Neolithic Pots, suppliers of the models of all our pottery. This ability to "mix and match" contributed greatly to the success of HTML on the World Wide Web, and there is no reason to suppose it will not succeed in VRML.

Another interesting side-effect of the `Inline` node is that it may be used[3] to *asynchronously* load sections of the scene not yet visible to the user. To put this into English, the content creator may explicitly specify the bounding box of the children of the `Inline` node as a "hint" to the browser that it may make optimizations on this node. In particular, if the bounding box in question isn't visible, then the loading of the children of the `Inline` node may be deferred until required, which can considerably speed up rendering in some situations. This idea is illustrated in Figure 3.3.

Levels of Detail And The `LOD` Node

A final trick we can use to optimize our scene graph is to build varying levels of detail of a model depending on the distance of that model from the current user's viewpoint. To elaborate, if we are a good distance from a neolithic pot, much of the detail on the pot is not likely to be discernible, if, in fact, the pot is actually visible at all! If the on-screen representation of a model is only going to be four pixels, why bother texture-mapping 400 polygons for that net result? Why not just render a small cube instead? No one would know the difference!

However, as we get nearer the pot, more detail becomes apparent, the engravings on the pot, the texture of the raw material the pot is constructed from, nicks in the pot, cracks and imperfections in the manufacture. These are all small features that add realism to our world, but, as stated above, are

---

[3]If the browser supports such a feature. This is not *required* behaviour in the *VRML97 Specification*.

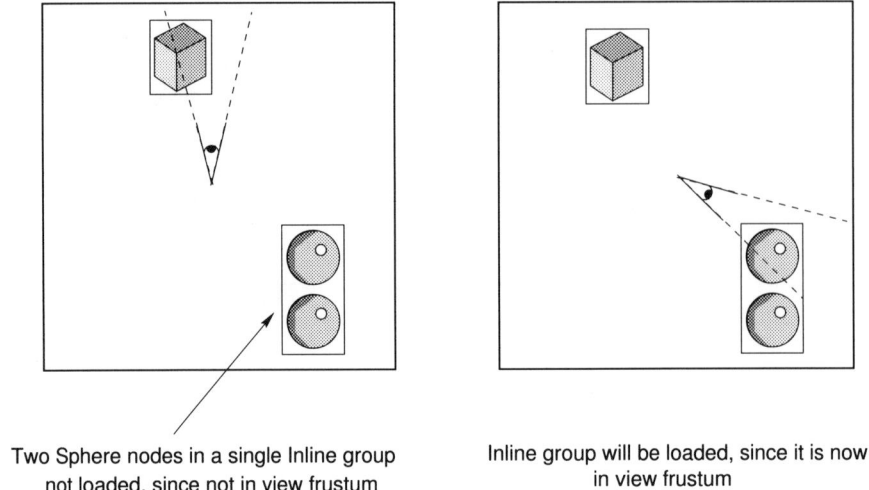

Two Sphere nodes in a single Inline group
not loaded, since not in view frustum

Inline group will be loaded, since it is now
in view frustum

Figure 3.3: Asynchronous Loading of `Inline` Nodes

hardly relevant to someone standing 100 feet away.

This principle is known as "level of detail" and is covered by the *VRML97 Specification*, which provides a handy node to do this sort of thing, namely the `LOD` node. The `LOD` node is fairly simple. It merely provides a framework for specifying children of a grouping node, but with the additional ability to specify a *distance* at which a given level of detail is used. Figure 3.4 illustrates a neolithic pot at various distances. In this example, the pot becomes less "rounded" as we get further away from it, which produces noticeable results in terms of saved processing time, if we look at Table 3.1 which details the number of vertices and polygons in each model at each range.

As you can see clearly from Table 3.1, the number of polygons drastically reduces as the object gets further away. This is quite an excellent saving, since the actual visual representation of the 82-polygon pot at range 15 is not much degraded from the 328-polygon pot at range 5. This is where careful use of the `LOD` node can enhance the navigability of our virtual worlds. Some sample code that creates a level-of-detail node is illustrated below.[4]

---

[4]This code has been simplified considerably, and can be found on the CD-ROM in full. Also, don't worry if you don't understand it! We're merely illustrating the `LOD` node here.

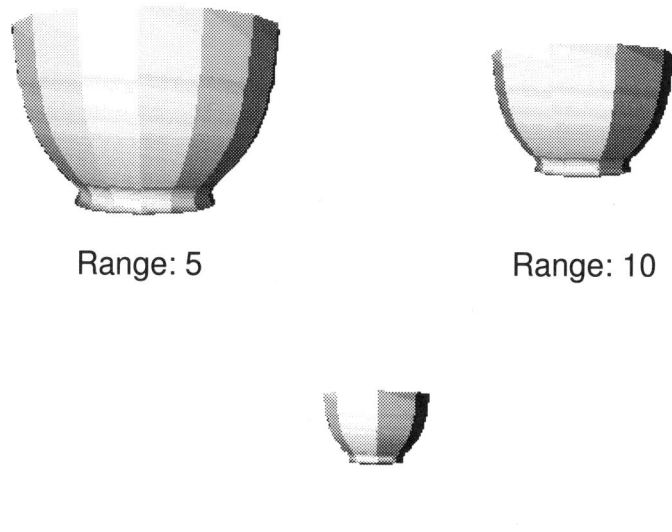

Range: 5   Range: 10

Range: 15

Figure 3.4: A Neolithic Pot At Various Distances

This LOD node sets up three ranges at which we change models. The ranges are specified in the **range** field, which is an array of floating-point numbers. The **levels** field contains an array of legal VRML nodes, *e.g.*, a grouping node or **Shape** node. The number of ranges specified in the **range** field must correspond to the number of nodes *plus 1* specified in the **range** field. If too few nodes are specified in the **levels** field, the last node specified will be used for each extra range.

```
#VRML V2.0 utf8
#
# Level-of-Detail node example

Transform {
    children [
        LOD {
            range [ 5, 10, 15 ]
            levels [
```

Distance	Vertices	Polygons
5	656	328
10	410	210
15	328	82

Table 3.1: Neolithic Pot At Various Distances

```
                # Here's a complete VRML node for range 5
                Shape USE VERYDETAILEDPOT

                # Here's a complete VRML node for range 10
                Shape USE DETAILEDPOT

                # Here's a complete VRML node for range 15
                Shape USE UNDETAILEDPOT
            ]
        }
    ]
}
```

A final caveat on the LOD node is that the values specified in the **range** field are merely *hints* to the browser telling it where the *ideal* range to switch between nodes is. The browser may choose to alter the range at which a switch may occur in order to maintain smooth rendering speeds. If the **range** field is not specified by the content creator, the browser will make the decision on where to switch between levels based on the heuristics of maintaining a smooth rendering speed and also to make the transition between models seamless and mostly invisible to the user.

Excellent optimization using the LOD node can be achieved by combining it with careful use of the **Inline** node. For example, if we create multiple level-of-detail versions of any given object, with each level of detail a separate **Inline** node, then, the amount of data to be loaded initially will be quite small. Only upon being within range of a different level of detail of an object in the scene will the new data be triggered to be loaded via the **Inline** node. Of course, this can have its downsides, since the network will be being constantly used as the user navigates the scene loading new **Inline** chunks, and requires a constant network connection.

Chapter 4

Virtual Lego

Natura vacuum abhorret

François Rabelais

Now that we are prepared with our basic scaffolding, we ought to investigate the materials we shall be using to build our worlds.

The *VRML97 Specification* defines a certain number of basic geometric primitives for building worlds with. These are quite rudimentary and unsophisticated objects in some cases, powerful and sophisticated in others.

However, all of these geometric nodes are united by their common heritage as *geometry* nodes, *i.e.*, nodes that, when rendered, produce a visual effect on the screen. To unify these disparate nodes together, a general "rendered object" node appeared called the `Shape` node.

Throwing Shapes

The `Shape` node is purely a construct to unify all the disparate geometric and `Appearance` node definitions that exist into a single node that can be used to define an object in the world that is to be rendered.

The `Shape` node has only two fields in it, being `appearance`, which contains a valid `Appearance` node; and `geometry`, which contains a valid geometrical node, *e.g.*, a `Box` or an `ElevationGrid`. We shall be discussing both the geometrical and `Appearance` nodes in much more detail shortly, but, for the sake of clarity, we shall illustrate the use of the `Shape` node within the scene graph as follows:

```
#VRML V2.0 utf8
#
# Short example of the Shape node
Transform {
    children [
        Shape {
            geometry Box {}
            appearance Appearance {
                material Material {
                    diffuseColor 1 1 1
                }
                texture ImageTexture {
                    url "http://somehost/sometexture.gif"
                }
            }
        }
    ]
}
```

As can be seen from this example, we have one object to render in the scene: a `Box` node, of default size, with the appearance of being white, with a texture mapped onto it.

And that's all there is to the `Shape` node! Now, on with the gory detail of the various geometrical nodes that are specified in the *VRML97 Specification*.

Basic VRML Geometrical Nodes

The most basic VRML objects are staple graphics *primitives*, *i.e.*, shapes that occur fairly regularly, probably due to their ease of creation, not to mention the fact they can be moulded together in a multitude of pleasing ways.

Box

The `Box` node is a cuboid, or, to quote the *VRML97 Specification*, "a rectangular parallelepiped box". The `Box` node's dimensions extend from its centre,

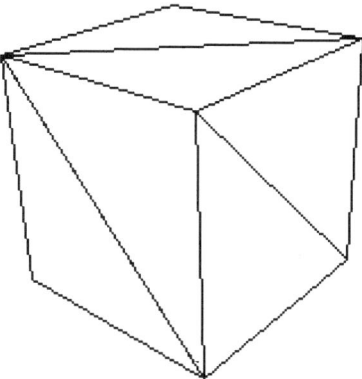

Figure 4.1: A Box Node

and not, say, the bottom-left corner, so if, for example, we create a `Box` of size $2 \times 2 \times 2$, its vertices will lie at $(1, 1, 1), (-1, 1, 1), (-1, 1, -1), (1, 1, -1)$. Again, be very careful about the fact that dimensions extend from the centre of the object, rather than from a given corner. This *must* be kept in mind, otherwise you'll start running into serious layout problems later on. Figure 4.1 shows a `Box` node in wire frame, with auto-triangulated faces.

Another major caveat of `Box` nodes is that they are considered to be *solid* objects, *i.e.*, you cannot "enter" the node through one of its "walls". If you do so, through either a lack of collision detection, or bad `Viewpoint` placement, the results are *undefined*. Generally this means that from the inside, the walls are back-face culled, which means that even though you are inside the `Box`, you won't be able to see it! This effect afflicts all *basic* VRML primitives, to varying degrees, as is discussed in each node below.

A short example scene that creates a single default-sized white `Box` node follows:

```
#VRML V2.0 utf8
#
# Simple scene containing a single white Box
Transform {
    children [
        Shape {
            geometry Box {}
```

```
            appearance Appearance {
                material Material {
                    diffuseColor 1 1 1
                }
            }
        }
    ]
}
```

Similarly, a non-defaulty-sized `Box` node could be written as:

```
#VRML V2.0 utf8
#
# Simple scene containing a single cuboidal Box
Transform {
    children [
        Shape {
            geometry Box {
                size 1 5 25
            }
            # Appearance node deleted for brevity
        }
    ]
}
```

Cone

The `Cone` node produces a conical object in the scene. The `Cone` is constructed of two separate parts, being the "side", which is the main cone body, and the "bottom", which is the base. Each part may be "switched off", if the scene creator so desires. The `Cone` node is regarded as being *solid*, and requires outside faces only. The results if viewed from inside are *undefined*. The cone is also sized from the centre, as per the `Box` node.

The `Cone` object is not particularly configurable, in that the only fields we can use to alter the geometry of the object are `bottomRadius`, which is the radius of the base of the `Cone`, and `height`, which is the distance from the centre of the base to the apex of the `Cone`.

The `Cone` object suffers the same deficiencies as the other basic VRML geometry primitives, in that it is regarded as being *solid*. If we were to

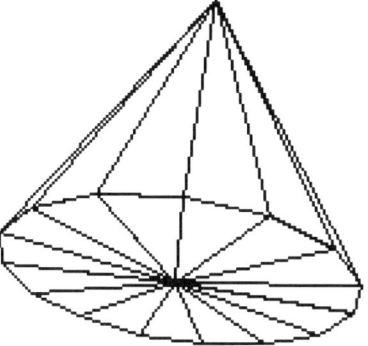

Figure 4.2: A Cone Node

specify that field `bottom` was `FALSE`, and then viewed the `Cone` from the same angle as per Figure 4.2, we would actually see not much at all. The majority of the node would have been back-face culled!

An example scene containing two `Cone` nodes, one of default size, the other not, follows:

```
#VRML V2.0 utf8
#
# Example scene containing two Cones, one of default size,
# the other not
Transform {
    children [
        Shape {
            geometry Cone {}
          }
        Transform {
            translation 4 0 0
            children [
                Shape {
                    geometry Cone {
                        radius 1.5
                        height 0.5
                      }
                  }
              ]
```

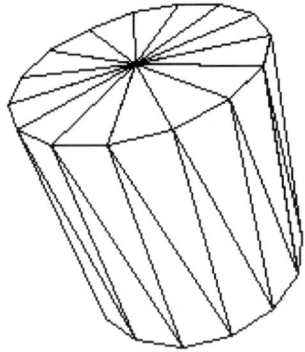

Figure 4.3: A Cylinder Node

```
            }
        ]
    }
```

Cylinder

The `Cylinder` node, rather unsurprisingly, creates a cylindrical object in the scene. The cylinder is constructed of three discrete parts, the "top" cap, the "bottom" cap and the "side", which is the tubing itself. Each part may be switched off by setting the appropriate flag in the node definition to **FALSE**. The `Cylinder`, as with the `Box` node, is regarded as being *solid*, so due care should be observed with usage. This node is sized from the centre.

The `Cylinder` has two main configurable fields with regard to geometry, being `radius`, which is the radius of the node; and `height`, which is the length of the "tube" part of the node, *i.e.*, the part of the node represented by the `side` field. Here's an example scene containing a `Cylinder` node.

```
#VRML V2.0 utf8
#
# Small example scene containing a Cylinder
Transform {
    children [
        Shape {
```

```
            geometry Cylinder {
                height 4
                radius 0.25
            }
            appearance Appearance {
                material Material {
                    diffuseColor 1 1 1
                }
            }
        }
    ]
}
```

The `Cylinder` node is certainly useful, but is somewhat crippled by the narrowness of its definition, in that we may only specify the **radius** of the `Cylinder` as being a uniform value.

A more useful general purpose `Cylinder` and `Cone` object could have been used with specification of both the top and bottom radii of the object. In the case of the `Cone`, the top radius would have been 0, *i.e.*, both sides coincide at a single centre point. Similarly, truncated cone objects could have been produced.

An example specification of a merged `Cylinder` and `Cone` node could be:[1]

```
Cylicone {
    field SFFloat topRadius 1.0
    field SFFloat bottomRadius 1.0
    field SFFloat height 1.0
    field SFBool top TRUE
    field SFBool bottom TRUE
    field SFBool side TRUE
    field SFBool solid FALSE
}
```

So, if we specify a small VRML scene as follows, we should get a scene as per Figure 4.4.

---

[1] An extension node that extends Liquid Reality to allow you to include `Cylicone` objects into your VRML files is on the CD-ROM.

Figure 4.4: A Cylicone Node

```
#VRML V2.0 utf8
#
# Cylicone object demonstration. This should produce
# a truncated cone.
Transform {
  children [
    Shape {
      appearance Appearance {
        material Material {
          diffuseColor 1 1 1
          }
        }
      geometry Cylicone {
        height 3
        topRadius 1
        bottomRadius 3
        }
      }
    ]
  }
```

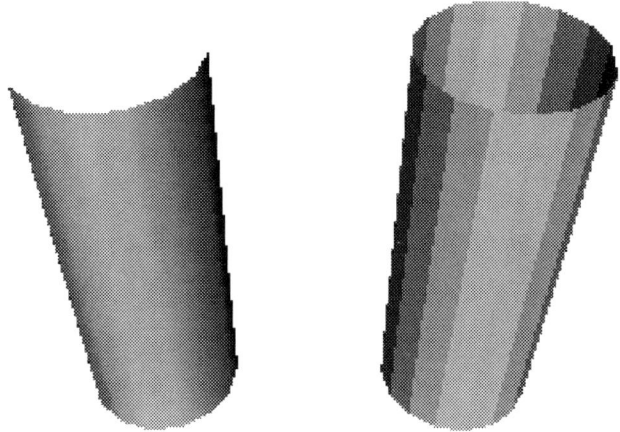

Figure 4.5: Wrong and Right Tubes

Another downside of the `Cylinder` is that whilst the various parts of the `Cylinder` can be removed, the node is always back-face culled, which is almost completely useless. If we remove a cap from a `Cylinder` by specifying `top FALSE` in our scene, then look down into the tube through the hole formed by the absence of the top cap, we get an effect that is certainly wrong, as shown in Figure 4.5 in the left-hand object. Things get notably worse if we want two disks floating in space, formed by specifying a `Cylinder` node with the `side` field set to `FALSE`. In this case, one of the disks would *always* be back-face culled! We would *never* get the effect we desired! The only real point of allowing the removal of parts of the node would appear to be to reduce the polygon count if those parts of the node were never visible, for example, we have a `Box` node sitting flush on top of a `Cylinder` node. In this instance, we could remove the cap at the end upon which the `Box` is attached to reduce the polygon count in the scene.

Needless to say, we have added the `solid` field back into the `Cylicone` node, which produces the correct behaviour for a tube, as shown in Figure 4.5 in the right-hand object.

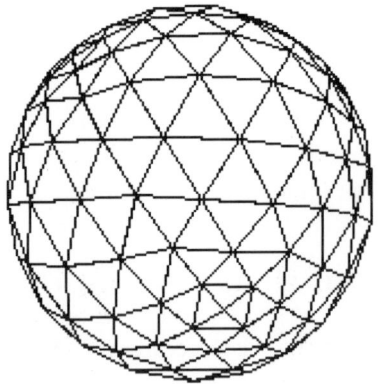

Figure 4.6: A Sphere Node

Sphere

The **Sphere** node encapsulates a spherical object in a scene with the given **radius**. There is very little that you can customize with a **Sphere** object since there is only one specified field in the node definition. The **Sphere** node is regarded as being *solid*, as per the other basic node types.

However, we can use a couple of tricks to get more for our money with the **Sphere** node. One of the most useful ones is to use the **scale** field of a **Transform** node to deform the shape of the **Sphere**; for example, to produce a pill shape, we can apply a non-uniform scale of 1 0.25 1 as shown in the following VRML.

```
#VRML V2.0 utf8
#
# Using a Transform node to generate pill shapes in
# conjunction with a Sphere node
Transform {
  scale 1 0.25 1
  children Shape {
    appearance Appearance {
      material Material {
        diffuseColor 1 1 1
      }
    }
    geometry Sphere {}
```

```
        }
    }
```

We can similarly use this trick to produce ellipsoidal shapes, although the scaling will be uniform from the centre, which makes generation of more complex shapes, for example, ovoids, impossible.

Thoughts On Basic Primitive Optimization

Now that we have discussed the basic geometric primitives that are built into the *VRML97 Specification*, we perhaps ought to discuss some of the pros and cons of using them. The most important of these issues boils down to the trade-off between *download time*, which is dependent on network speed, and *frame rate*, which is dependent mostly on the configuration of the user's machine.

Primitives are seductive to use because of their compactness in terms of file size. Constructing a sphere of about 500 polygons can be achieved merely with one **Sphere** node. However, as mentioned before, the content creator is at the mercy of the VRML browser implementor as to exactly how many polygons are actually created with a **Sphere** node, or any other type of basic primitive. There is no way to control this.

In some cases, for example, where a sphere is embedded into a cylinder to make a rough rotary quern as shown in Figure 4.7, we are actually rendering half the sphere that will *never* be seen. Now, given we have a sphere with, say, 512 polygons, that's 256 polygons per frame we're rendering that will never be seen. This is the essential core of the problem of trading off CPU resources to render additional polygons that may never be seen against file size, which is limited by network bandwidth.

Returning to the problem of rendering the basic primitives, there is light at the end of the tunnel, in that we should recall that the basic primitives are regarded as being solid; that is, they enclose a bounded volume of space. This means they are back-face culled. This means, the polygons embedded inside our rotary quern shown in Figure 4.7 have a very good chance of never being rendered anyway. However, the fact remains that those polygons must still be tested to see if they are facing towards or away from the viewer, which is still unnecessary computation.

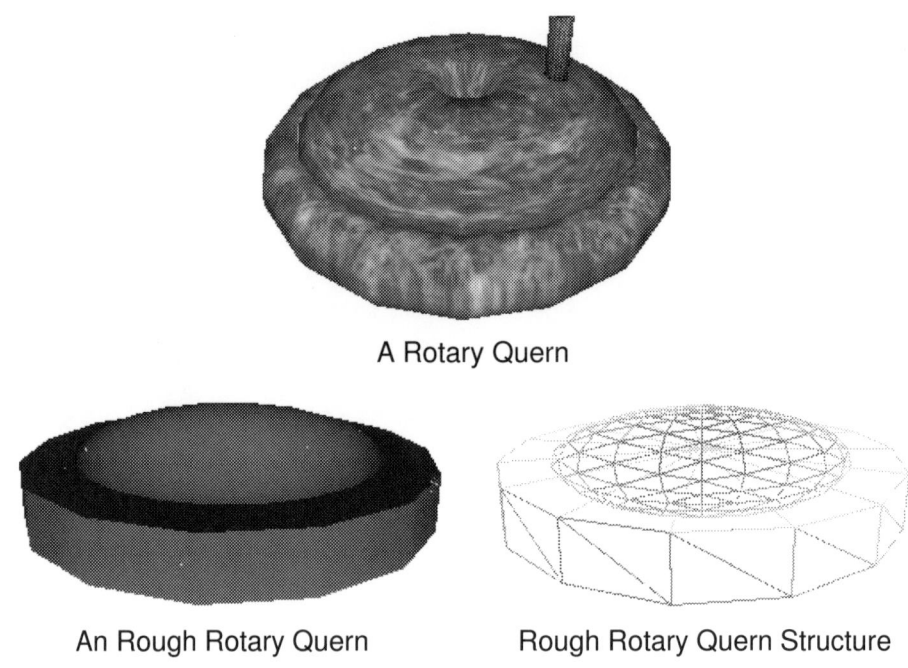

A Rotary Quern

An Rough Rotary Quern   Rough Rotary Quern Structure

Figure 4.7: Rotary Querns

A possible solution is to hand-generate `IndexedFaceSet` nodes[2] for each primitive, corresponding to the desired basic primitive. This method of generating basic primitives makes the file size of the VRML scene much larger, but can drastically reduce the number of polygons in a scene, which considerably helps less powerful machines render scenes at a more acceptable frame rate to the user.[3]

For example, if we look at the two cones in Figure 4.8, we can see that the smooth-shaded cones look fairly similar. However, the polygon counts are radically different, as seen in Table 4.1. We may also examine the flat-

---

[2] See below for more information on the `IndexedFaceSet` node.

[3] A small Java utility that allows the user to experiment with generating basic primitives with a given polygon count can be found on the CD-ROM.

Number of Facets	Number of Vertices	Number of Polygons
8	10	16
16	18	32
32	34	64

Table 4.1: Polygon And Vertex Counts Of Cones

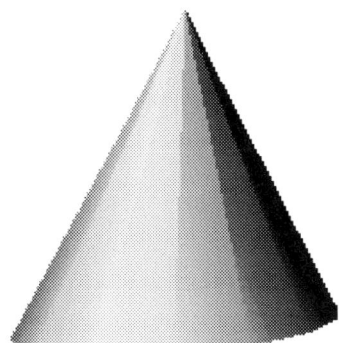

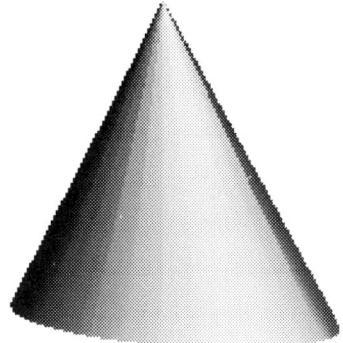

16-Facet Cone   32-Facet Cone

Figure 4.8: Smooth-Shaded 16- And 32-Facet Cones

shaded cones in Figure 4.9 which shows the difference in tessellation of the cones.

This merely shows that there is a valid cut-off point at which more polygons in a model does *not* increase the perceived realism of that model. In most browsers, 16 facets are used to generate the basic primitives, and that value, coupled with smooth shading, results in fairly realistically curved models, rather than using 32 facet models, which, although increase realism, even in a flat-shaded pipeline, may cost more computationally to render. This problem, unfortunately, is not an easy one to solve, since so much is dependent on the user's perception of the objects within the scene.

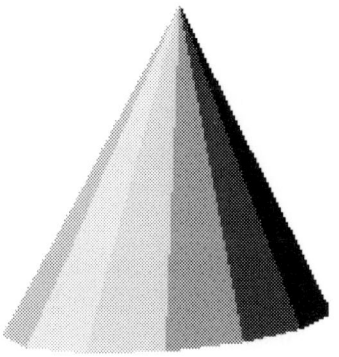 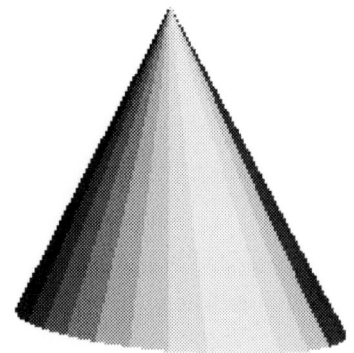

16-Facet Cone   32-Facet Cone

Figure 4.9: Flat-Shaded 16- and 32-Facet Cones

Controlling Points and Polygons

Out of the various "complex" geometrical nodes defined in the *VRML97 Specification*, `IndexedFaceSet` and `IndexedLineSet` may be the first ones that the content creator is interested in, since they allow you to create arbitrary three-dimensional models. This is of particular note if the content creator is used to using 3D modelling tools or CAD packages. Therefore, we shall deal with these two nodes in their own section, and shall discuss the other, more specialized, nodes later.

IndexedFaceSet

The `IndexedFaceSet` node is most likely to be the first "complex" built-in VRML node that the budding world designer will encounter, as it allows you to create arbitrary polygons from a set of given coordinates. This gives you complete power over exactly *how* an object is represented in three-dimensional space; you are now no longer at the mercy of what the browser author deemed to be a good idea. Suppose we have a cylinder modelled with 16 facets, *e.g.*, as shown in Figure 4.3, we might find that a world that heavily uses the `Cylinder` node runs appallingly slowly. Therefore, we would rather have our

Cylinders constructed with eight facets instead of 16, since that halves the number of polygons in the scene. Great idea, but, sorry, it's not possible. The content creator simply does not have that level of control over what the browser renders regarding the basic built-in VRML nodes.

However, one way, albeit painstakingly slow, is to construct a cylinder using the IndexedFaceSet node.

The more usual and less pathological case for using the IndexedFaceSet node is where we wish to construct a shape that is *not* representable with the built-in primitives, *e.g.*, a hexcone, a humanoid or an aircraft.

The following example shows a simple IndexedFaceSet that constructs a pyramid.

```
#VRML V2.0 utf8
#
# Pyramid constructed from IndexedFaceSets
Transform {
  children [
    Shape {
      appearance Appearance {
        material Material {
          diffuseColor 1 1 1
        }
      }
      geometry IndexedFaceSet {
        coord Coordinate {
          point [ 0 0 0,
                  1 0 0,
                  1 0 -1,
                  0 0 -1,
                  0.5 0.5 -0.5 ]
        }
        coordIndex [ 3, 2, 1, 0, -1,
                     0, 1, 4, -1,
                     1, 2, 4, -1,
                     2, 3, 4, -1,
                     3, 0, 4, -1 ]
      }
    }
  }
}
```

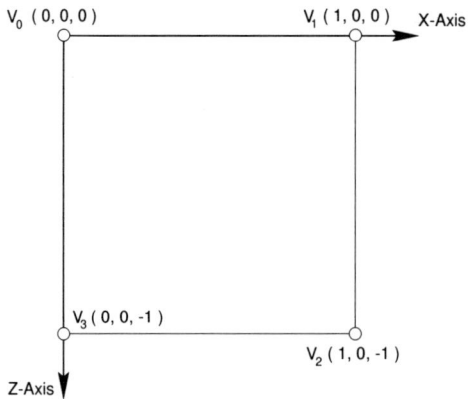

Figure 4.10: The `ccw` Field In Action!

```
        ]
    }
```

Now, in addition to being able to explicitly specify the points and polygon composition of our shapes, we can also do some other more interesting things. By now, you'll hopefully have loaded the pyramid scene up and wiggled it around a bit. If you walk into it, you'll find it suffers from the same problem as the basic built-in primitive nodes, in that, when viewed from the inside, you'll see nothing, because those polygons have been back-face culled. This isn't much use, especially if you've built a house, and people look through a door or a window only to see your living-room wall has gone missing!

One of the fields in `IndexedFaceSet` that we can now specify to request the renderer to *disable back-face culling on this object* is `solid`. The `solid` field defines whether or not the polygons defined in the `IndexedFaceSet` bound a volume completely or not. In the case of the pyramid they do, so the default setting of `solid TRUE` is fine. But in the case of our house, the polygons don't completely bound a volume, so by setting `solid` to `TRUE`, our living-room wall will reappear!

Another useful field that is contained within the `IndexedFaceSet` definition is that of `ccw`, which specifies the direction that vertices are defined in in the `coordIndex` field. If we look at Figure 4.10, we can see that if we specify the vertices in anti-clockwise order, *i.e.*, a `coordIndex` field of

```
coordIndex [ 0, 1, 2, 3 ]
```

then the face will be facing us. If we set **ccw** to be **FALSE**, then the vertex order will assume to be *clockwise*, which will cause the polygon to behave as if it was facing *away* from us, and, if **solid** is not set to **FALSE**, then the polygon will be back-face culled.[4]

To illustrate a final additional field, **creaseAngle**, that we may experiment with to enhance the geometry of the **IndexedFaceSet** node, we shall build a new scene containing a hexcone.

```
#VRML V2.0 utf8
#
# Hexcone. For demonstrating creaseAngle
Transform {
  children [
    Shape {
      appearance Appearance {
        material Material {
          diffuseColor 1 1 1
        }
      }
      geometry IndexedFaceSet {
        coord Coordinate {
          point [ 0 0 1,
                  0.866 0 0.5,
                  0.866 0 -0.5,
                  0 0 -1,
                  -0.866 0 -0.5,
                  -0.866 0 0.5,
                  0 2 0 ]
        }
        coordIndex [ 5, 4, 3, 2, 1, 0, -1,
                     0, 1, 6, -1,
                     1, 2, 6, -1,
                     2, 3, 6, -1,
                     3, 4, 6, -1,
                     4, 5, 6, -1,
                     5, 0, 6, -1 ]
```

---

[4]In actuality, the **ccw** field's effect is to reverse the order of vertices used to compute the polygon normal, which results in the normal being flipped 180deg on all axes.

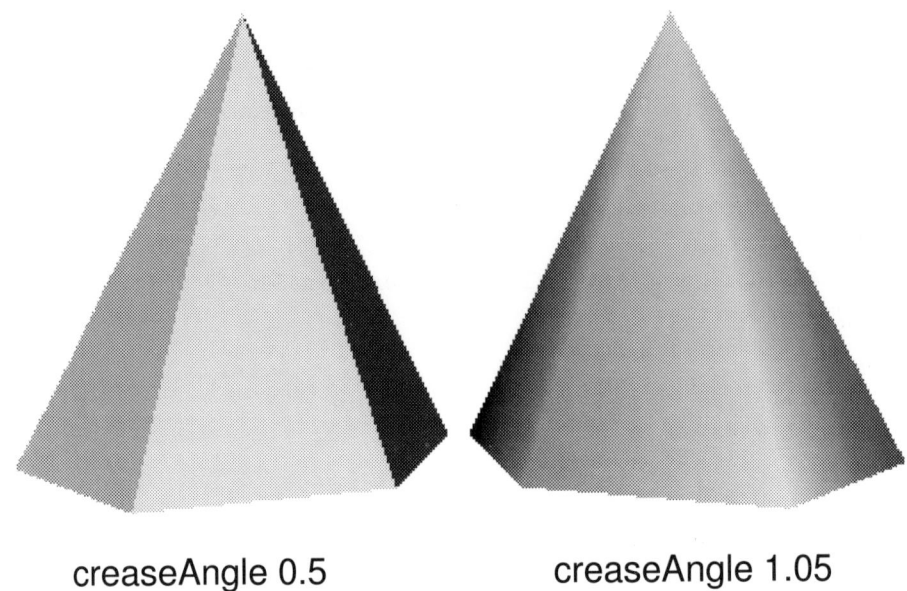

creaseAngle 0.5   creaseAngle 1.05

Figure 4.11: `creaseAngle` In Action

```
#               creaseAngle 0.5    # Uncomment for flat shading
#               creaseAngle 1.05   # Uncomment for smooth shading
            }
          }
        ]
      }
```

The `creaseAngle` field specifies the maximum angle at which the renderer should smooth-shade the adjacent faces to blend them together. An angle between adjacent faces of more than the value of the `creaseAngle` field will cause a visible crease to appear. The angle being tested against is the one between the polygon normals of the adjacent faces, and the `creaseAngle` field, when specified, may be used to automatically generate normals unless normals as explicitly specified in the `normal` field of the `IndexedFaceSet` node. Figure 4.11 shows the two renderings of the hexcone scene with the different `creaseAngle` settings.

IndexedLineSet

The `IndexedLineSet` node behaves in a similar way to the `IndexedFaceSet`, except it allows us to build wire-frame models instead of solid models. For example, our pyramid example from above as an `IndexedLineSet` node would read as follows:

```
#VRML V2.0 utf8
#
# Pyramid constructed from an IndexedLineSet
Transform {
  children [
    Shape {
      appearance Appearance {
        material Material {
          diffuseColor 1 1 1
        }
      }
      geometry IndexedLineSet {
        coord Coordinate {
          point [ 0 0 0, 1 0 0, 1 0 -1, 0 0 -1,
                  0.5 0.5 -0.5 ]
        }
        coordIndex [ 3, 2, 1, 0, -1,
                     0, 1, 4, -1,
                     1, 2, 4, -1,
                     2, 3, 4, -1,
                     3, 0, 4, -1 ]
      }
    }
  ]
}
```

which is pretty much identical except for the node type changing. It should be noted that the additional fields of `ccw`, `creaseAngle`, `convex`[5] and `solid` do not apply to `IndexedLineSet` nodes.

Wire frame is still an extremely useful rendering pipeline to use, especially if used cunningly in conjunction with the `LOD` node, since it is far faster than any

---

[5] We shall discuss the `convex` field below.

of the filled polygon pipelines, and can produce some desirable performance boosts.

Some Thoughts On `Indexed{Face,Line}Set` Optimization

A common line of discussion regarding `IndexedFaceSet` and `IndexedLineSet` nodes regards their efficiency, and in what cases performance drags can occur through poor use of them.

Vertex Sharing

Automatic *vertex sharing* is a technique used by several rendering engines nowadays to automatically detect whether or not a vertex has already been defined in a scene, prior to adding it into the scene. If the vertex already exists, then a pointer[6] is returned to that existing vertex, otherwise a new vertex is created. In an example of a badly crafted `IndexedFaceSet` or `IndexedLineSet`, we aim to define a cube as being comprised of six polygons, but, instead of adding eight vertices and joining them up to define polygons, we shall define four vertices per face.

```
#VRML V2.0 utf8
#
# An example of how *not* to build a cube
Transform {
    children [
        Shape {
            appearance Appearance {
                material Material {
                    diffuseColor 1 1 1
                 }
            }
            geometry IndexedFaceSet {
                coord Coordinate {
                    point [ -0.5 -0.5 -0.5, # The base
                            -0.5 -0.5 0.5,
                            0.5 -0.5 0.5,
```

---

[6]By pointer, we don't mean this in a C "pointer" or Java "reference" way. We just mean the renderer lets you know where the original is.

```
                                  0.5 -0.5 -0.5,
                                  -0.5 0.5 -0.5, # The top
                                  -0.5 0.5 0.5,
                                  0.5 0.5 0.5,
                                  0.5 0.5 -0.5,
                                  -0.5 -0.5 0.5, # Left side
                                  -0.5 0.5 0.5,
                                  -0.5 0.5 -0.5,
                                  -0.5 -0.5 -0.5,
                                  -0.5 -0.5 -0.5, # Back
                                  -0.5 0.5 -0.5,
                                  0.5 0.5 -0.5,
                                  0.5 -0.5 -0.5,
                                  0.5 -0.5 0.5, # Front
                                  0.5 0.5 0.5,
                                  -0.5 0.5 0.5,
                                  -0.5 -0.5 0.5,
                                  0.5 -0.5 -0.5, # Right side
                                  0.5 0.5 -0.5,
                                  0.5 0.5 0.5,
                                  0.5 -0.5 0.5
                              ]
                  }
          coordIndex [ 3, 2, 1, 0, -1,       # The base
                       4, 5, 6, 7, -1,       # The top
                       8, 9, 10, 11, -1,   # Left side
                       12, 13, 14, 15, -1, # Back
                       16, 17, 18, 19, -1, # Front
                       20, 21, 22, 23, -1  # Right side
                     ]
              }
          }
      ]
  }
```

As you can see just from the length of the code, that this is probably not the most efficient way to build a cube! However, if vertex sharing was present in the renderer, then the addition of duplicate vertices *would not matter*. A renderer behaving in that way would be far more tolerant of poorly specified **IndexedFaceSets** or **IndexedLineSets**. This example may seem rather pathological, but imagine a world constructed with many cubes defined in this manner.[7] Now, imagine calculating 16 duplicate vertex transformations more *per cube* for each rendering. If we had 100 cubes, we would be doing 1600 unnecessary calculations per frame. And that's just on a model as simple as a cube!

To Separate, Or Not To Separate ...

The question here is whether or not it makes a difference in performance to specify polygons of `IndexedFaceSet`s or `IndexedLineSet`s as separate nodes. The answer to this question can be quite a difficult one to adhere to since, as with many things in software, the benchmarks are rather difficult to reproduce. The fundamental issues can be separated down into RAM usage and bounding box optimization.

RAM Usage Specifying a model in the form of one `IndexedFaceSet` or of one `IndexedLineSet` node *per polygon* has the effect of creating far more nodes in the scene graph than if we had specified all the polygons in a single node. This could conceivably cause fairly large problems in the cases where we are attempting to load either large, high-polygon models or lots of smaller models in a single scene.

Bounding Box Optimization Specifying a model in the form of one `IndexedFaceSet` or `IndexedLineSet` node *per polygon* could be beneficial if the renderer practises bounding box culling, as discussed above. In this case, the model can be culled very cheaply at a polygon level, speeding the rendering process up fairly dramatically. On large models, in terms of the amount of space occupied in the world, this can produce fairly beneficial speed increases. This also helps when models are very close to the current camera in the scene, *i.e.*, the model fills a good proportion of the viewport, since a high percentage of the polygons in the model are likely to lie outwith the view frustum.[8]

So, to conclude, in some cases it may be beneficial to split each polygon into a separate node whilst, in others, it will perhaps cause performance problems!

---

[7]This is especially the case with many modelling tools, which do not optimize their VRML output into VRML built-in primitives, but export everything as large `IndexedFaceSet`s or `IndexedLineSet`s. Fortunately, this tide is turning.

[8]Unless we're looking at a large model end-on, at which point we are back to testing each polygon, which is not much worse than the usual case.

Helping the Renderer

An additional field that is sometimes specified in the `IndexedFaceSet` node is that of `convex`. The `convex` field specifies whether or not all the polygons in the node are *convex*, and if so, the renderer may perform optimizations. If nothing is known about the convexity of the polygons, the `convex` field should be set to `FALSE`.

Complex VRML Geometrical Nodes

The complex geometry nodes built into VRML2.0 are a fairly eclectic collection of shapes and effects and require a little more explanation, but, if used carefully, can produce some truly spectacular effects with little effort on the part of the content creator. We shall look at each of these nodes more closely.

ElevationGrid

An `ElevationGrid` is a succinct geometry node that describe a variable-height[9] array of coordinates and polygons between these coordinates.

What this basically means is that we have a grid of $x \times y$ points which are interconnected. If we alter the height of one of the points, it deforms the grid into producing a contour. If we alter the heights of a few more points in the `ElevationGrid`, we can build effects that resemble terrain or rippling water or a flapping flag.

We can illustrate this more clearly with an example and Figure 4.12 shows the output.

```
#VRML V2.0 utf8
#
# Basic ElevationGrid node
Viewpoint {
  position 14.8235, 16.2256, 31.7256
  orientation -0.910245 -0.120415 -0.396176 0.742914
  }

Transform {
  children [
```

---

[9]In the y-direction.

```
Shape {
  geometry ElevationGrid {
    xSpacing 2
    zSpacing 2
    xDimension 10
    zDimension 10
    height [
      0.3,  0.29, 0.47, 0.19, 0.32,
            0.13, 0.15, 0.38, 0.47, 0.17,
      0.06, 0.22, 0.3,  0.43, 0.32,
            0.15, 0.11, 0,    0.2,  0.46,
      0.08, 0.09, 0.23, 0.36, 0.21,
            0.41, 0.33, 0.4,  0.4,  0.47,
      0.37, 0.39, 0.11, 0.02, 0.14,
            0.05, 0.22, 0.13, 0.31, 0.04,
      0.33, 0.32, 0.33, 0.12, 0.17,
            0.26, 0.44, 0.04, 0.3,  0.45,
      0.33, 0.31, 0.47, 0.28, 0.03,
            0.33, 0.2,  0.31, 0.21, 0.19,
      0.21, 0.16, 0.42, 0.17, 0.13,
            0.16, 0.36, 0.49, 0.49, 0.03,
      0.41, 0.03, 0.1,  0.27, 0.35,
            0.47, 0.42, 0.35, 0.33, 0.01,
      0.3,  0.48, 0.33, 0.04, 0.28,
            0.45, 0.31, 0.4,  0.47, 0.13,
      0.22, 0.02, 0.38, 0.14, 0.32,
            0.44, 0.4,  0.33, 0.05, 0.44
    ]
  }
  appearance Appearance {
    material Material {
      diffuseColor 1 1 1
    }
  }
}
]
}
```

ElevationGrid nodes are absolutely excellent for producing fast, simple and usefully realistic terrain and landscape surfaces since the underlying polygon

Figure 4.12: An `ElevationGrid` Node

creation calculations are hidden to the content creator. This is of utmost relevance to GIS systems, where VRML could be used as a portable format between GIS systems, and other visualization systems.

A more potentially interesting use of the `ElevationGrid` node is to generate "wave" effects, by perturbing the heights of the vertices that comprise the grid by random values. We shall take a closer look at VRML and behaviour in a later chapter.

Extrusion

The `Extrusion` is, in this writer's opinion, the most complex and powerful built-in primitive the VRML Specification has to offer. It provides the capability to construct and manipulate completely free-form shapes, based on stretching, twisting, bending and tapering objects. To explain the separate possibilities more clearly, we shall resurrect our previous example of a hexcone, except in this case we only require the hexagonal base to work with.

The `Extrusion` node defines a field called `crossSection` which we use to define the 2D shape, in the XZ plane, that we plan on manipulating, in our

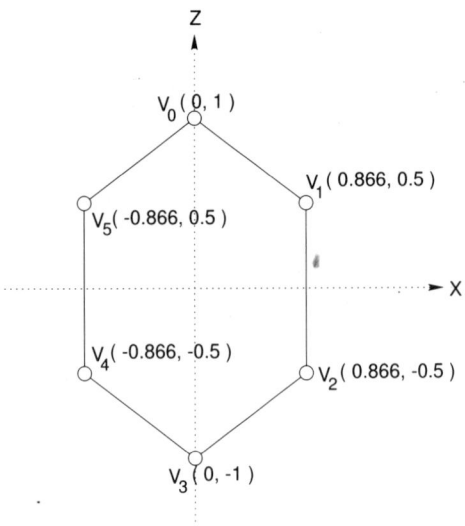

Figure 4.13: A Hexagonal `Extrusion` `crossSection`

case, the hexagon. Figure 4.13 shows the hexagon, with the calculated vertex positions. The corresponding `crossSection` would read

```
crossSection [ 0 1, 0.866 0.5, 0.866 -0.5,
               0 -1, -0.866 -0.5, -0.866 0.5, 0 1
           ]
```

"Stretching"

The simplest operation that we can achieve with the `Extrusion` node is to "stretch" the `crossSection` along the 3D curve specified in the `spine` field. For example, to stretch the hexagon into a hexoid shape, we can specify it as

```
#VRML V2.0 utf8
#
# A hexoid, created by Extrusion
Transform {
  children [
    Shape {
      appearance Appearance {
```

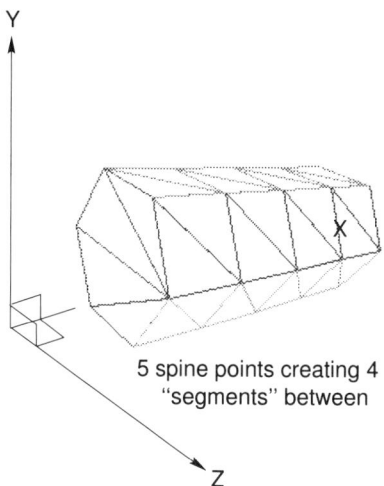

Figure 4.14: Hexagon Extruded Along A Straight Spine

```
          material Material {
            diffuseColor 1 1 1
            }
        }
      geometry Extrusion {
        crossSection [ 0 1, 0.866 0.5, 0.866 -0.5,
                       0 -1, -0.866 -0.5, -0.866 0.5, 0 1 ]
        spine [ 0 0 0, 1 0 0, 2 0 0, 3 0 0, 4 0 0 ]
        }
      }
    ]
  }
```

which can also be seen in Figure 4.14. What we have done here is *pull* the hexagon along the spine, and, at each spine point, a new hexagon is created and joined to the previous one.

The points in the **spine**, as you will have noticed, are specified in three dimensions, which implies that we can stretch shapes defined in the **crossSection** through tortuous hoops, if desired, as shown in Figure 4.15.

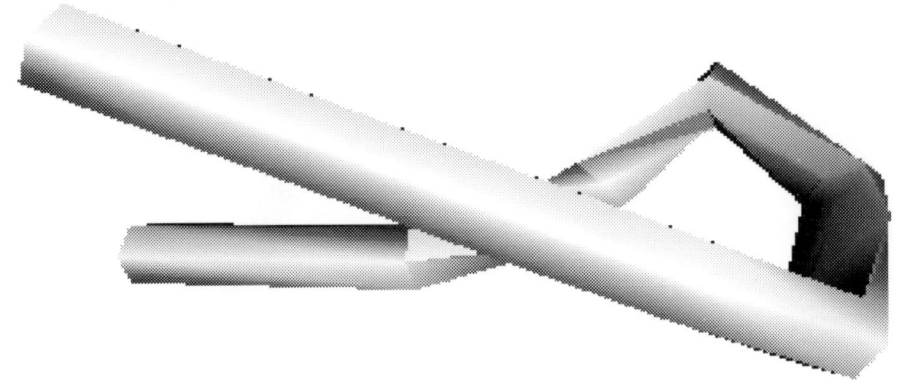

Figure 4.15: Hexagon Extruded Along A Twisted Spine

Now, this is all very well, but what about twisting and tapering objects? Easy! If we recall the concept of spine points that we discussed earlier, we find that we are allowed to apply an arbitrary rotation and/or an arbitrary scale *at each spine point*. This is a very important idea.

Tapering

Let's look at tapering our hexoid into a hexcone. We have specified five points in the `spine`, to which we can apply separate `scale` values as designated in the `scale` fields. The scalings are given as two-dimensional values, *i.e.*, they apply the scale to the `crossSection`. Thus, to produce a taper effect, we merely reduce the `scale` value at each scale point until the final point, which will be 0 0 if we wish to taper to a point. The number of values in the `scale` field should correspond to the number of points in the `spine`. This principle is illustrated in Figure 4.16, as is the resulting hexcone that the VRML listed below produces.

```
#VRML V2.0 utf8
#
# A hexcone, created by Extrusion
Transform {
  children [
    Shape {
```

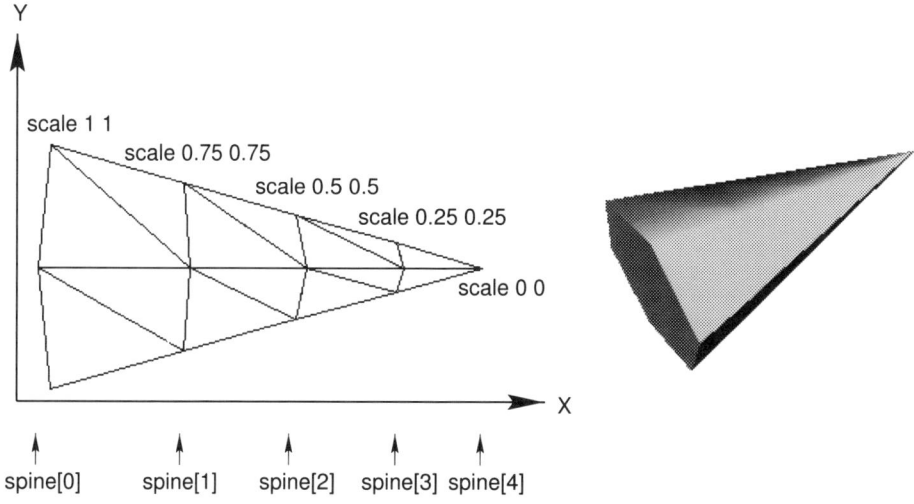

Figure 4.16: Hexagon Extruded Along A Straight Spine With Tapering

```
appearance Appearance {
  material Material {
    diffuseColor 1 1 1
    }
  }
geometry Extrusion {
  crossSection [ 0 1, 0.866 0.5, 0.866 -0.5, 0 -1,
                 -0.866 -0.5, -0.866 0.5, 0 1 ]
  spine [ 0 0 0, 1 0 0, 2 0 0, 3 0 0, 4 0 0 ]
  scale [ 1 1, 0.75 0.75, 0.5 0.5, 0.25 0.25, 0 0 ]
  creaseAngle 1.05
  }
 }
]
}
```

We can also use tapering in a way similar to that of a wood carver's *lathe*.[10]
All this basically is is pulling the **crossSection** along a straight spine, scaling each spine point as you go, to simulate the differing depths of the tool

---

[10]**lathe**[1] (leið) *n*. **1.** a machine for shaping, boring, facing or cutting a screw thread in metal, wood, etc., in which the workpiece is turned about a horizontal axis against a fixed tool. (*Collins English Dictionary*)

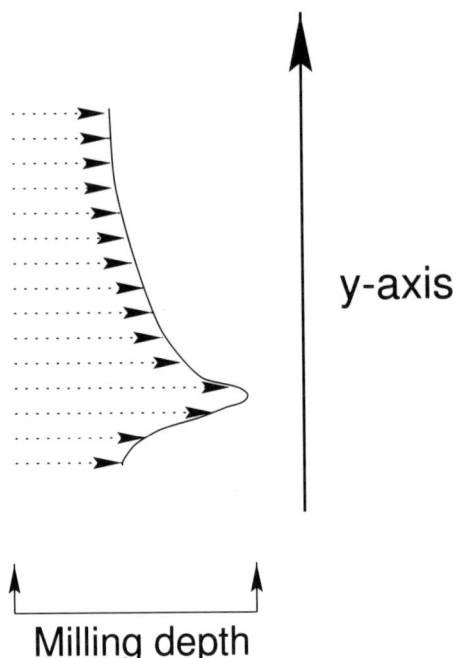

Figure 4.17: The Lathe Concept

against the surface being "milled".

The potter in Skara Brae sits down at his wheel every morning to throw pots. The wheel spins rapidly around, the potter shaping the clay delicately, not to disrupt and break the tenuous shape that is forming.

Figure 4.17 illustrates the principle, which is exactly the same as that of a lathe, albeit a tad messier.

Given that we have a straight spine, and that we know how many spine points there are on the pot's "outline" as seen in Figure 4.17, we can construct an `Extrusion` node to model that pot very quickly. Figure 4.18 shows the outline of the pot, the spine points and the required amount of scale we have to apply to each spine point to produce the effect we desire. This outline would translate into the following `Extrusion` node.

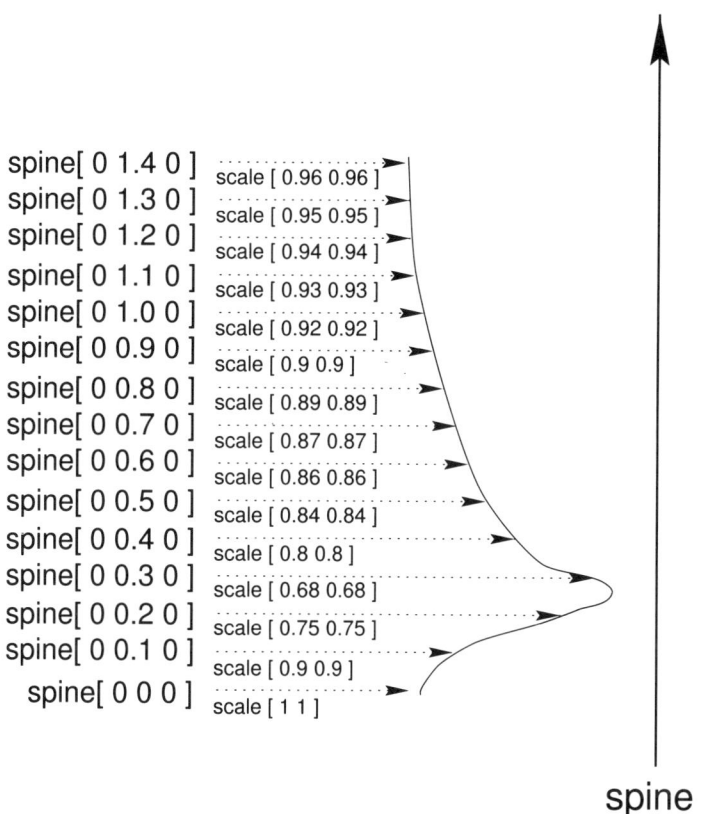

Figure 4.18: A Neolithic Pot with Lathe Values

```
#VRML V2.0 utf8
#
# A very rough Neolithic pot
Transform {
    children [
        Shape {
            geometry Extrusion {
                crossSection [
                    0 1, 0.866 0.5, 0.855 -0.5, 0 -1,
                    -0.866 -0.5, -0.866 0.5, 0 1
                ]
                spine [
                    0 0 0, 0 0.1 0, 0 0.2 0, 0 0.3 0,
                    0 0.4 0, 0 0.5 0, 0 0.6 0, 0 0.7 0,
                    0 0.8 0, 0 0.9 0, 0 1.0 0, 0 1.1 0,
                    0 1.2 0, 0 1.3 0, 0 1.4 0
                ]
                scale [
                    1 1, 0.9 0.9, 0.75 0.75, 0.68 0.68,
                    0.8 0.8, 0.84 0.84, 0.86 0.86, 0.87 0.87,
                    0.89 0.89, 0.9 0.9, 0.92 0.92, 0.93 0.93,
                    0.94 0.94, 0.95 0.95, 0.96 0.96
                ]
                creaseAngle 1.05
                beginCap TRUE
                endCap FALSE
                solid FALSE
            }
            appearance Appearance {
                material Material {
                    diffuseColor 1 1 1
                }
            }
        }
    ]
}
```

This pot, as you will see when you load it up and as shown in Figure 4.19, isn't particularly good. The potter was having an off-day. But, if you look at the points we have chosen along the outline of the pot, you can see why. Similarly, we only chose 15 spine points to model the pot, so the detail level would never

Figure 4.19: A Roughly Thrown Neolithic Pot

be particularly high. Use of some sort of line drawing tool is recommended here for calculating both accurate `scale` values, *i.e.*, the distance from the outline to the `spine`, and accurate `spine` values, *i.e.*, the distance along the `spine` of each `spine` point. The following VRML file is a far more realistic Neolithic pot, since it has far more `spine` points, and the `scale` values were calculated accurately. It also has a 16-segment `crossSection` field instead of the hexagonal `crossSection` of the roughly thrown pot above. You can see the results of this VRML in Figure 4.20.

```
#VRML V2.0 utf8
#
# Copyright (c)1997 Alligator Descartes <descarte@hermetica.com>
#
# Neolithic pot modelled with Extrusion node.
# 16 segment cross-section.
Transform {
    children [
        Shape {
            appearance Appearance {
```

Figure 4.20: A Well-Thrown Neolithic Pot

```
      material Material {
         diffuseColor 1 1 1
       }
      texture ImageTexture {
         url "terracotta01.jpg"
       }
      textureTransform TextureTransform {
         scale 1 1
       }
   }
geometry Extrusion {
   crossSection [
       1 0, 0.927184 0.374607, 0.71934 0.694658,
       0.406737 0.913545, 0.0348995 0.999391,
       -0.34202 0.939693, -0.669131 0.743145,
       -0.898794 0.438371, -0.997564 0.0697565,
       -0.951057 -0.309017, -0.766044 -0.642788,
       -0.469472 -0.882948, -0.104528 -0.994522,
       0.275637 -0.961262, 0.615661 -0.788011,
       0.866025 -0.5, 1 0
     ]
   spine [
```

```
                0 0.75 0, 0 0.56 0, 0 0.48 0, 0 0.41 0,
                0 0.35 0, 0 0.31 0, 0 0.27 0, 0 0.23 0,
                0 0.17 0, 0 0.11 0, 0 0.05 0, 0 0 0,
                0 -0.04 0, 0 -0.08 0, 0 -0.12 0, 0 -0.17 0,
                0 -0.23 0, 0 -0.30 0, 0 -0.36 0, 0 -0.41 0,
                0 -0.45 0, 0 -0.48 0, 0 -0.50 0, 0 -0.51 0,
                0 -0.53 0, 0 -0.55 0, 0 -0.57 0, 0 -0.59 0,
                0 -0.61 0, 0 -0.63 0, 0 -0.65 0, 0 -0.67 0,
                0 -0.69 0, 0 -0.71 0, 0 -0.72 0, 0 -0.73 0,
                0 -0.74 0, 0 -0.74 0, 0 -0.74 0, 0 -0.74 0,
                0 -0.74 0
            ]
        scale [
                1.17 1.17, 1.15 1.15, 1.14 1.14,
                1.13 1.13, 1.126 1.126, 1.123 1.123,
                1.11 1.11, 1.09 1.09, 1.08 1.08,
                1.07 1.07, 1.05 1.05, 1.03 1.03,
                1.01 1.01, 1.00 1.00, 0.98 0.98,
                0.95 0.95, 0.91 0.91, 0.86 0.86,
                0.81 0.81, 0.77 0.77, 0.73 0.73,
                0.70 0.70, 0.68 0.68, 0.66 0.66,
                0.64 0.64, 0.62 0.62, 0.61 0.61,
                0.60 0.60, 0.59 0.59, 0.60 0.60,
                0.60 0.60, 0.61 0.61, 0.63 0.63,
                0.60 0.60, 0.54 0.54, 0.47 0.47,
                0.39 0.39, 0.30 0.30, 0 0, 0 0, 0 0, 0 0
            ]
        creaseAngle 1.05
        beginCap FALSE
        endCap TRUE
        solid FALSE
        }
    }
  ]
}
```

Twisting

Twisting objects is just as easy as tapering them. The only difference here is that we specify the **orientation** field in place of the **scale** field, *i.e.*, at each

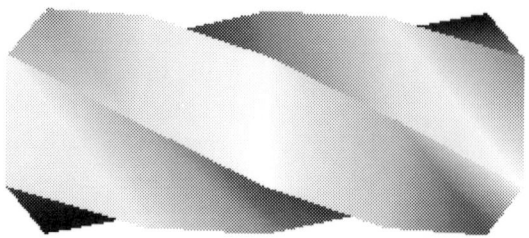

Figure 4.21: Hexagon Extruded Along A Straight Spine With Twisting

Figure 4.22: A Dutch Cheese

spine point, we specify the new orientation of the object, so, for example, to produce a twisted hexoid that looks like a loosely threaded screw, we could specify an `orientation` field of

```
orientation [ 1 0 0 0.52, 1 0 0 1.04, 1 0 0 1.56,
              1 0 0 2.08, 1 0 0 2.607 ]
```

in the VRML listed above in the tapering section. This would produce an object similar to Figure 4.21.

"Surfaces of Revolution"

The "surface of revolution" concept is similar to that of lathing objects, except, instead of spinning a conceptual solid block around an axis quickly whilst applying a milling tool against it, as happens with lathing, we take the outline of the object and spin it around the spine causing a solid object to be formed. To help visualize this process, imagine a Dutch cheese, as shown in

Figure 4.22. This cheese is formed not by a cheesification-of-milk process as you may have imagined, no! What actually happens is that we take a cheese outline, as shown in Figure 4.22, and revolve that outline around an axis for 360deg, or, in the case of the cheese in Figure 4.22, 290deg. The resulting solid object is formed by the "surface of revolution" principle.

This is fairly similar in theory to the lathing idea we explored above, but differs in terms of the form that we can produce more complex shapes in with this technique. Unfortunately, there is also an exponential increase in difficulty in generating the shapes!

The potter, one day, decides he's made more than enough pots for people to store food, objects, fish and knick-knacks in, and, beginning to worry about how he shall continue his livelihood, tries his hand at throwing a pottery drinking goblet. This fails dismally since the technique for throwing pots and the technique for making a goblet are quite different, although, in principle, very similar.

If we look at Figure 4.23, you will see a drinking goblet, and the outline used to create it with a surface of revolution. Now, this goblet is quite special in that the bottom of the cup of the goblet is not basically the flip-side of the outside of the goblet. The cup is actually *thick*, which adds realism to the object.[11] Now, if we used the milling concept from above by scaling each `spine` point in the model, we would not be able to create the goblet in the form that we require. We would only be able to create a "hollow" object, in which we could see down into the stem. The cup would have no bottom. This is where the surface of revolution concept comes into its own. Unfortunately, building a surface of revolution is slightly more complicated than the neat trick we used for lathing surfaces before. In this case, we have to build a complex `crossSection` in the form of the outline we wish to revolve, then stretch that outline along a circular `spine`. For example, if we take the default `crossSection` of a square, and apply that to a hexagonal spine,[12] we will get a hexagonal drum object, rather like our hexoid above. The code to build this object is given below:

```
#VRML V2.0 utf8
#
```

---

[11]To demonstrate this, load up a neolithic pot model and spin it until you can see the fact that the sides of the bowl are actually paper-thin!

[12]An incredibly rough approximation of a circle!

Figure 4.23: A Drinking Goblet

```
# Surface of revolution used to form a hexagonal ''drum''
Transform {
    children [
        Shape {
            geometry Extrusion {
                spine [
                    0 0 1, 0 0.855 0.5, 0 0.855 -0.5, 0 0 -1,
                    0 -0.866 -0.5, 0 -0.866 0.5, 0 0 1
                    ]
            }
            appearance Appearance {
                material Material {
                    diffuseColor 1 1 1
                }
            }
        }
    ]
}
```

Further Notes on Extrusion

Some final points concerning the Extrusion node as a whole regard the use of the ccw, convex, creaseAngle and solid fields, which operate in the same way as defined for IndexedFaceSet.

There are, however, two fields specific to the Extrusion node, being beginCap and endCap. These two fields are Boolean and indicate whether or not a cap should be affixed to the given "end" of the Extrusion. These fields behave in the same way as the capping fields previously discussed in the Cylinder node. It should also be noted that if we remove a cap from the Extrusion, then look into it, it will produce an effect similar to that shown in Figure 4.5, but unlike in the Cylinder node, we can specify solid FALSE, which will stop back-face culling occurring!

PointSet

The PointSet node allows the content creator to construct a set of the points in three-dimensional space. This is also known as a *point cloud* in some circles.

Point clouds are not particularly useful for rendering, since it is wellnigh impossible to fathom out what shape is represented by the point cloud. However, point clouds can be useful for graph plotting and other data visualization needs, since they could be used to plot three-dimensional scatter graphs, especially in light of the fact that points in a PointSet node can be arbitrarily coloured. This facility enables us to draw convincing graphs quite easily.

Text

The Text node allows the content creator to easily place textual strings into a VRML world. The polygons that the rendered text comprises are automatically two-sided and are flat, *i.e.*, are not "solid" three-dimensional objects. The content-creator has a fairly wide range of control over the overall style that the Text node will use to render text, in that the actual font typeface, language, spacing, justification, direction and more can be configured through a subsidiary node called the FontStyle node. The actual layout rules for the FontStyle node are carefully described in the *VRML97 Specification*, and are not worth reproducing here.

Figure 4.24: A Trilithon

PROTO Nodes

VRML2.0, although fairly powerful with careful usage of the built-in geometry nodes, allows the content creator to arbitrarily extend the language by
defining *prototype*s. A prototype node, or PROTO, can be likened to a member
of a library of shapes which the content creator may dip into at any point, using and reusing the same component parts to create new and different worlds.
In essence, PROTOs are no different to the built-in nodes, and are subject to
exactly the same grammar and syntax. The only real difference is that they
have not been formally specified, and therein lies the power of VRML2.0, as
a scene description language.

The understanding of PROTO nodes lies in the knowledge that, during the
parsing phase of the VRML scene being loaded, each node is defined when
the parser correctly parses it. In the case of built-in nodes, such as Box or
Transform, some internal code that builds the definition of the node is executed. In the case of PROTOs, the URL referring to the file in which the PROTO

is defined is read, and the VRML in that is parsed as per the built-in nodes. This concept is central to the principle we discussed above, because nodes are infinitely reusable.

At our neolithic village of Skara Brae, the villagers, after having a particularly good season of having no foul weather, decided to erect a ritual monument. Being neolithic, the monument is planned to take the shape of four massive trilithon structures with a central pillar of stone. The local astronomer-priest was consulted as to the building plan, and it was eventually decided that they would erect *one* trilithon and base the other ones on that design. The central pillar would be added at the end, once the really heavy work had been completed. This plan met with general approval, and work on the first trilithon proceeded apace.

After a period of five years, the first trilithon was erected (Figure 4.24), and the villagers decided that the plan was sound. Unfortunately, none of the villagers could be bothered spending another 15 or so years finishing the monument.[13] The monument fell into disrepair, and after a few more years, collapsed and was consumed by the earth.

Many years later, a wise man visited the village, bringing with him a miraculous mould which, if you poured in molten stone, would create exact replicas of trilithons in a matter of days! The villagers were overjoyed, and in the space of two weeks had erected their monument.

And so it is with reusable PROTOs and rekeying pages of text. If we have a look at the basic trilithon VRML, we can see that to rekey that four times would be extremely tedious, error-prone and would increase the size of the VRML file being passed across the network. It would also lengthen parsing times for the file, for, instead of a PROTO node being parsed once, and once only, no matter how many times it is reused, the trilithon code would have to be repeatedly reparsed, even if only a **translation** field was different between each trilithon.

```
#VRML V2.0 utf8
#
# Rudimentary trilithon
PROTO trilithon [] {
  Transform {
```

---

[13]This accounts for the lack of megalithic remains around Skara Brae.

```
children [
  ### The left-hand side pillar
  Transform {
    translation 0 1.25 0
      children [
        Shape {
          appearance DEF STONE Appearance {
            material Material {
              diffuseColor 0.4375 0.5 0.5625
            }
          }
          geometry Box {
            size 1.3 2.5 1
          }
        }
      ]
  }
  ### The right-hand side pillar
  Transform {
    translation 2 1.25 0
    children [
      Shape {
        appearance USE STONE
        geometry Box {
          size 1.3 2.5 1
        }
      }
    ]
  }
  ### The lintel stone
  Transform {
    translation 1 2.75 0
    children [
      Shape {
        appearance USE STONE
        geometry Box {
          size 3.55 0.6 1.1
        }
      }
    ]
```

```
            }
          ]
        }
      }
```

As can be seen, the trilithon is fairly short, but then it is a very simple node. If we had modelled it using a modelling tool, it could have run for several more pages. Imagine rekeying that each time!

The important line to note in the above listing is

```
      PROTO trilithon [] {
```

which states that this VRML represents a node called `trilithon`, and that each use of the node in an external VRML file should result in the code contained within that node being substituted in. This statement has a corollary in the file which wishes to use the PROTO node in EXTERNPROTO, which specifies the URL of the PROTO node, *e.g.*, the scene that represents the entire ritual monument looks like this:

```
#VRML V2.0 utf8
#
# A basic circular arrangement of trilithons
# with a central pillar

EXTERNPROTO trilithon [] "trilithon.wrl"

Transform {
  children [
    ### The four trilithons at the
    ### cardinal points
    Transform {
      translation 10 0 0
      rotation 0 1 0 1.57
      children trilithon {
       }
    }
    Transform {
      translation 0 0 10
      children trilithon {
       }
    }
```

```
Transform {
  translation -10 0 0
  rotation 0 1 0 -1.57
  children trilithon {
   }
 }
Transform {
  translation 0 0 -10
  children trilithon {
   }
 }
### A central pillar
Transform {
  translation 0 1.5 0
  children Shape {
    appearance Appearance {
      material Material {
        diffuseColor 1 1 1
       }
     }
    geometry Cylinder {
      radius 0.25
      height 3
     }
   }
 }
### Disc the scene sits on
Transform {
  children Shape {
    appearance Appearance {
      material Material {
        emissiveColor 0.5 0.85 0.5
       }
     }
    geometry Cylinder {
      bottom FALSE
      side FALSE
      radius 12
      height 0.01
     }
```

Figure 4.25: A Megalithic Setting Of Four Trilithons

```
        }
      }
    ]
  }
```

As you can see, the **EXTERNPROTO** line matches the **PROTO** line. A rendering of this scene can be seen in Figure 4.25, to help you visualize what the VRML is doing.

However, this leads nicely on to a more complex use of **PROTO** nodes, in that we can set fields within a node, just as we can set field values in the built-in nodes. For example, if we wanted to be able to set the size of the lintel stone, then we would specify the **PROTO** and **EXTERNPROTO** lines as:

```
PROTO trilithon [ field SFVec3f lintelSize 3.55 0.6 1.1 ]
EXTERNPROTO trilithon [ field SFVec3f lintelSize ]
                "trilithon.wrl"
```

Again, note carefully that the node definitions match. The value specified in the PROTO definition is the *default* value that is given to that field if you decide not to specify one. Now, this leads us to another problem. How do we use these defined fields? Well, in exactly the same way as we would use fields in built-in nodes. Instead of referencing a trilithon as:

```
trilithon {}
```

we can refer to it using the field as:

```
trilithon {
  lintelSize 4.5 1 1.1
}
```

which would create us a new trilithon with a much bigger lintel. Or would it? Well, no. It wouldn't. And, it wouldn't because we haven't actually *used* the value of the parameter anywhere. VRML does not automatically read your mind and build scenes accordingly, you need to *tell* it where to use that value. This brings us to a keyword in the VRML syntax which, like PROTO and EXTERNPROTO, does not define a node. The keyword in question is IS. The IS keyword associates the value of a field given in the PROTO with a field *within the* PROTO *code itself.* For example, to actually use the lintelSize field in the PROTO definition of our trilithon node, we would change the line in the lintel definition that declared the size as

```
Transform {
  translation 1 2.75 0
  children [
    Shape {
      appearance USE STONE
      geometry Box {
        size 3.55 0.6 1.1
      }
    }
  ]
}
```

to

```
Transform {
  translation 1 2.75 0
  children [
    Shape {
```

```
      appearance USE STONE
      geometry Box {
        size IS lintelSize
       }
     }
   ]
 }
```

which would set the field `size` to the value of the field specified in the `PROTO` definition. Again, note that if the field `lintelSize` *hadn't* been specified, then the default value would have been used, even if we had defined another value somewhere for the lintel size in the `PROTO`.

As you can see, using `PROTO` nodes is a powerful way of building modular objects which can be used many times, in many places, without causing overcomplication and bloating in VRML scenes.

Chapter 5

The Illusion of Reality

"**Socrates:** *And if he similarly asked what colour is, and you answered whiteness, and the questioner rejoined, Would you say that whiteness is colour or a colour? you would reply, A colour, because there are other colours as well.* "

Plato, *Meno*

We have now discussed all the geometrical aspects of building VRML scenes, but, certain things are still lacking from the worlds we build: colour, texture, lighting and atmosphere.

Our worlds up until this point have looked fairly drab in shades of white, albeit very nicely shaded white, but unless we're modelling snowscapes for a living, we might want to splash a little bit of colour about. This section will tell you how to get the most for your money regarding colouring the world.

We shall also be discussing the topics of atmospheric effects using the `Fog` node, multiple camera positioning using the `Viewpoint` node, background texturing with the `Background` node and giving hints to the renderer with the `NavigationInfo` node.

To finish off, we shall examine lighting in the world using the lighting nodes defined in the *VRML97 Specification*.

Appearances Can Be Deceptive

The `Appearance` node in VRML is the way in which we add colour and textures to objects. The node itself is quite simple, since it merely provides "hooks" to other more complex property definitions, *e.g.*, the `Material` node which allows you to specify various colour effects and properties, a texture node (`ImageTexture`, `MovieTexture` or `PixelTexture`) which specifies a texture map to apply to the object, and a `TextureTransform` node which allows you to scale and rotate the specified texture.

We shall look more closely at each of these types of `Appearance` properties.

Splashing Colour Around

Adding colour to a scene makes an immediate and immense difference. It adds highlights to objects, gives depth and, most importantly, looks far more interesting and realistic. Of course, that's if you do it properly! Adding colour without much forethought is rather like decorating your house without thinking about the effects of contrast and blending neighbouring colours. However, if you want psychedelic, we can do that too!

Colour in VRML is added to objects by specifying a `Material` node within an `Appearance` node which is applied to the object. In the case of basic VRML primitives, such as `Box`, `Cone` and so on, the colour is applied across the entire object uniformly. However, in the case of the more complex VRML primitives, such as `IndexedFaceSet` and `ElevationGrid`, we can apply a technique known as *per vertex colouring*, which means that a separate colour may be applied to each vertex in the primitive, and that the space between the vertices is coloured with an interpolated value. We shall discuss per vertex colouring more extensively below.

"Solid" Colouring

"Solid" colouring is the simplest way of adding colour into a scene, but is not, in itself, simple. There are several "types" of colour that can be applied to an object, depending on the effect that you wish to produce. We shall look at each type of colouring in detail.

Diffuse Colour

The `diffuseColor` is generally regarded as being the colour reflected by a surface, which, depending on the angle of the light to that surface, will darken and lighten accordingly.

The diffuse component of the lighting equation is only one part of a complex set of algorithms for calculating realistic lighting effects, but is the most commonly implemented in rendering software.

Ambient Intensity

The `ambientIntensity` field of the `Material` node is used to indicate the quantity of light from the scene that is to be reflected from the object to which the `Material` is attached. To allow the object to be coloured with the colour specified in the `diffuseColor` field, the `ambientIntensity` field should be specified as `1.0`, which is the default. To "dull" an object, or "mute" its colour, you can reduce the `ambientIntensity`. The *ambient colour* can be calculated from the equation of `ambientIntensity` $\times$ `diffuseColor`.

Emissive Colour

The `emissiveColor` is the colour that an object *emits* and can be used to modify the final colour seen by the viewer after the diffuse colour and any textures are combined. The emissive colour of an object is displayed irrespective of lighting in the scene. It is extremely useful for applying colour to objects that are themselves light sources, *e.g.*, the sun or a light-bulb.

Specular Colour

The `specularColor` field of the `Material` node specifies the colour of the highlights on an object, as generated by the environmental lighting effects.

Shininess

The `shininess` field of the `Material` node specifies the intensity of the specular highlights. For example, a high `shininess` value will produce sharp highlights, for example, those reflected off metallic or plastic surfaces, whereas lower shininess values will produced a more "glowing" highlight, as on dull or burnished metal, matt varnished woods or other organics.

Transparency

The `transparency` field of the `Material` node specifies the opacity of an object, *i.e.*, how "solid" it looks to the viewer. The `transparency` field can be effectively used to simulate glassy surfaces,[1] "ghostly" apparitions and clouds.

Per Vertex Colouring

We touched on per vertex colouring earlier, in that it is a technique of applying colour to an object non-uniformly. To illustrate the concept more clearly, Figure 5.1 shows an `IndexedFaceSet` with four vertices laid out in the shape of a square. We have applied the colour *red* (1 0 0) to vertex 1, the colour *green* (0 1 0) to vertex 2 and vertex 4 and, finally, the colour *blue* (0 0 1) to vertex 3. Here, the red blends towards green in the middle, since

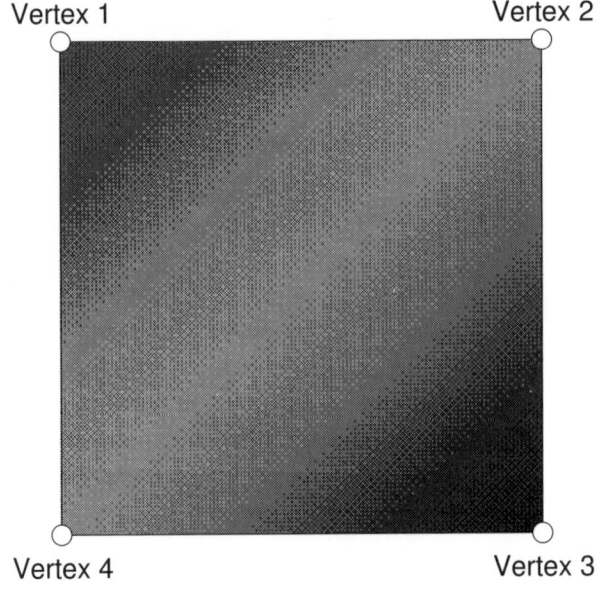

Figure 5.1: Per Vertex Colouring Of An `IndexedFaceSet`

there are two green vertices running diagonally across the polygon, and then it blends towards blue in the bottom right corner. Therefore, each colour

---

[1]In conjunction with `shininess` and `specularColor` values.

on each vertex exerts a "pull" towards its colour, which causes variance in the pixel colour. The VRML that produced the effect in Figure 5.1 is listed below.

```
#VRML V2.0 utf8
#
# Fiddles with per vertex colouring
Transform {
  children [
    Shape {
      appearance Appearance {
        material Material {
          diffuseColor 1 1 1
          }
        }
      geometry IndexedFaceSet {
        coord Coordinate {
          point [ 5 5 0, 5 -5 0, -5 -5 0, -5 5 0 ]
          }
        coordIndex [ 0, 1, 2, 3, -1 ]
        solid FALSE
        colorPerVertex TRUE
        color Color {
          color [ 0 1 0, 0 0 1, 0 1 0, 1 0 0 ]
          }
        }
      }
    ]
  }
```

More interesting effects can be produced if we increase the number of variables in the colour blending process, *i.e.*, we add more vertices to the object being colourized. The ElevationGrid node is perfect for this sort of deranged behaviour, simply because it automatically creates a lot of vertices for you. Of course, we don't need to use the contour producing functionality of the ElevationGrid node at all, we're merely wanting its usefulness at producing vertices.

Figure 5.2 shows a more psychedelic usage of per vertex colouring. We have applied a random colour value to each vertex in the ElevationGrid node, which then causes this chaotic splash of colour. The example code for this can be found on the CD-ROM, and is pretty much identical to the example above, except we use a 10×10 `ElevationGrid` node instead of an `IndexedFaceSet`. In a later chapter, we shall look at ways in which we can produce more unusual

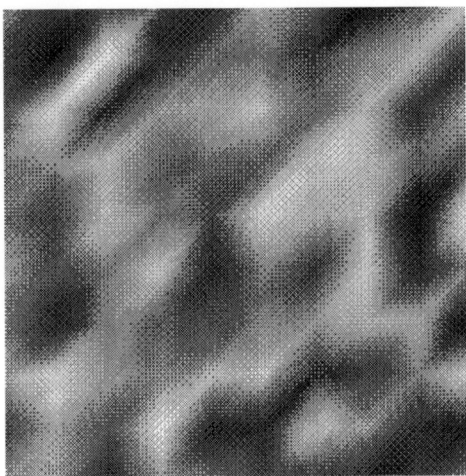

Figure 5.2: Random Per Vertex Colouring Of An `ElevationGrid`

special effects using colour *via* the powerful `Script` node extensions.

Texturing

Texture mapping, as discussed in Chapter 2, is a tremendously important aspect of building good scenes. The potential uses for texture mapping are immense, as are the drawbacks if it is done incorrectly.

There are three different types of texturing available in VRML2.0, which we shall take a more in-depth look at separately.

ImageTexture

`ImageTexture` will most probably be the most common type of texturing used in VRML scenes since it represents an image in a standard format that can be texture-mapped onto the object in question.[2] The image is fetched

---

[2] By standard format, we mean GIF, JPEG or PNG images.

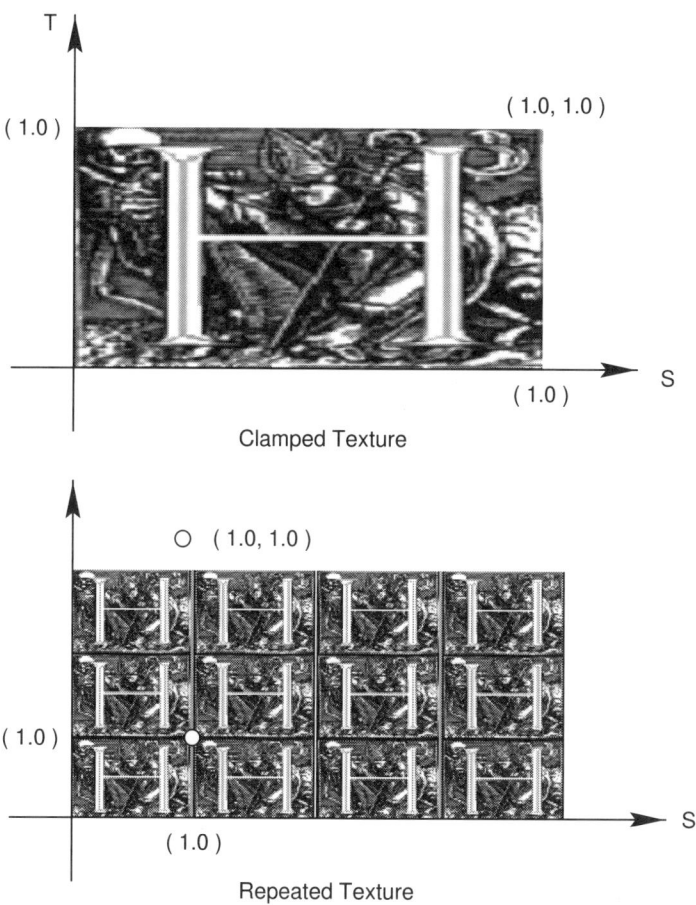

Figure 5.3: Clamped and Repeating Textures

from the URL specified in the `url` field. We may apply two other parameters to textures, being the `repeatS` and `repeatT` values, which specify the tiling behaviour of the texture across objects. For example, if we specify `repeatS` to be `TRUE`, as is the default, then the texture will repeat in the S direction across the object until the whole object is textured. If `repeatS` is set to `FALSE`, then the texture coordinates are *clamped*, or stretched to be in the $(0,0)$ to $(1,1)$ range. Figure 5.3 illustrates the principle. We have a single rectangular `IndexedFaceSet` node, which has the texture co-ordinates marked on it. If we were to apply our texture to the image with `repeatS` equal to `TRUE`, we would get the result shown in the top diagram. With `repeatS` set to `FALSE`, we will see the effect in the lower diagram. Some example code to texture-map a square polygon with a non-repeating texture follows.

```
#VRML V2.0 utf8
#
# Example showing a non-repeating texture applied to a
# square polygon
Transform {
    children [
        Shape {
            geometry IndexedFaceSet {
                coord Coordinate {
                    point [
                        0 0 0, 10 0 0, 10 10 0, 0 10 0
                    ]
                }
                coordIndex [ 0, 1, 2, 3, -1 ]
                texCoord TextureCoordinate {
                    point [ 0 0, 0.5 0, 0.5 0.5, 0 0.5 ]
                }
                texCoordIndex [ 0, 1, 2, 3, -1 ]
            }
            appearance Appearance {
                material Material {
                    diffuseColor 1 1 1
                }
                texture ImageTexture {
                    url "holbeinH.gif"
                    repeatS FALSE
                }
                textureTransform TextureTransform {
```

```
                    scale 4 4
                  }
              }
          }
      ]
  }
```

The same effects apply to setting `repeatT` as with `repeatS`, except that the axis in the texture map that operations are applied to changes.

Textures can be further distorted by using a `TextureTransform` value in the `Material` node that contains the current `ImageTexture` node.

MovieTexture

The `MovieTexture` node is one of the more sophisticated nodes described in the *VRML97 Specification*, in that it allows content creators to play video clips on to the surfaces of objects, in place of static graphical texture maps. This can be used to fairly stunning effect, for example, if someone wanted to model a television set playing live streaming video. The `MovieTexture` node is described in exactly the same way as the `ImageTexture` node, in that the URL of the video clip to play is specified in the `url` field. However, there are some additional fields particular to the `MovieTexture` node that control various aspects of the video playback.

The simplest of the fields specific to the `MovieTexture` node is the rather obviously named `SFBool loop FALSE` field, which informs the browser, when the video clip finishes, whether or not it should replay it from the beginning or not.

Another important field for content creators will be the field entitled `SFFloat speed 1`, which regulates the speed of playback of the video clip. For example, the default speed of 1 implies the video clip will play back at the speed at which it was recorded; a speed of 2 implies the video will play back at double the speed at which it was recorded. In reality, video clips can be recorded at speeds of up to 30 frames per second, which would imply that our rendering engine would need to be rendering the VRML scene at 30 frames per second also to ensure the `MovieTexture` node is playing at its correct speed. To manage double-speed playback, we would need to achieve 60 frames per second, which is a quite unimaginable speed unless we have an extremely powerful processor, lots of RAM and a hardware-accelerated graphics card! And for this calculation, we are assuming that the cost of decoding the video clip is nil! Therefore, our maximum video playback speed is realistically bounded by the speed at which our renderer can render the scene, unless the browser chooses to have "lossy video", *i.e.*, the video is decoded *faster* than it can be displayed, causing frames to "go missing". Similarly, a video can be given a negative speed, which implies that the video clip plays *backwards*. For example, a speed of -1 implies the video clip is played backwards at the speed at which it was recorded. Given that the supported video type required by the *VRML97 Specification* is MPEG-1, and this video format does not support reverse playback, this feature should not be relied upon.

Furthermore, the amount of resource, in terms of both processing power and memory, required by the `MovieTexture` node makes it a "luxury" node to include in your worlds. It can be used to glorious effect, but the inclusion of such a node may grind your worlds to a complete standstill.

PixelTexture

The `PixelTexture` node is one which allows the content creator to specify an image in terms of an `SFImage` field. The primary use for this node is to create "on-the-fly" images internally, instead of reading images from URLs. This node can provide rudimentary textural animation facilities, akin to GIF animation, as opposed to a true `MovieTexture` node.

The `SFImage` datatype represents a single uncompressed two-dimensional picture. Various colour models may be implemented by a `SFImage` node, and therefore we specify a set of information in the declaration of the field as to the size and colour model used by the `SFImage`. This field is declared as:

```
someImageField <width> <height> <num> <pixels>
```

To elaborate, the `width` and `height` values are specified as integer values, and represent the width and height of the image represented by the `SFImage` field. The `num` value informs us how many colour components there are *per pixel* in this image. The final field in the declaration contains the actual hexadecimal values representing each pixel. These values are decoded in the colour model specified by the `num` field, which can be interpreted as follows:

1. A single-byte component has a value between 0x00 and 0xFF, or 255. Therefore, a pixel value of 0xFF would indicate a full intensity *i.e.*,

white, and a pixel value of 0x00 would indicate no intensity, *i.e.*, black. A single-component SFImage is regarded as being greyscale.

2. A two-byte component can be interpreted as being an intensity contained in the first byte and an opacity, or transparency, value contained in the second byte. A two-byte component SFImage is a greyscale image.

3. A three-byte component can be interpreted as being an RGB triple, with the red component being contained in the first byte, the green component being contained in the second byte and the blue component specified in the third and final byte of each pixel value. Three-byte component SFImage fields are RGB coloured, but have no transparency capabilities.

4. A four-byte component can be interpreted as being an RGB triple, as discussed above, with an opacity value specified in the final byte. SFImages specified with four-byte pixel values have full RGB colouring and support transparency.

For example, an SFImage of a 1×2 dimensioned image of a white pixel followed by a black pixel would be specified as:

```
someSFImage 1 2 1 0xFF 0x00
```

A more complex SFImage would be a fully specified RGBA (red, green, blue, alpha—alpha is the opacity/transparency) texture which would be described as:

```
someSFImage 1 2 4 0xFF00FFFF 0x00FF007F
```

which would be an initial pixel fully opaque and coloured magenta, (255, 0, 255) and alpha value 0xFF, followed by a green half-transparent pixel, (0, 255, 0) with alpha 0x7F. A point to note carefully is that the image data specified in an SFImage field should be specified *upside-down*, *i.e.*, the bottommost scanline in the image should be listed first and the topmost scanline listed last.

At last! Illumination!

Now that we have discussed the various ways in which we can colour a scene, we should turn to the thornier topic of lighting the scene. Lighting can be used to completely alter the mood of a scene, hard white light can be used to convey an atmosphere of minimalism, softly toned diffuse and ambient light can produce feelings of relaxation. The effects of lighting in the real world are generally accepted, and the same precepts can be applied in our virtual worlds. Of course, lighting, like everything else, is a can of worms just waiting to be opened.

There are three different light nodes in VRML2.0, being `DirectionalLight`, `PointLight` and `SpotLight`. Most VRML browsers support the concept of a *headlight* mounted on the current user's "head", which provides light in the direction that the user is facing. Each type of light has subtly different properties, and can be used elegantly to produce a wide variety of effects.

A further bonus with lighting in VRML is that lights are subject to *transformations*, which means that we can apply motion to lights to produce spectacular effects, such as the sun rising, fireflies flitting around the sky or the flare from falling stars...

We shall discuss these advanced topics in Chapter 7.

PointLight

A `PointLight` provides a single light source from which light radiates in all directions. An excellent analogy for a `PointLight` is an unshielded lightbulb. Figure 5.4 illustrates the principle more clearly.

A `PointLight` node is designed for producing radiating light sources, *e.g.*, light-bulbs, flares, fires, the sun or even explosions! The possibilities are many.

As an example, we shall illuminate the megalithic setting that we created in the previous chapter with simulated sunrise and sunset. The sun acts as a mobile `PointLight`, which alters the lighting on the scene as the sun follows its path through the sky. Two images showing the different lighting effects cast onto the scene from different `PointLight` positions can be seen in Figure 5.5.

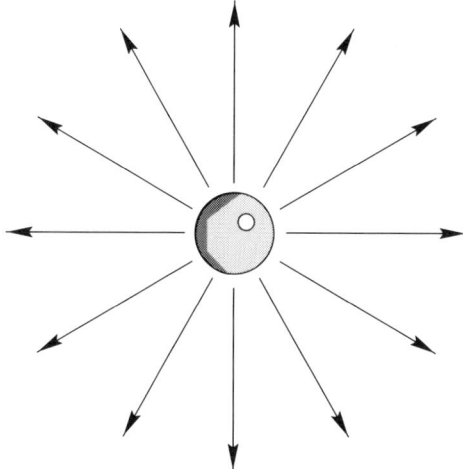

Figure 5.4: `PointLight`

DirectionalLight

A `DirectionalLight` provides ambient lighting flowing in a given direction, *i.e.*, it doesn't originate from any particular source *per se*, it just flows along parallel rays in the given direction. Figure 5.6 illustrates the principle more clearly.

A `DirectionalLight` node is ideal for generating "all over" light, *i.e.*, light coming in a window from "outside", or dulled lighting that has no obvious source, but has a distinct direction, i.e., you could place a `DirectionalLight` node outside a room, but cause the light to flow into the room. This differs from the idea of a `PointLight` which has a defined three-dimensional volume that it illuminates, which is illustrated in Figure 5.7.

SpotLight

A `SpotLight` is basically a `PointLight` with a focused beam of light comprising an arc of light, as opposed to infinitely large light radiation. Figure 5.8 shows the cross-section from above of the lighting effects of various parts of the beam.

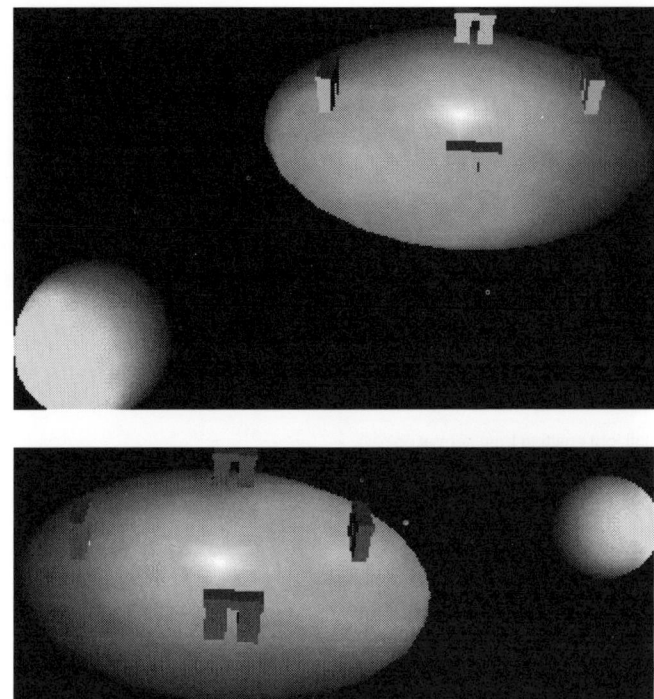

Figure 5.5: An Orbiting `PointLight`

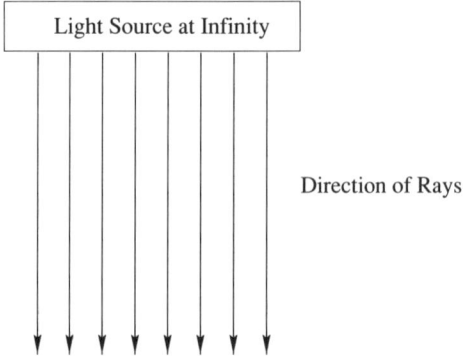

Figure 5.6: `DirectionalLight`

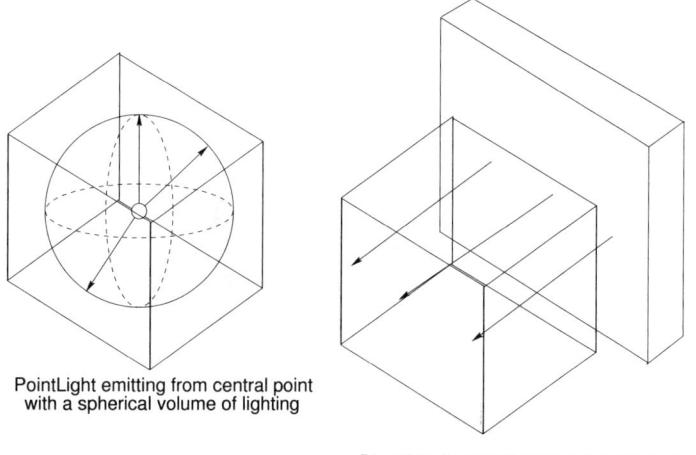

Figure 5.7: `PointLight` versus `DirectionalLight`

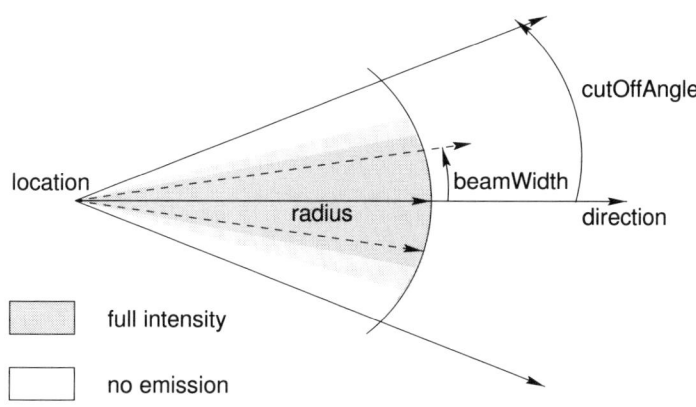

Figure 5.8: `SpotLight`

The beam is split into several separate parts, which blend together. The core, brightest part of the beam exists in the space between the `location` and the `radius` along the axis of the `direction`, and a distance `beamWidth` to either side of the axis at the `radius`. To either side of the bright core light along the axis of `direction`, the light "fades", or gets less bright, until the angle equals `cutOffAngle`. Below `cutOffAngle`, there is no light. The brightness of the light in the "fade" area is interpolated between no light at `cutOffAngle` and full light at `beamWidth`. If the `attenuation` field is specified, then the brightness of the light *beyond* `radius` along the axis of direction in the core section fades according to the values specified.

Camera-derie And The `Viewpoint` Node

One of the more interesting aspects of navigating three-dimensional space via a computer model is that we can arbitrarily move around in that space without the usual restrictions, such as gravity, or having to physically position ourselves in a location and orientation to see what the world looks like from that angle. VRML2.0 supports the concepts of *multiple viewpoints, i.e.*, locations and orientations in the world that the user can "jump" to at any given time. A fair analogy of the multiple viewpoint concept is that of a teleporter in which the user appears to be transported from one location to another.

Similarly, in a CAD simulation, multiple viewpoints might be defined in the world allowing users who wish to look at various parts of the model to zoom there immediately, without having to wobble through a potentially confusing three-dimensional space.

Looking at the `Viewpoint` node description, you will see that we can not only define the `position` and `orientation` of the new viewpoint, but also specify some parameters for getting to that viewpoint, whether by smoothly moving from our current position to the new position, or "jumping"; and the "aperture" or *field of view* of the camera at that viewpoint.

The ability to move smoothly from viewpoint to viewpoint is extremely useful, and we can use this ability to produce effects such as automatic directed "tours" through the scene, a glass élevator ride up the side of a building or even a plane on auto-pilot. This smooth navigation between viewpoints is achieved by setting the field `jump` to the value of `FALSE`. To produce an effect such as the transporters in *Star Trek* where you are instantly teleported from one location to another, you would set the `jump` field to value `TRUE`.

The other main configurable option in the `Viewpoint` node that we should be interested in is the `fieldOfView` field, which describes the angle that our viewpoint encompasses. For example, a small `fieldOfView` value would correspond to a telephoto lens, whereas a large `fieldOfView` value would correspond to a wide-angle or panoramic lens.

Atmospheric Effects

Atmospheric effects can play a major part in the effectiveness of a scene. Take a world set in Sherlock Holmes' time or based on H.P. Lovecraft or Edgar Allen Poe's fiction. Now, imagine those worlds without fog and gloom. We can simulate the gloom of those worlds with careful use of lighting, but you can still clearly see distant objects in the scene, and that rather destroys the terror of things leaping out of fog banks at you! Thus, the `Fog` node.

The `Fog` node is capable of two different types of fog effect, *linear* and *exponential*. Linear fog is where the amount of fog colour blended with the original object colour is subject to a linear calculation resulting in a *depth cueing* effect: the object fades out into the distance. More natural fog, that all encompassing pea-souper, can be simulated with exponential fog which is where the fog colour is blended with the original object colour using an exponential function.

Let's take a look at some example code, which should help clarify usage of the `Fog` node. We have defined a street lamp in a prototype node that we shall refrain from listing here for brevity. The code can be found on the CD-ROM.

```
#VRML V2.0 utf8
#
# A street scene
EXTERNPROTO streetLamp [] "lamp.wrl"

Viewpoint {
  position 0 2 10
 }
```

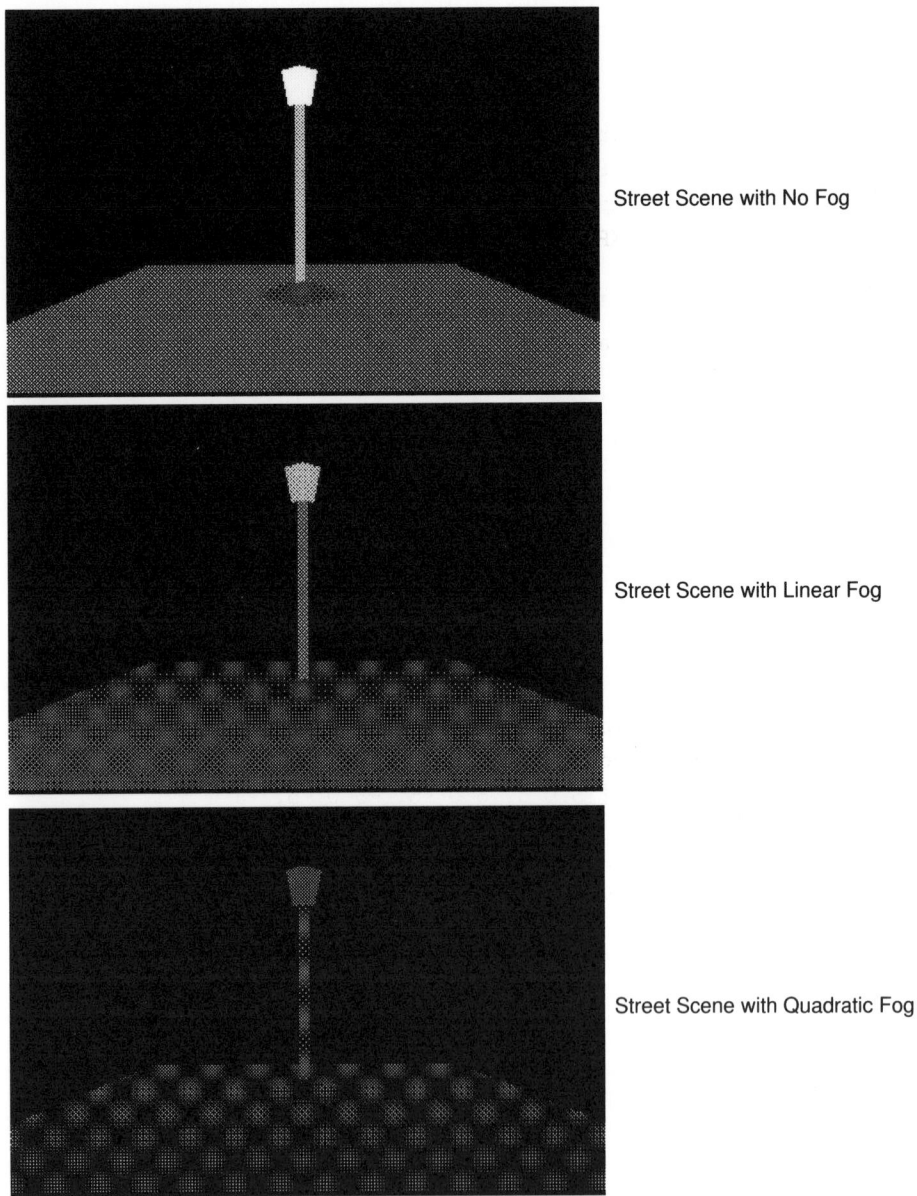

Street Scene with No Fog

Street Scene with Linear Fog

Street Scene with Quadratic Fog

Figure 5.9: Various Fog Node Scenes

```
       Transform {
         children [
           ### The Fog node
           Fog {
             color 0 0 0
             visibilityRange 25
             fogType "LINEAR"
#            visibilityRange 0              # This disables fog
#            fogType "EXPONENTIAL"
           }

           ### A street lamp
           streetLamp {}

           ### The ground
           Transform {
             children Shape {
               appearance Appearance {
                 material Material {
                   emissiveColor 0.2 0.2 0.1
                 }
               }
               geometry IndexedFaceSet {
                 coord Coordinate {
                   point [ 5 0 5, 5 0 -5, -5 0 -5, -5 0 5 ]
                 }
                 coordIndex [ 0, 1, 2, 3, -1 ]
                 ccw FALSE
               }
             }
           }
         ]
       }
```

This example code should produce a set of scenes as in Figure 5.9, which shows the scene as seen from the defined `Viewpoint` with various fog settings.

Now imagine a many-tentacled beast lurking just behind the fog bank...

A secondary use for the `Fog` node it to provide smooth blending of ob-

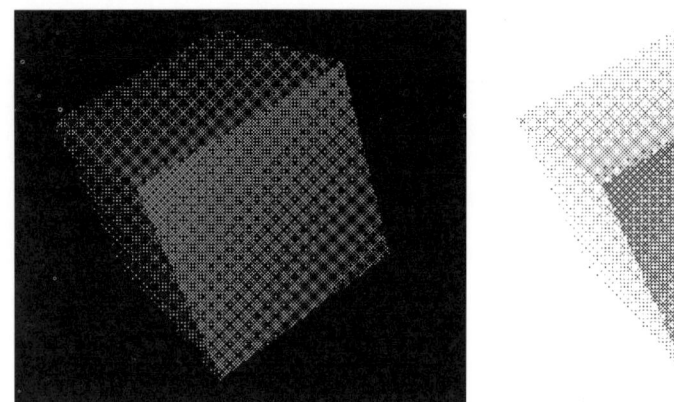

Far Clipping Plane and Fog Blending

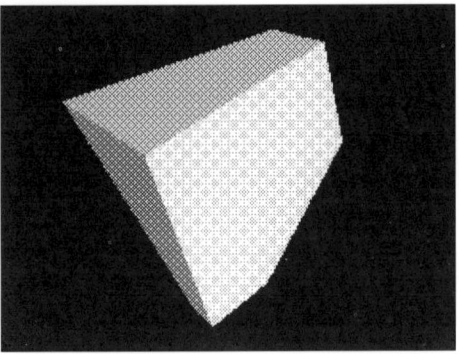

Far Clipping Plane and No Fog Blending

Figure 5.10: Far Clipping Plane Blending With The Fog Node

jects into the far clipping plane, which produces a far more realistic and atmospheric effect than objects disappearing into the distance! Setting the `visibilityRange` field of the `Fog` node to be just in front of the far clipping plane's distance as specified in a `NavigationInfo` node will produce this effect, which is quite desirable. For the best results, the `fogType` field of the `Fog` node should be set to *LINEAR*, *i.e.*, the depth-cueing effect is the one we want to use and, to complete the effect, the `fogColor` field should be match the background colour of the display. Figure 5.10 shows two scenes, one with no fog blending and the other with. The difference is quite noticeable. It should be noted that to show that we're not tricking you here, we've included a reverse video picture of the `Fog` blended cuboid in the top right-hand image which clearly shows that no far plane clipping has occurred yet, but that the cube does appear to have "disappeared" off into the distance.

A final use for the `Fog` node that may not immediately spring to mind is to use it to simulate nightfall.

In Skara Brae, lights at the distant edges of the village and the sea will become harder to see as darkness settles on the world, possibly aided by fog banks rolling in off the nearby bay. Nightfall can be simulated using the `Background` node, as we demonstrated above, but the concept of night falling simulated by an ever-decreasing `Fog` node `visibilityLimit` is extremely appealing. This use of `Fog` produces an effect that is quite powerful and convincing. Coupling the techniques of modifying the `skyColor` field of a `Background` node and modifying the `fogColor` and `visibilityLimit` fields of a `Fog` node can produce splendid atmospheric effects that add immensely to the enjoyment of navigating worlds.

Chapter 6

Have You Heard The One About...

The soul may be a mere pretense,
the mind makes very little sense.
So let us value the appeal
Of that which we can taste and feel.

PIET HEIN
"A Toast", *Grooks* (1966)

Where's The Sense In Virtual Reality?

Virtual reality has been around in some form or other for some time now (although, admittedly, not very long on the geological scale of things), and yet just how close has it come to realizing its aims?

Of course, in order to answer this we need to know what the aims of virtual reality are. As there has been no international treaty ratified by all the countries of the world, we have to accept that this is a somewhat unanswerable question; virtual reality will have different aims for different people (ranging from saving the universe to playing games where you can imagine you are saving the universe). But maybe there are some general and incomplete answers...

Surely a major aim of virtual reality is to be able to create computer-generated worlds which are realistic. Or, given that some of the virtual worlds have no basis in reality whatsoever, the aim is to be able to create worlds which are *believable.*

It is certainly possible with expensive computers—and, increasingly, with cheaper computers—to produce images which are sufficiently believable. But is that good enough? Is a feast for the eyes sufficient to satisfy when what I want is a feast?

If I walk into a computer-generated world containing the neolithic village of Skara Brae I can see the low, thick-walled houses, the waste middens, small fields of weather-beaten crops.

And then add more senses.

My face and ears tingle as the storm wind rushes by (but only gently—I want the sensations at a level that makes the world believable, not uncomfortable). There is a distant noise of rock striking rock. I turn to the right and the noise is a little clearer...that way! The wind shifts and the smell of peat smoke and burning meat catches my attention. As I pass the entrance to a house, the sounds of stone-carving are that much clearer...it must be coming from inside.

Visually, that scene is unchanging; yet there is life there from the "movement" that the other senses can "see". Computer control of taste, smell, touch, balance, localized temperature (put your hand near a fire and the fingertips get warm), and more—having these modelled in a realistic way in the virtual environment may be a little way off yet.[1] But sound—that is, believable 3D sound—may be a little closer.

---

[1]Why not consider one or more of these as a research topic, if you are that way inclined?

Sound In VRML

Basic VRML Sound

In a simplified view of the world, there are two kinds of sound source: undirected sounds and directed sounds.

Throw a brick into a lake. As in Figure 6.1, the sound propagates equally in all directions—if you are 100 metres away from the splash, the "plop" will be just as loud whether you are positioned towards the top of the lake or towards the lower right. The only factor in the volume of the sound is the distance from the source.

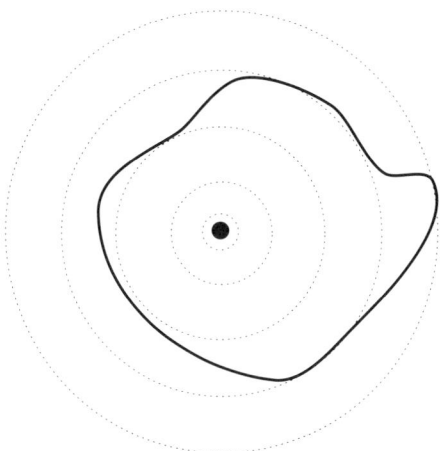

Figure 6.1: Sound From A Stone Thrown Into A Lake Radiates Equally In All Directions

In earlier drafts of VRML, an undirected sound was represented by the PointSound node. This has now been replaced with the Sound node which is a little more complex—however, it is simple to use the Sound node to create a PointSound node, and as the PointSound node is so useful, this is what we will do.

```
#VRML V2.0 utf8


# Prototype for an undirected point-source sound
```

```
PROTO PointSound [
  field SFString description ""
  field MFString url         []
  field SFFloat  intensity   1
  field SFVec3f  location    0 0 0
  field SFFloat  maxRange    10
  field SFFloat  minRange    1
  field SFFloat  priority    0
  field SFBool   loop        FALSE
  field SFTime   start       0
  field SFTime   stop        0
  ]
{
  DEF audioSource AudioClip {
    description IS description
    loop IS loop
    pitch 1.0
    startTime IS start
    stopTime IS stop
    url IS url
  }

  Sound {
    direction 0 0 1
    intensity IS intensity
    location IS location
    maxBack IS maxRange
    maxFront IS maxRange
    minBack IS minRange
    minFront IS minRange
    priority IS priority
    source USE audioSource
  }
}
```

This PointSound node can be used to create our "stone thrown into a lake" model, for example:

```
#VRML V2.0 utf8
```

```
Transform {
  children [

    PointSound {
      name "http:plop.wav"
      description "Watery Splash"
      intensity 1
      location 0 0 0
      minRange .05
      maxRange 500
      loop FALSE
      start now
    }
  ]
}
```

which uses the sound file `plop.wav` to actually create the sound. At the location of the splash, and within 0.05 metres of the splash, the sound is at full intensity.

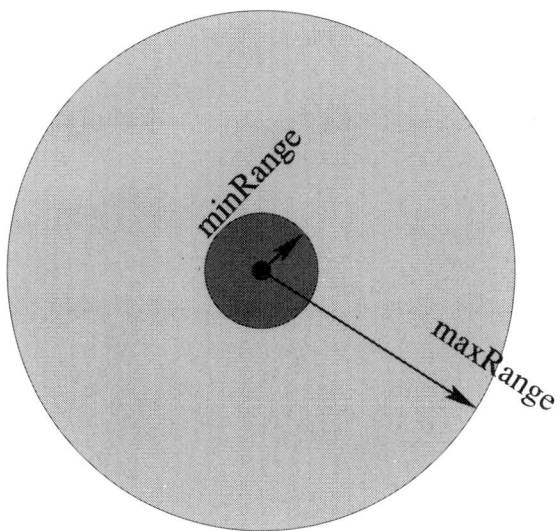

Figure 6.2: VRML Undirected Sound

Whenever the listener is within a radius of `minRange` from the `location` of the sound (Figure 6.2), then the sound is heard at the given `intensity`, where an intensity of 1 is the intensity at which the sound was recorded (*i.e.*, the maximum intensity) and 0 is silence. The intensity of sound falls off the further away you get from the `location` of the splash, until you go beyond the `maxRange` (here, 500 metres) when you would no longer be able to hear the sound.

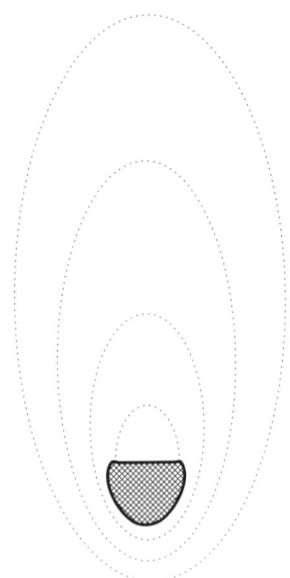

Figure 6.3: Sound From A Megaphone Radiates More Strongly In The Direction The Horn Is Pointed

A megaphone, on the other hand, does not produce an even volume of sound in all directions (Figure 6.3). Standing in front of the horn you will hear a much louder sound than standing to the side or behind the horn.

Similarly, if you stand in front of me when I am speaking then you will hear me more clearly than if you stand behind me—although the effect will be much less pronounced than with the megaphone.

In earlier drafts of VRML, this was modelled by using the `DirectedSound` node. In version 2.0, a directed sound is modelled using the slightly different `Sound` node.

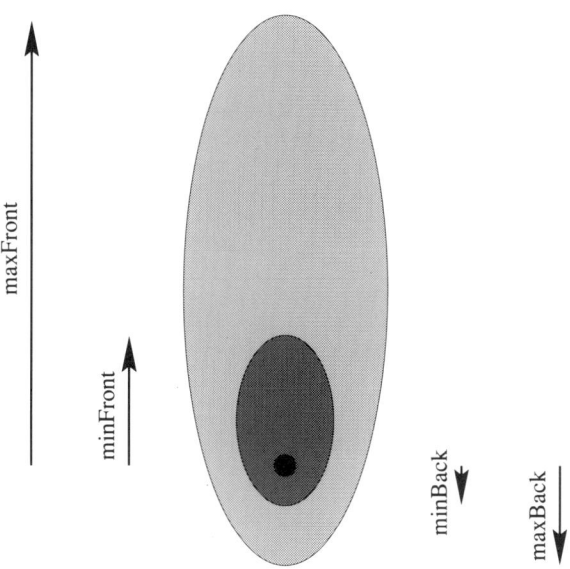

Figure 6.4: VRML Directed Sound

In a `Sound` node (Figure 6.4), the sound field is not represented as a circle with the source of the sound at the centre (as in the undirected sound) where the volume falls off equally in all directions, but as an ellipse with the source at the sound at one focus of the ellipse (that is, with the source towards one end of the ellipse).

The sound can be not so directional (as in Figure 6.5), then the source is nearer to the centre and the values of `maxFront` and `minFront` are fairly similar to the values of `maxBack` and `minBack` respectively. This might be a good model for a person speaking—you can hear them better to the front, but not a lot better.

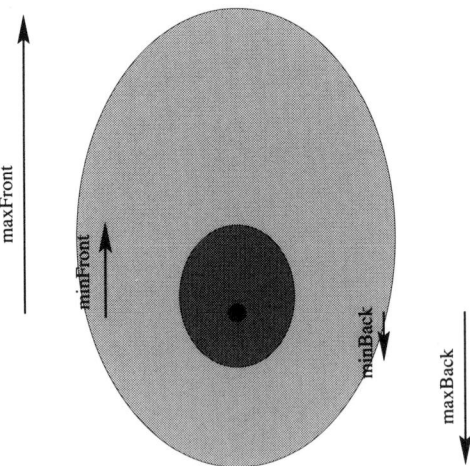

Figure 6.5: VRML Not Very Directed Sound

Or the sound can be very directional (as in Figure 6.6) where the source is very near to one end of a long, thin ellipse and the values of `maxFront` and `minFront` are very different from the values of `maxBack` and `minBack`. This might be a good model for a sound from a megaphone.

This Sound Thing Is Great...Isn't It?

All this sounds really good. And it *is* really good. But there's a long way to go before we achieve any kind of realism. VRML2.0 gives a level of sound realism which, in visual realism terms, might be compared to wire-frame graphics with depth-cueing.[2]

To give a clearer idea of the limitation, consider the brick thrown into the lake again. This time there is one person standing on the virtual lake shore to the north and another person standing on the virtual lake shore to the south,

---

[2]Wire-frame graphics give you an idea of visual depth. The addition of depth-cueing, where drawn pixels are coloured in such a way that those that are "further into" the screen are drawn with darker colours, much like VRML sounds, gives a sense of depth by reducing the volume the further away you are from the source of that sound.

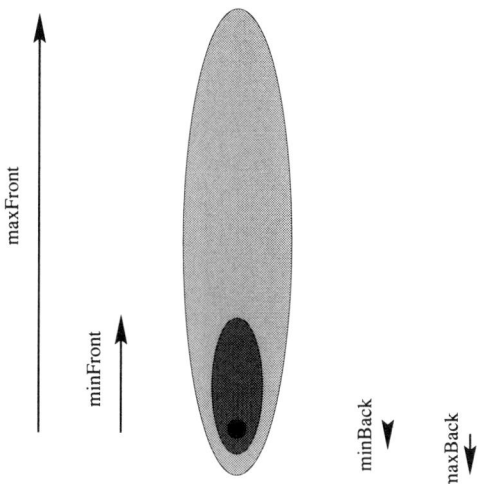

Figure 6.6: VRML Very Directed Sound

but this latter person is standing inside a virtual house. In the VRML-created world, the only factor in determining the volume of the sound is the distance from the source, so both observers will hear the sound at the same volume. In a believable world, the person to the north would hear a louder splash than the person to the south, who may not even hear it at all. How the sound is transmitted to the person on the south shore depends on quite a number of factors such as what the walls of the house are made of, what the windows are made of and whether the door to the house is open. This can be compared with the visual problems of hidden-surface removal, shadows and reflections, not to mention transparency of materials.[3]

Making It More Realistic

With a little care, some things can be done to improve the realism of the VRML sound model. This requires a little planning and forethought, and in all but the simplest cases you might want to consider whether the extra work

---

[3]Have you ever noticed how you can always hear the bass notes when the person in the next room has the music on too loud (*too loud*, of course, being another way of saying *at the correct volume* if you are that way inclined)? This is because lower-frequency notes generally travel more easily through solid materials. For believability, the sound model should take this into account as well.

is worth the effort, given the effect that it achieves. Hopefully you *will* think that it is worth the effort—getting closer to believability (if not realism) can be very satisfying.

Consider our Skara Brae village again. You will recall that there was a house in which a stone-carver was working and from which the sound of tapping stone could be heard—particularly when passing by the doorway.

At the simplest level, we can put an undirected sound source at the centre of the house. If the `minRange` is set to be the same as the radius of the house then the tapping will be at full volume everywhere within the house, and will get progressively quieter as the distance from the house increases, as in Figure 6.7.

Figure 6.7: Propagation Of Sound From A Stone-Carver in Skara Brae House 7

Not too bad, and this might be quite adequate for your world. But it is possible to do a *lot* better for not a lot of extra work.

In our first improvement, let's assume that the sound cannot pass through the walls of the house. This isn't a bad assumption in this case as the walls of the Skara Brae houses are really quite thick. If the values for `minRange` and `maxRange` are *both* set to be the same as the radius of the house then the volume will be loud everywhere inside, but it will drop abruptly to zero when you leave the house. From outside the house the source of the sound does not appear to be the stone-carver. Instead the sound would appear to come from the entrance to the house. So we can add a second undirected sound at the entrance to the house, as in Figure 6.8. This should be at a lower intensity than the sound inside the house, and should also be synchronized with it. (We shall consider synchronizing sound sources a little later).

So from outside the house, the sound will appear to be emanating from the entrance to the house. On stepping inside the entrance, the sound will get significantly louder. Much more believable! But, if you want, still more improvement can be made.

To improve the effect still further, the sound should get noticeably louder as you pass the entrance to the house even if you don't go inside. This can be modelled by adding a third synchronized sound source—this would also be sited at the entrance to the house, but we now use a directed sound so that the volume is greater along the axis of the doorway, as in Figure 6.9.

Two very directional sounds back-to-back could give a fairly convincing model for a sound generated in the corridor of a building with solid walls. Here you want the sound to propagate well down the length of the corridor—where there is nothing to impede the soundwaves—but not seep through the walls, as in Figure 6.10. The sound gradually decreases in volume along the corridor, as you would expect, with a suitably large value for `maxFront`; but a small value for both `maxBack` and `minBack` causes the sound to propagate very little to the sides, and so the sound cannot be heard through the walls.

This corridor effect is demonstrated in the VRML example below:

```
#VRML V2.0 utf8

# Prototype for a wall of the corridor
```

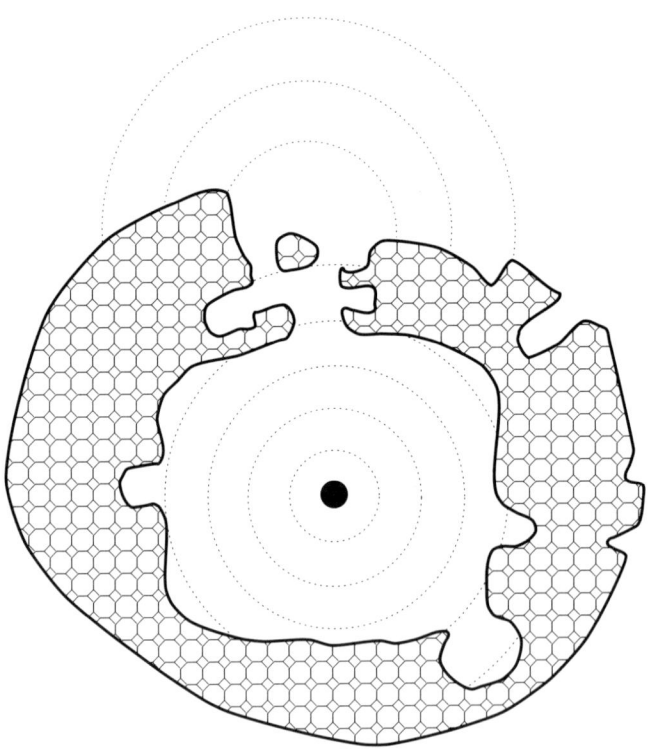

Figure 6.8: Better Propagation Of Sound From A Stone-Carver in Skara Brae House 7

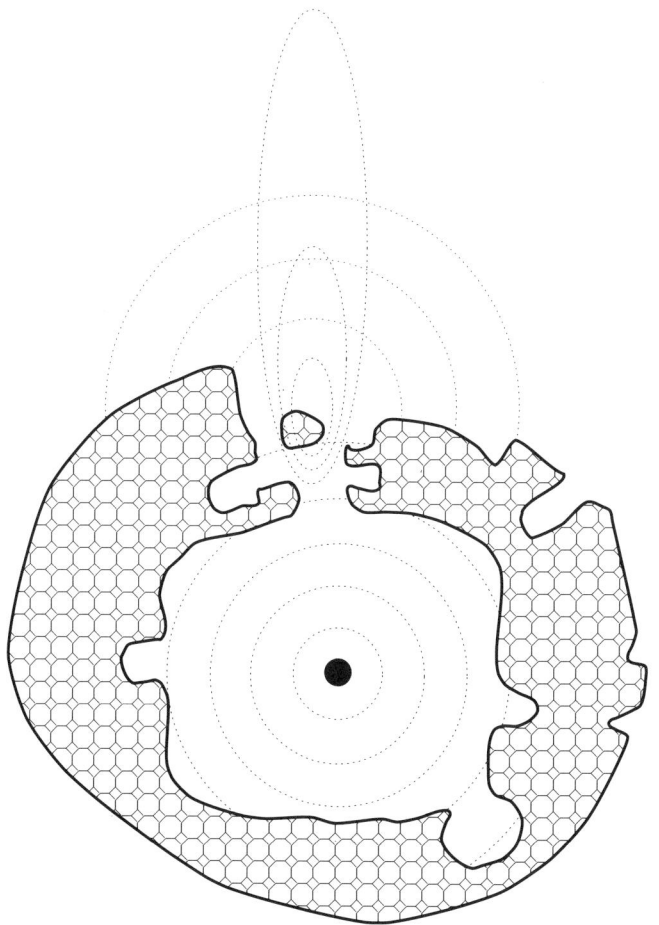

Figure 6.9: Final Model Of Propagation Of Sound From A Stone-Carver in Skara Brae House 7

```
PROTO Wall [ field SFFloat wallPos 0.0 ]
{
  Transform {
    translation wallPos 0 0
      children
        Shape {
          appearance Appearance {
            material Material {
              diffuseColor 1 0 0
            }
          }
          geometry Box { size .1 2 10 }
        }
  }
}

DEF Talk AudioClip {
  description "Sound of a Person Talking"
  loop TRUE
  url "talk.wav"
}

Transform {
  children [
    Wall { 0.0 }
    Wall { 2.0 }
    Transform {
      translation 1 1 5
      children [
        # two back-to-back sounds.  Identical in all
        # but the direction in which they point
        Sound {
          direction 0 0 1
          maxFront 5
          minFront .5
          maxBack  .1
          minBack  .01
          source USE Talk
        }
```

```
        Sound {
          direction 0 0 -1
          maxFront 5
          minFront .5
          maxBack  .1
          minBack  .01
          source USE Talk
        }
      ]
    }
  ]
}
```

This effect is illustrated in Figure 6.10.

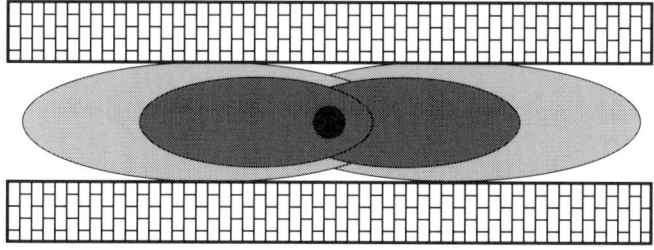

Figure 6.10: Model Of Propagation Of Sound In A Solid-Walled Corridor

To give the impression of sound seeping through thinner walls, `maxBack` can be increased so that the limit at which the sound can be heard is slightly beyond the boundary of the corridor, as in Figure 6.11. Here, the intense sound is still within the confines of the corridor, but some quieter sound can still be heard near the walls from the outside of the corridor.

Ideally, you would be able to shape a sound to the shape of the space in which that sound is created, and you would be able to set the lever of audio transparency and refractivity for each type of obstacle through which the sound might pass. But even with the limits imposed by the VRML implementation of sound nodes, believable effects can be created with a small amount of effort.

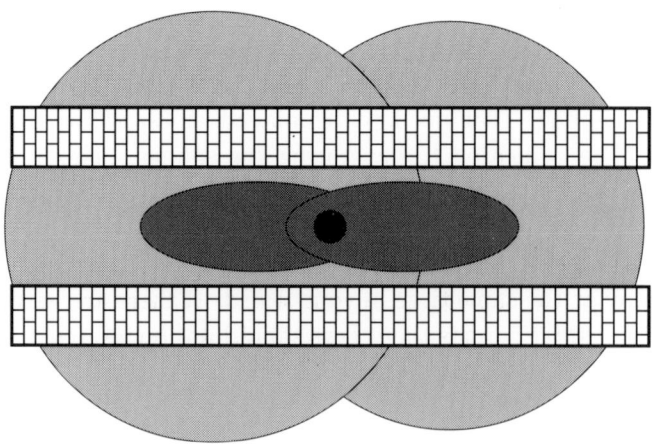

Figure 6.11: Model Of Propagation Of Sound In A Thin-Walled Corridor

Can You Hear Me, Mother?

Having argued the case for using plenty of sounds to add realism—or at least believability—to a scene, I must now argue for a certain degree of caution and even restraint.

There are three main reasons for this restraint, and they are all dependent on capabilities of the computer and software used to view the world that you have created. In a closed environment—such as on a local network in a small office—where you know exactly what the capabilities of the viewing machines are, you can tailor your models to take full advantage of their strengths and not over-stretch their weaknesses. In an open environment—such as over the Internet—you may want to tailor your models to be usable (and believable) on as wide a variety of machines as possible.

So what are these limitations that need to be considered?

Coping With Limited Computing Power

First of all, there is the computing power of the machine on which the model is to be displayed. Playing a sound can take up a fair bit of processing power,[4] and the more sounds that need to be played at once, the more processor time needs to be dedicated to generating the sounds. This might leave insufficient processor time to generate realistic graphics at an acceptable speed.

The simple answer here is to make sure that there are never lots of sounds which will play at the same time in your world. If there are never more than, say, four or five active sounds then there should not be too much of a problem.

An *active* sound is one which can be heard from your current location. That is, you are within the circle of radius `maxRange` (for an undirected sound) or within the `maxFront/maxBack` ellipse (for a directed sound). Any sounds that are not active will not have an effect on the speed of the viewer.

Returning to our stone-carver in Skara Brae...

At the doorway to house 7, we have three active sounds: one generated inside the house, and two generated in the doorway. So if there are things which can be heard from other parts of the village it might be a good idea to try to organize the world such that we can only hear one or two of these other sounds at any one time. For example, if there are robot tour-guides walking around the village explaining items of archaeological interest to visitors it would be sensible to make sure that only one approaches a visitor at any one time.

But I Really Need Ten Sounds

As always, though, there are better solutions if you have the time and are willing to make the effort. "Four or five sounds" is a good rule of thumb, but remember that it is no more than a rule of thumb! Having more sounds playing at once may degrade the speed at which the graphics can be drawn; so if you *need* a lot of sounds to be playing, reduce the detail in the surrounding visual models. In a world consisting of a single cube you can probably get

---

[4]Of course, this depends to some extent on the capabilities of the sound-generating hardware. Getting realistic sound out of the internal speaker of a PC takes *much* more processor effort than getting realistic sound out of dedicated, intelligent sound-generating chips.

away with having the processor concentrate on much more audio complexity.

Conversely, in areas where the visual complexity is much more significant (and much more important) you may need to reduce still further the number of audio clips that are active.

Coping With Limited Bandwidth

Then there is the available bandwidth of the network over which the sounds must be transmitted. A megabyte of CD-quality sound might give a truly wonderful and realistic sense of a stone splashing into a lake, but if it takes an hour to transfer onto a machine over a slow modem link would it not be better to have a noise which sounds vaguely like a splash and which can be transferred in a matter of seconds?

Use small sounds as much as possible. If an insect buzzes past, keeping within earshot for maybe 30 seconds, then consider using a looped audio clip of a buzz which lasts only one second but repeats 30 times rather than a more convincing 30-second clip. How many people are going to take that much notice of your incidental sounds, anyway? (Of course, if you are building a world where people *do* need to take notice of incidental sounds then give much more priority to the quality of your audio clips).

Raw audio files can be very large and produce very little effect. As with graphics formats (where a JPEG encoded image, for instance, can take up *much* less bandwidth than a raw bitmap image, but at the expense of increasing loss of quality as you decrease the number of bytes needed to represent the image) there are audio formats which can store the sound information in much less space. Unfortunately, the only format that a VRML viewer *must* be able to handle in order to conform to the *VRML97 Specification* is an uncompressed wave format. The VRML specification *recommends* that a VRML viewer also supports the MIDI file type 1 sound format, although you certainly can't rely on this format being supported. But if you know that more efficient formats are being used by the VRML viewers that will be accessing your virtual world, make good use of them.

Coping With Limited Software

Finally, there are limitations of the software that is used to view the model. To comply with the VRML version 2.0 specification, a VRML viewer need only be capable of handling three active sounds at any one time. That might sound like not very much, but if you are battling for believability it can be even worse than you think...

Let's go back to our stone-carver in Skara Brae. Standing in the entrance to his house, we can hear him chipping away. But remember that there are three active sounds making up this chipping noise, even though it sounds like just one: there is the undirected sound coming from the stone-carver's actual position in the centre of the house; there is another undirected sound coming from the doorway; and there is a directed sound pointing outwards from the doorway. Of course, this is not a problem as our minimal VRML viewer can happily handle three sounds. Then three midges fly into earshot. Your viewer is now being asked to handle six active sounds, which means that it has to ignore three of them. Maybe it will ignore the three sounds of the stone-carver. That would be a terrible choice if this world is intended to be an archaeological reconstruction in which the midges are simply there to add a bit of atmosphere. Maybe it will ignore the three midge sounds, which would be equally terrible if this world is part of an adventure game in which the player has been given a clue that they should follow the midges to a hard-to-find swamp.

Chapter 7

Behave Yourself!

πάντα χωρεῖ, οὐδεν μένει

Heraclitus

Imagine yourself standing in Skara Brae village looking all around you. What's missing? Life, energy, movement and, most importantly, *realism*.

The worlds that we have built in the previous chapters may have been rendered smoothly and looked fantastic, but nothing reacted to your presence in that world. Bumping into things made you float ethereally through them and any attempts to pick up objects resulted in frustration as your "hands" passed silently through them.

On a historical note, this is the position that VRML1.0 reached, in that worlds could be defined geometrically, but could not be infused with any energy.

In this chapter, we shall explore the possibilities which VRML2.0 creates for us in terms of infusing worlds with energy and vitality using the sensor nodes, interpolator nodes and the `Collision` node all carefully linked together by an invisible web of events being relayed around the scene.

Passing the Event Horizon

Central to the concept of interactivity, reaction and behaviour in VRML2.0 is the idea of an *event. Collins English Dictionary* defines *event* as:

> **e-vent** (ɪ'vɛnt) *n.* **1.** anything that takes place or happens, esp. something important...[C16: from Latin *eventus* a happening, from *evenire* to come forth, happen, from *venire* to come]

It follows from this that we can see that the concept of "something happening" is fairly central to the way things work. What we need to define more clearly, however, is when these events occur and what we do with them once we realize they have occurred.

Events are generated by various nodes by default, *e.g.*, the `TouchSensor` node will generate various events depending on the values of fields within that node. To elaborate further, if we look at the *VRML97 Specification*, we can see that the `TouchSensor` node has six separate fields defined as `eventOut`. These fields will contain the values generated by the node, which can then be used. Therefore, each node that contains an `eventOut` field will generate events. The corollary of this is that each node that contains an `eventIn` field will *react* to external stimuli. This is the heart of the behaviour model in VRML2.0.

However, we now have events occurring in the world, but how do we send these events to other nodes that have `eventIn` fields? For this, we need to look at the `ROUTE` construct.

ROUTEs

ROUTEs are not nodes, but syntactic constructs that are defined in the scene to pass events from `eventOut` fields to `eventIn` or `exposedField` fields. For example, if we wish to make a cube rotate on the spot over a period of time, we would plan on using a `TimeSensor` node to generate `eventOut`s, then ROUTE that field into an `eventIn` field in the Box node.[1]

This brings up some important points, namely, that the fields being ROUTEd together must be of the same type, which we shall discuss in more detail in

---

[1]This is an over-simplification: the exact process would require an `OrientationInterpolator` node as well.

Tables 7.1 and 7.2, and that the node being ROUTEd to must contain the desired field. In the case of our Box node from above, there is no way of setting a rotational value. For that, we must look to the nearest enclosing Transform node, and apply the ROUTEd event to that instead.

The VRML code below will display a blue cube which, if you click on then drag the mouse, you will interact with, and it will spin. Figure 7.1 shows the event mechanism in action.

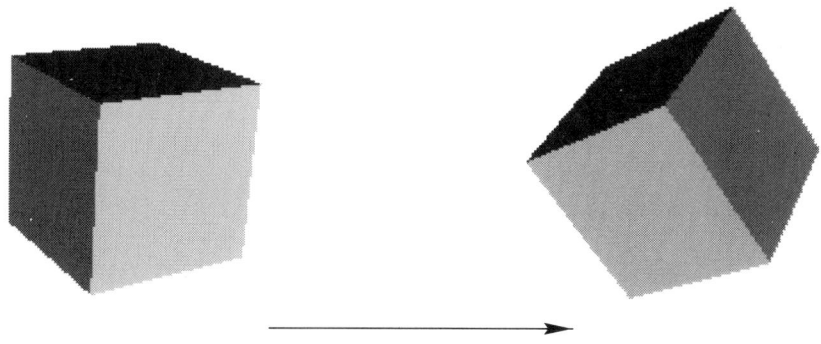

SphereSensor:
rotation_changed

Transform:
set_rotation

Figure 7.1: Dragging A Cube

```
#VRML V2.0 utf8
#
# Spins a cube by clicking and dragging
Transform {
  children [
    DEF S SphereSensor { autoOffset TRUE }
    DEF T Transform {
      children Shape {
        appearance Appearance {
          material Material {
            diffuseColor 1 1 1
```

```
        }
      }
    geometry Box {}
    }
  }
 ]
 ROUTE S.rotation_changed TO T.set_rotation
}
```

VRML Datatypes

As you may have noticed from the various VRML node definitions that we
have been using, each node contains several fields which we may manipulate.
To be more exact, there are four distinct types of field within any node:

`field` which is initialized at the time the node is created. This value is
non-modifiable and is considered *private* to this node.

`exposedField` which is initialized at the time the node is created. However, this value may be modified after the creation of the node, and
is actually a compound of the following types. Given that we have an
`exposedField` of *blah*, it is actually treated as

```
    eventIn set_blah
    field blah
    eventOut blah_changed
```

which is to say, a `ROUTE` may set the value of an `exposedField`, and an
`exposedField` will produce an `eventOut` containing its new value.

`eventIn` which is an input event to the node which has been `ROUTE`d from
another node.

`eventOut` which is an output event from the node, which may be `ROUTE`d to
another node.

However, this is not all there is to VRML datatyping! You will also have
noticed that in addition to the type of field, there is also a datatype which
indicates the sort of data contained within a field. The defined datatypes are
described in Tables 7.1 and 7.2.

VRML datatype	What it means
SFBool	This datatype represents a single Boolean value, *i.e.*, a value that is either **TRUE** or **FALSE**. If the field is an SFBool eventOut, its initial value will be **FALSE**.
SFColor	This datatype represents a single RGB colour triple, *i.e.*, a value containing three floating-point numbers between 0 and 1.0, representing the mix red, green and blue primary colours. If the field is an SFColor eventOut, its initial value will be (0 0 0), which corresponds to the colour black.
SFFloat	This datatype represents a single single-precision floating-point number written in ANSI C floating-point format, *e.g.*, 1.0, -100.4e-4 or .00005. If the field is an SFFloat eventOut, its initial value will be 0.0.
SFInt32	This datatype represents a single integer value, *i.e.*, a number that has no decimal places. This value will be 32 bits long, and may be specified as either decimal or hexadecimal, *e.g.*, 13 or 0xaf. Hexadecimal values are prefixed with the standard 0x characters. If this field is an SFInt32 eventOut, its initial value will be 0.
SFNode	This datatype represents a single VRML node, correctly specified as per the syntax of that node. For example:

```
field SFNode Transform {
    children [
        Shape {
            geometry Box {}
        }
    ]
}
```

If the field is an SFNode eventOut, its initial value will be NULL.

Table 7.1: Single-Value VRML Datatypes

VRML datatype	What it means

SFImage | This datatype represents a single uncompressed two-dimensional picture. Various colour models may be implemented by an SFImage node, and therefore we specify a set of information in the declaration of the field as to the size and colour model used by the SFImage. This field is declared as:

```
someImageField <width> <height> <num>
                              <pixels>
```

To elaborate, the width and height values are specified as integer values, and represent the width and height of the image represented by the SFImage field. The num value informs us as to how many colour components there are *per pixel* in this image. The final field in the declaration contains the actual hexadecimal values representing each pixel. These values are decoded in the colour model specified by the num field, which can be interpreted as follows:

1. A single-byte component has a value between 0x00 and 0xFF, or 255. Therefore, a pixel value of 0xFF would indicate a full intensity *i.e.*, white, and a pixel value of 0x00 would indicate no intensity, *i.e.*, black. A single-component SFImage is regarded as being greyscale.

2. A two-byte component can be interpreted as being an intensity contained in the first byte and an opacity, or transparency, value contained in the second byte. A two-byte component SFImage is a grayscale image.

Table 7.1: Single-Value VRML Datatypes *continued...*

VRML datatype	What it means
`SFImage`	3. A three-byte component can be interpreted as being an RGB triple, with the red component being contained in the first byte, the green component being contained in the second byte and the blue component specified in the third and final byte of each pixel value. Three-byte component `SFImage` fields are RGB coloured, but have no transparency capabilities.
	4. A four-byte component can be interpreted as being an RGB triple, as discussed above, with an opacity value specified in the final byte. `SFImage`s specified with four-byte pixel values have full RGB colouring and support transparency.
	For example, an `SFImage` of a 1×2 dimensioned image of a white pixel followed by a black pixel would be specified as:
	`someSFImage 1 2 1 0xFF 0x00.`

Table 7.1: Single-Value VRML Datatypes *continued...*

VRML datatype	What it means
SFRotation	This datatype represents a single rotation value specified as an axis of rotation plus a right-handed angle of rotation. This is written as four floating-point values, separated by white space, *e.g.*, 0 1 0 3.14, which represents a 180deg rotation around the *y*-axis. The axis of rotation is *normalized*. If the field is an SFRotation eventOut, its initial value is 0 0 1 0.
SFString	This datatype contains a string of characters formatted with the UTF-8 universal character set. This character set provides a rich syntax for specifying characters from many languages accurately, without the limitations of standard ASCII formatting. The format of an SFString is that it will be written as a sequence of UTF-8 bytes enclosed within double-quote (") characters. In the case of an SFString being used as an eventOut, the initial value is "".
SFTime	This datatype represents a single time value specified as a double-precision floating number in ANSI C format, as described above. Time values are specified as the number of seconds from Jan 1, 1970, 00:00:00 GMT. If an SFTime field is being used as an eventOut, its initial value will be −1.
SFVec2f	This datatype represents a two-dimensional vector, specified as two single-precision floating-point values separated by white space. If being used as an eventOut, an SFVec2f value will have an initial value of (0 0).
SFVec3f	This datatype represents a three-dimensional vector, specified as three single-precision floating-point values separated by white space. In the case of an SFVec3f value being used as an eventOut, its initial value will be (0 0 0).

Table 7.1: Single-Value VRML Datatypes *continued...*

VRML datatype	What it means
MFColor	This datatype represents an array of SFColor values. We can specify this array as a list of comma-separated SFColor values, *e.g.*: `someMFColor [ 1 1 1, 0.5 0.5 0.5, 0 0 0 ]`
MFFloat	This datatype represents an array of SFFloat values. We can specify this array as a list of comma-separated SFFloat values, *e.g.*: `someMFFloat [ 3.14, 0.0004, 3e-10 ]`
MFInt32	This datatype represents an array of SFInt32 values. We can specify this array as a list of comma-separated SFFloat values, *e.g.*: `someMFInt32 [ 1, 3, 5, 2, 1 ]`

MFNode	This datatype represents an array of SFNode values. We can specify this array as a list of comma-separated SFNode values, *e.g.*:
	
	`someMFNode [ Transform { translation 1 0 0 }`
	`             DEF CUBE Box{}`
	`             USE CUBE,`
	`             USE SOME_OTHER_NODE ]`

MFRotation	This datatype represents an array of SFRotation values. We can specify this array as a list of comma-separated SFRotation values, *e.g.*: `someMFRotation [ 0 1 0 3.14, 1 0 0 0.78 ]`

Table 7.2: Multiple-Value VRML Datatypes

VRML datatype	What it means

MFString	This datatype represents an array of SFString values. We can specify this array as a list of comma-separated SFString values, *e.g.*:
	
	`someMFString [ "String A",`
	`            "String B",`
	`            "String C" ]`

MFVec2f	This datatype represents an array of SFVec2 values. We can specify this array as a list of comma-separated SFVec2f values, *e.g.*: `someMFVec2f [ 1 1, 0 1, 15 3, 10 10 ]`
MFVec3f	This datatype represents an array of SFVec3f values. We can specify this array as a list of comma-separated SFVec3f values, *e.g.*: `someMFVev3f [ 1 1 1, 10 2 8, 5 5 5, 6 6 6 ]`

Table 7.2: Multiple-Value VRML Datatypes *continued...*

Sensors

Sensor nodes are the user's way of directly interacting with the world, *e.g.*, clicking on a cuboid in the scene will cause it to start spinning, or change colour or morph into a sphere.

Sensors can be broken into three categories, being:

- *Touch Sensors*
  Sensors in this category provide ways of tracking input from the user using an input device, usually in the form of a mouse. The sensors in this group are:

  - `TouchSensor` which reacts to mouse clicks and releases.
  - `CylinderSensor` which maps the input device motion into a rotation across the surface of an invisible cylinder that surrounds the user's viewpoint in the world. Rotational values are calculated using either the *side* of the invisible cylinder, or the *caps*.
  - `PlaneSensor` which maps the input device motion into "flat" motion across an invisible two-dimensional surface placed in front of the user's viewpoint in the world.
  - `SphereSensor` which maps the input device motion into a rotation across the surface of an invisible sphere which surrounds the user's viewpoint in the world.

- *Spatial Sensors*
  Sensors in this category provide sensory data with regard to the world, *e.g.*

  - `ProximitySensor` which reacts to motion of the avatar in the world when the avatar enters, moves in or leaves the volume bounded by the `ProximitySensor` in three-dimensional space.
  - `VisibilitySensor` which reacts to the visibility of a volume in three-dimensional space with regard to the current viewpoint position and orientation of the avatar.

- *Temporal Sensors*
  There is only one type of temporal sensor, and that is the `TimeSensor` node which generates events over specified time periods and at regular specified time intervals across those periods.

We shall now look at each category and, more specifically, each sensor type in more depth.

TouchSensor

The `TouchSensor` node is the general purpose pointing device tracking sensor which will sense when the user clicks on any node within the grouping node to which the `TouchSensor` node belongs. Furthermore, the `TouchSensor` will also sense when the user moves the mouse over any node within the current grouping node. This is a powerful and useful thing to be able to do!

The sensor `TouchSensor` is a more generic sensor type than, for example, the sensor `PlaneSensor`, which is similar in that it detects movement over a two-dimensional surface, since the `TouchSensor` can generate events based on whether or not the pointing device is currently over an object and whether or not the pointing device has activated[2] over an object. The `PlaneSensor`, in direct comparison, may only detect the *translation* between the point on the sensor's "surface" where the pointing device was activated and the point on the sensor's surface where the pointing device was released.[3]

The events generated by an activated `TouchSensor` node are numerous, and include:[4]

`isActive` This `eventOut` signifies that the pointing device was activated over an object that has an attached `TouchSensor` node.

`isOver` This `eventOut` signifies that the location in the viewport that the pointing device is currently pointing at has an object with an attached `TouchSensor` underneath it.

`touchTime` This `eventOut` contains the *timestamp* that an object with an attached `TouchSensor` node was pointed at or moved over with the pointing device.

As we have discussed above, these events may be `ROUTE`d to other nodes, for example, to start an animation running by clicking on an on-screen button or to switch on a light by clicking on the light switch.

---

[2]For example, clicking a mouse button.

[3]For example, letting go of the mouse button.

[4]The *VRML97 Specification* lists all the `eventOut` fields and contains some more information on them.

Figure 7.2 shows the various events of the `TouchSensor` being generated and the conditions under which they will be generated:

1. The cursor is dragged over the `Box` node. This will generate the following events:

   - `hitPoint_changed`
   This event will contain the three-dimensional co-ordinate of the point on the surface over which the pointing device rests.

   - `hitNormal_changed`
   This event will contain the surface normal vector at the point on the surface over which the pointing device rests.

   - `hitTextureCoord_changed`
   This event will contain the texture co-ordinates of the point on the surface over which the pointing device rests.

   - `isOver`
   This event will be set to `TRUE` when the pointing device moves over an object in the scene to which the `TouchSensor` is attached.

   Between the points specified at 1 and 2, the `TouchSensor` will continue to emit the above events for each and every movement of the mouse until point 2.

2. The cursor is dragged past the `Box` node into empty space. This will generate the following event:

   - `isOver`
   When the pointing device moves off of an object in the scene to which the sensor is attached, an `isOver` event with value `FALSE` will be emitted. This signifies that the mouse is no longer over an "interesting" object.

   Also, it should be noted that the other `eventOut` fields of the `TouchSensor` node at this point will contain either `NULL` or *undefined* values.

3. The cursor is dragged over the `Sphere` node. This will generate the same events as in 1 above.

   However, if we were to *activate* the pointing device at a point between the current one and the point specified by 4, then the `touchTime` event would be generated.

4. The cursor is dragged past the `Box` node into empty space. This will generate the same events as in 2 above.

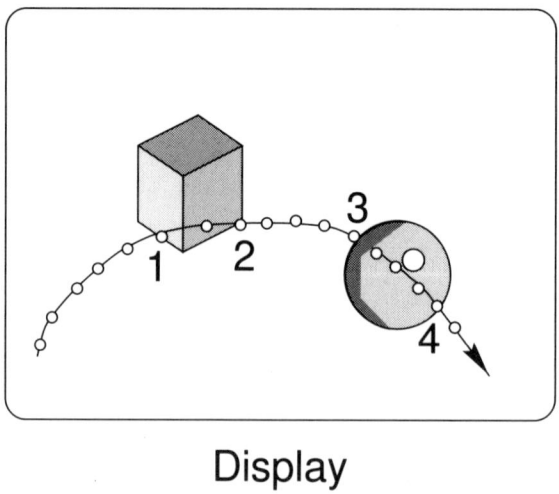

Display

Figure 7.2: The TouchSensor Node

CylinderSensor

The `CylinderSensor` node is a more specialized touch sensor node than `TouchSensor` itself. This node maps dragging motion with the pointing device onto the surface of the inside of an invisible cylinder, which allows rotation of objects with attached `CylinderSensor` nodes.

However, to confuse matters, different parts of the invisible cylinder can be used to calculate the rotational values, *i.e.*, the *caps* of the cylinder, or the *side* or tubing of the cylinder. Figure 7.3 illustrates the anatomy of a

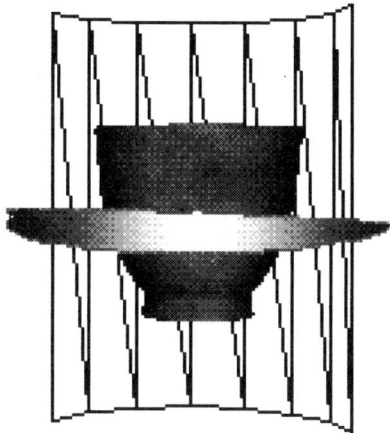

Figure 7.3: The `CylinderSensor` Node Acting On A Neolithic Pot

`CylinderSensor` node.

To provide "incremental dragging", *i.e.*, smooth dragging from the point at which the pointing device was activated to the point at which the pointing device was deactivated, the `autoOffset` field should be set to `TRUE`. This field keeps track of the last position at which the pointing device was deactivated and calculates the relative offset of the pointing device from that location. An example of using a `CylinderSensor` node to rotate a cube around its Y-axis follows:

```
#VRML V2.0 utf8
#
# Rotates a cube by using a CylinderSensor node
Viewpoint {
  position 0 0 10
 }

Transform {
  children [
    DEF CS CylinderSensor {
```

```
        autoOffset TRUE
      }
    DEF BOX Transform {
      children Shape {
        geometry Box {
          }
        appearance Appearance {
          material Material {
            diffuseColor 0 0 1
            }
          }
        }
      }
    }
  ]
  ROUTE CS.rotation_changed TO BOX.set_rotation
}
```

By clicking and dragging on the cube that should be in the centre of the viewport, you can rotate it around its Y-axis. If you try spinning it around its X-axis, *i.e.*, try to rotate it either towards or away from you you'll find that this isn't possible. To do this, we shall need to look at the `SphereSensor` node.

SphereSensor

The `SphereSensor` node allows full six-degrees-of-freedom rotation of objects that a `SphereSensor` node is attached to. This allows us to rotate objects round any axis at all, in behaviour akin to that of the "examiner viewer" present in most VRML browsers. From a conceptual point of view, the `SphereSensor` acts along the same lines as a "trackball" input device, which is operated by rolling your hand across the surface of the ball to produce rotation.

The `SphereSensor` operates in an almost identical way to the `CylinderSensor` in terms of information emitted via `eventOut` fields, but is far simpler in terms of configurability. The `autoOffset` field behaves like other sensor nodes. An example of rotating a cube on the spot with a `SphereSensor` follows.

```
#VRML V2.0 utf8
#
# Rotates a cube by using a SphereSensor node
```

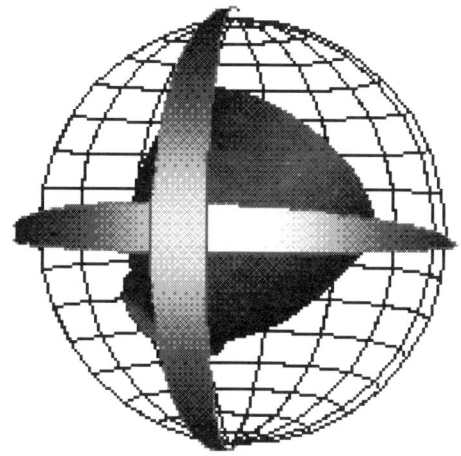

Figure 7.4: The SphereSensor Node Acting On A Neolithic Pot

```
Viewpoint {
  position 0 0 10
  }

Transform {
  children [
    DEF SS SphereSensor {
      autoOffset TRUE
      }
    DEF BOX Transform {
      children Shape {
        geometry Box {
          }
        appearance Appearance {
          material Material {
            diffuseColor 0 0 1
            }
          }
        }
      }
    }
```

```
    ]
    ROUTE SS.rotation_changed TO BOX.set_rotation
}
```

As you have no doubt noticed after trying the example out, the cube will now spin on all its axes instead of just around the Y-axis, as with the `Cylinder Sensor` node.

PlaneSensor

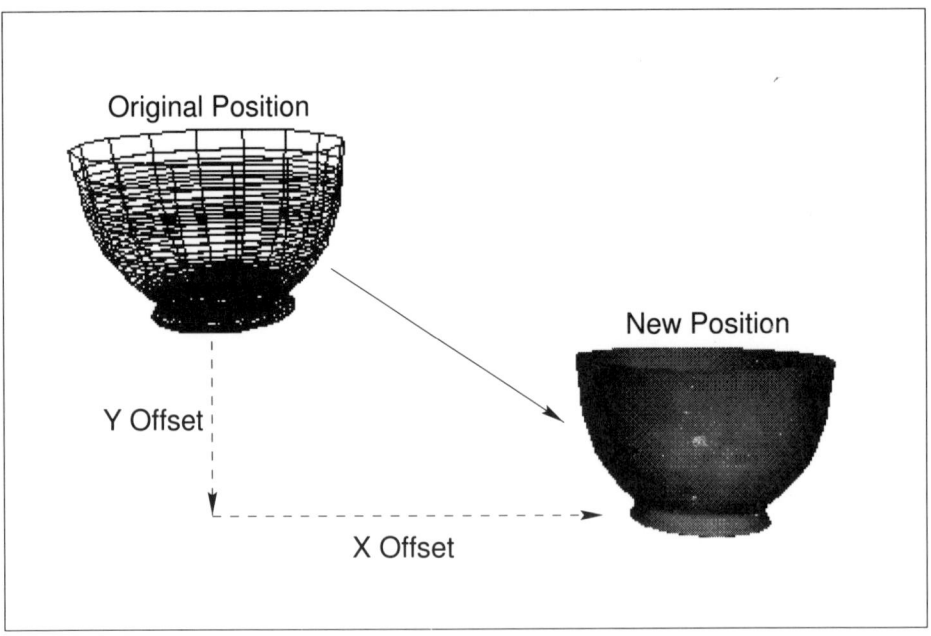

Figure 7.5: The `PlaneSensor` Node Acting On A Neolithic Pot

The `PlaneSensor` node is the corollary sensor type for the `CylinderSensor` node, in that it handles *translational* motion whereas the `CylinderSensor` handles *rotational* motion in the world. Both differ from the `SphereSensor` which provides rotation around the centre of the object. Hence the `PlaneSensor` is useful for moving objects *around* the world, at least in two dimensions.

The following code demonstrates the usage of a `PlaneSensor` node to move a `Box` node around the screen.

```
#VRML V2.0 utf8
#
# Demonstrates usage of a PlaneSensor
Viewpoint {
  position 0 0 10
 }

DEF T Transform {
  children [
      DEF PS PlaneSensor {}
      Shape {
        appearance Appearance {
          material Material {
            diffuseColor 1 1 1
          }
        }
        geometry Box {}
      }
    ]
  }


    ROUTE PS.translation_changed TO T.set_translation
```

The `PlaneSensor` motion corresponds to acting as if the viewport was a two-dimensional screen. It isn't possible within VRML2.0 to move objects wrapped in a `PlaneSensor` around in three-dimensional space. To accomplish this, you must move the object in one plane, then rotate your position by 90deg, then make the positional changes in another plane!

ProximitySensor

The `ProximitySensor` is the first *spatial* sensor node that we shall look at.

The `ProximitySensor` tracks interaction between the user and a defined re-gion of three-dimensional space, *e.g.*, when the user enters, exits or moves within that region in space. The region of space in question is defined as a cuboid with its dimensions specified in the `size` field, and its centre spec-ified in the `center` field. The cuboid is orientated along the three axes in

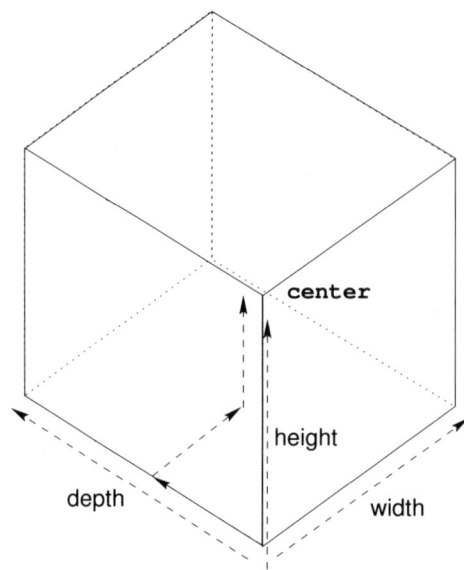

Figure 7.6: The `ProximitySensor` Node

the local co-ordinate system, and therefore is subject to the cumulative rotations down through the parent `Transform` nodes. Figure 7.6 illustrates the `ProximitySensor` node's geometry.

Furthermore, `ProximitySensors` may intersect each other, providing non-cuboid spatial regions in which user tracking is enabled, *e.g.*, as illustrated in Figure 7.7.

The important events generated by the `ProximitySensor` node for `ROUTE`ing into other nodes are as follows:

`position_changed` This `eventOut` contains an `SFVec3f` value that indicates the current location in three-dimensional space of the user in the current local co-ordinate system. This value can be used to inform other connected users in a multi-user world where a certain user is in the world.

`orientation_changed` This `eventOut` contains an **`SFRotation`** value that indicates the current orientation, or facing, of the user in the current local co-ordinate system.

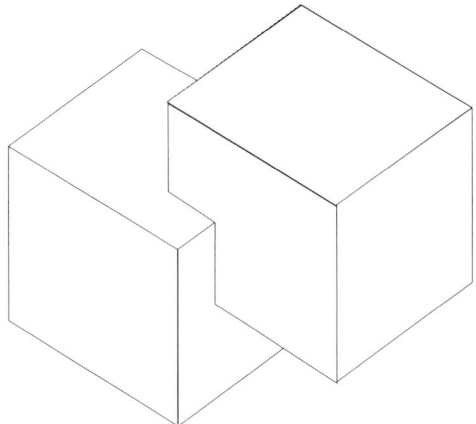

Figure 7.7: A `ProximitySensor` Union

`enterTime` This `eventOut` contains an `SFTime` value that represents the time that the user entered the volume bounded by the current `Proximity-Sensor` node. This event will also be emitted when the user *moves* within the sensor-bound volume.

`exitTime` This `eventOut` contains an `SFTime` value that represents the time that the user left the volume bounded by the current `ProximitySensor` node.

For user tracking in the world, for example in a multi-user situation, we could create a `ProximitySensor` node that encloses the entire world. In this case, any time the user moves will generate various events that can inform other connected users as to the exact position and orientation in the world of the moving user.

VisibilitySensor

The `VisibilitySensor` is another spatial node that informs the world whenever a specified region of three-dimensional space becomes either visible to the user, or invisible. This is particularly useful for disabling or enabling parts of the world depending on whether or not the user can see them; for example, if the user cannot see the rolling waves of the sea, then we can disable the `Script` node that generates the new waves, which will enhance performance. Similarly, visual cues may be added into the world depending on whether or not the user can see them. A more sophisticated use of the `VisibilitySensor` node would be to add and remove sections of the world's geometry as it becomes invisible to the user. This would in theory greatly increase performance; however, the cost of removing and adding data continuously would probably nullify any gains made!

The region of space that is bounded by a `VisibilitySensor` node is defined in exactly the same way as that for a `ProximitySensor` node, in that two fields, `center` and `size`, are used to fix the location of the centre of the region in space and to calculate the volume bounded by the region.

The `VisibilitySensor` will emit various `eventOut` events according to various criteria. These events are:

isActive The `isActive eventOut` is generated whenever the user, or the world, moves, or by any other event that causes a potential change in the visibility of the region of space bounded by a `VisibilitySensor`. If the region of space is visible, *i.e.*, is being rendered, then an `isActive` event is emitted with the value **FALSE**. If the region of space is *not* visible to the user, an `isActive` event of value **FALSE** is emitted.

enterTime This `eventOut` is generated whenever the `isActive` event is generated with the value **TRUE**.

exitTime This `eventOut` is generated whenever the `isActive` event is generated with the value **FALSE**.

TimeSensor

The `TimeSensor` node is the only node within the *VRML97 Specification* that allows you to control activity in the world according to the time at which you wish something to occur. For example, the potter in Skara Brae would start his wheel spinning when he starts pressing the pedal with his foot, or, to translate into VRML, when he clicked on the pedal. We would use a `CylinderSensor` for this. However, he must keep pedalling to keep the wheel spinning, just as we must continue dragging the mouse. Now, one day, the potter decides he's fed up with this, and he invents the perpetual motion potter's wheel, that, once started, will rotate at a steady speed. Similarly, he may invent a device that starts the wheel spinning every day at 9 a.m.

exactly. This is where the `TimeSensor` comes in useful.

The `TimeSensor` node functions on the principle that the sensor has a "cycle" in seconds, through which it elapses. This cycle is bounded by a starting time and a finishing time, both of these specified in the `SFTime` datatype, as discussed in Table 7.1. The `TimeSensor` then starts running from the time specified in the `startTime` field for the duration specified in `cycleInterval`, or the time specified in `stopTime`, whichever comes first.

We shall now take a more detailed look at the component fields of the `TimeSensor` node, explaining each, and illustrating some of their potential uses.

cycleInterval The `cycleInterval` field specifies the duration, in seconds, for which the `TimeSensor` will be enabled and generating events.

startTime The `startTime` field specifies an absolute time in `SFTime` format that the `TimeSensor` is to become enabled at, and therefore begin generating `eventOuts`.

stopTime The `stopTime` field specifies an absolute time in `SFTime` format that the `TimeSensor` is to become disabled at, and stop generating `eventOuts`.

loop The `loop` field specifies simply whether or not the `TimeSensor` will loop back and continue running after it reaches a stop point, *e.g.*, either when `cycleInterval` seconds have elapsed, or the system time is greater than or equal to `stopTime`.

Furthermore, the `TimeSensor` node has a plethora of `eventOut` fields that are populated with information the content creator can use. These are as follows:

cycleTime This `eventOut` is generated whenever the time of `cycleInterval` seconds + `startTime` has been reached, and the `TimeSensor` is still active. This field is intricately tied up in the interpolator nodes which we shall discuss in a later section. It can also be usefully used to perform periodic activities, such as playing a chiming bells audio clip once per hour.

fraction_changed The `fraction_changed` `eventOut` is generated every "tick", where a tick is a browser-dependent quantum of time. This `eventOut` is most useful for driving continuous behaviour, such as the rising and setting of the sun, where each tick will slightly alter the position of the sun, for example. The values emitted through this field are in the closed interval of 0 to 1 inclusive, and represent the completed fraction of the current cycle specified by `cycleInterval`; *e.g.*, in a `TimeSensor` node with `cycleInterval` of 5, at 2.5 seconds a `fraction_changed` `eventOut` with a value of 0.5 would be emitted.

`time` The `time` `eventOut` is generated every "tick", as per `fraction_changed`. It contains an `SFTime` value holding the absolute time of the current "tick".

We shall explore `TimeSensor` nodes in more detail as we discuss the next type of behavioural construct given to us in the *VRML97 Specification*, namely, *interpolators*.

Interpolators

Interpolator nodes provide the second behavioural construct in the *VRML97 Specification*. They are used to produce linear interpolated values in a certain range using a set of keys which are used to calculate the value of the interpolator. Interpolators are extremely useful for building keyframed animations. Each interpolator type follows the same definition, in that they all have a single `eventIn` entitled `set_fraction`, which specifies the input value to be used to calculate the output value, which is emitted out through the `value_changed` `eventOut`.

There are six forms of interpolator node, each producing interpolations of different VRML datatypes. To wit

`ColorInterpolator` The `ColorInterpolator` node interpolates colour values specified in the `SFColor` datatype. This node is extremely useful for providing smooth colour shifting of objects; *e.g.*, in a set of traffic lights, a `ColorInterpolator` node could be used to animate the blinking on and off of the lights, but instead of the lights having two discrete states, on and off, you could smoothly fade between the two colours.

`CoordinateInterpolator` The `CoordinateInterpolator` node interpolates co-ordinate values specified in the `MFVec3f` datatype, *i.e.*, an array of co-ordinates is produced instead of a single value. This node is used primarily for altering the geometry of objects, *e.g.*, in *morphing* between shapes.

NormalInterpolator The NormalInterpolator node interpolates normal values specified in the MFVec3f datatype, *i.e.*, an array of normals is produced instead of a single value. The NormalInterpolator node is useful for producing unusual surface effects, *e.g.*, making light strike a polygon at strange angles.

OrientationInterpolator The OrientationInterpolator node calculates interpolated values specified in the SFRotation datatype. The OrientationInterpolator node is used to produce rotational values which may be applied to Transform nodes to produce smooth rotational animation of objects.

PositionInterpolator The PositionInterpolator node interpolates SFVec3f values that may be used in the translation field of a Transform node for producing smooth motion between two locations in three-dimensional space.

ScalarInterpolator The ScalarInterpolator node interpolates scalar values, which are represented by the SFFloat datatype. This node is useful for altering single-value exposedFields of various nodes, such as a Fog node's visibilityRange or the radius of a SpotLight node's beam.

Having briefly introduced each type of interpolator node that is available to the content creator, we shall describe and illustrate each one in more detail.

Firstly, we shall take some time to explain the general concept involved in specifying key values, and producing interpolated values from an interpolator node, no matter what its type.

All interpolator nodes have two fields that are used to describe the interpolation. These fields are:

key which contains the range of valid input values which can be used for calculating an interpolation value.

keyValue which contains the range of valid output values that are interpolated using key.

To elaborate on this further, if we supply a value through the `eventIn` associated with each interpolator node, this value is compared to the values specified in the `key` field to find its "position". For example, if we have a node described in the following way:

```
ScalarInterpolator {
    key [ 0.0, 0.5, 1.0 ]
    keyValue [ 0, 50, 100 ]
}
```

and we `ROUTE` a value of `0.25` into its `eventIn`, we can see that the value that will be interpolated lies between `0.0` and `0.5` in the `key` field. This corresponds to values in the `keyValue` field between 0 and 50. Therefore, we can interpolate the output value in the following way:

```
eventOut SFFloat value_changed 25
    = 0 + ( ( 50 - 0 ) / ( 0.5 - 0.0 ) ) * 0.25
```

which is to say, the output value has been interpolated from the relationship between the `key` and the `keyValue` fields.

ColorInterpolator

The `ColorInterpolator` node, as described above, is used to produce smooth blending between colours, the number of which is as specified in the interpolator definition.

For example, we can use a `ColorInterpolator` node to make the surface colour of a `Box` node "pulse" between the three primary colours as time passes, as can be seen in the example below.

```
#VRML V2.0 utf8
Viewpoint {
  position 0 0 7
}

Transform {
  rotation 1 1 1 0.78
  children [
    Shape {
      geometry Box {
        }
```

```
        appearance Appearance {
          material DEF MATERIAL Material {
            diffuseColor 1 1 1
            }
          }
        }
      DEF CINTERP ColorInterpolator {
        key [ 0, 0.5, 1.0 ]
        keyValue [ 1 0 0, 0 1 0, 0 0 1 ]
        }
      DEF CLOCK TimeSensor {
        cycleInterval 1.0
        stopTime 0
        startTime 1
        loop TRUE
        }
    ]
  ROUTE CLOCK.fraction_changed TO CINTERP.set_fraction
  ROUTE CINTERP.value_changed TO MATERIAL.set_diffuseColor
  }
```

This example program is driven by a **TimeSensor** node which continuously emits **fraction_changed** events containing an **SFFloat** value, which we can use as a **key** value in our **ColorInterpolator**. As can be seen, the **ColorInterpolator** is defined to interpolate a colour between either red and green, or green and blue.

CoordinateInterpolator

The **CoordinateInterpolator** is an extremely powerful node, in that you can carry out arbitrary mesh deformation in a controlled manner. This node produces an array of new co-ordinates which may be used, *e.g.*, in an **IndexedFaceSet** node to produce morphing effects on an object.

For example, if we define a cube using the **IndexedFaceSet** node, we can apply some interesting effects to it using interpolated co-ordinate values.

```
#VRML V2.0 utf8
#
# Morphs a square into something else!
Viewpoint {
```

```
    position 0 0 5
  }

Transform {
  children [
  Shape {
    geometry IndexedFaceSet {
      coord DEF COORDINATES Coordinate {
        point [ -0.5 -0.5 0, 0.5 -0.5 0,
                0.5 0.5 0, -0.5 0.5 0 ]
      }
      coordIndex [ 0, 1, 2, 3, -1 ]
    }
    appearance Appearance {
      material Material {
        diffuseColor 1 1 1
      }
    }
  }
  DEF CLOCK TimeSensor {
    cycleInterval 5.0
    stopTime 0
    startTime 1
    loop TRUE
  }
  DEF CINTERP CoordinateInterpolator {
    key [ 0.0, 0.33, 0.66, 1.0 ]
    keyValue [ -0.5 -0.5 0, 0.5 -0.5 0,
               0.5 0.5 0, -0.5 0.5 0,
               -1.0 -1.0 0, 1 -1 0,
               1 1 0, -1 1 0,
               -0.5 -0.5 0, 0.5 -0.5 0,
               1 1 0, -1 1 0,
               -0.5 -0.5 0, 0.5 -0.5 0,
               0.5 0.5 0, -0.5 0.5 0 ]
  }
  ]
ROUTE CLOCK.fraction_changed TO CINTERP.set_fraction
ROUTE CINTERP.value_changed TO COORDINATES.set_point
}
```

This demonstration shows the square polygon growing to twice its size, then the bottom edge halves in size, with the top following suit until the square is its original size again. This is an extremely simple example, but you can see the potential power inherent in the `CoordinateInterpolator` node. Notice also the smooth transition between each frame of animation.

However, sharp cookies will have spotted a potential problem or two with this node. To provide four frames of animation of a simple, and single, square polygon, we have had to *respecify every co-ordinate per frame.* This is important! Now, imagine a complex model, say, a dinosaur, and imagine the amount of data required to produce animation on that. The mind truly boggles. Given that we can assume three floating-point values *per vertex* in the model, and that each floating-point value is going to average, say, three bytes, a single frame of animation would come out at roughly *10,800 bytes* per frame of animation! And that's if we remove all the white space out of the frame definitions. More importantly, the work involved in calculating each of the co-ordinates for each new frame realistically places use of this node into the realms of editing programs, and not hand-crafted VRML scenes.

A second potential beartrap is that for each frame of animation, an entire new model may require to be created, which will replace the previous model in the scene. This is quite a costly operation involving calculation of polygon normals, texture co-ordinates, not to mention memory allocation issues and destruction of the previous model. This problem is more subtle since the content creator may not readily spot the undesired impact of this node.

NormalInterpolator

The `NormalInterpolator` is probably the interpolator node that will be used the least, possibly due to the fact that a lot of content creators will work the default generated normals, and not experiment heavily with them.

The `NormalInterpolator` node allows you to specify a new set of normals for use in, *e.g.*, the `IndexedFaceSet` node. This will produce the effects you would hope for when you alter vertex normals, *e.g.*, the lighting of a polygon will alter, since you are changing the direction the polygon is facing, without actually moving the polygon. This can be quite a useful effect. It should perhaps be noted that the `NormalInterpolator` node generates an `eventOut` of datatype `MFVec3f`, which means you must list enough normals for each vertex in the `IndexedFaceSet` for as many frames as you have specified in the `key` field of the `NormalInterpolator`, otherwise errors will occur.

An example of the `NormalInterpolator` node in action is shown below.

```
#VRML V2.0 utf8
#
# Wiggles normals around
Viewpoint {
  position 0 0 5
 }


Transform {
  children [
    Shape {
      geometry IndexedFaceSet {
        coord Coordinate {
          point [ -0.5 -0.5 0, 0.5 -0.5 0,
                   0.5 0.5 0, -0.5 0.5 0 ]
           }
          normal DEF NORMALS Normal {
            vector [ 1 0 0, 1 0 0, 1 0 0, 1 0 0 ]
            }
          coordIndex [ 0, 1, 2, 3, -1 ]
          normalIndex [ 0, 1, 2, 3, -1 ]
          }
        appearance Appearance {
          material Material {
            diffuseColor 1 1 1
            }
          }
        }
      }
      DEF CLOCK TimeSensor {
        cycleInterval 5.0
        stopTime 0
        startTime 1
        loop TRUE
        }
      DEF CINTERP NormalInterpolator {
        key [ 0.0, 0.5, 1.0 ]
        keyValue [ 1 0 0, 1 0 0, 1 0 0, 1 0 0,
```

```
                    0 0 1, 0 0 1, 0 0 1, 0 0 1,
                    1 0 0, 1 0 0, 1 0 0, 1 0 0 ]
        }
      ]
      ROUTE CLOCK.fraction_changed TO CINTERP.set_fraction
      ROUTE CINTERP.value_changed TO NORMALS.set_vector
    }
```

The example demonstrates the normals moving from being aligned along the
x-axis, which will result in the polygon being totally dark, to being aligned
along the *z*-axis, which will cause the polygon to "fade in" until completely
bright. The normals will then turn back round to become aligned with the
x-axis again, thereby causing the polygon to darken and "fade out".

OrientationInterpolator

The `OrientationInterpolator` node provides a capability to the content
creator to rotate objects smoothly along any of an object's axes. This is an
extremely useful thing to be able to do, since it removes the need for the content creator to calculate sequences of rotational values. The `value_changed`
`eventOut` generated by the `OrientationInterpolator` node is ROUTEd, typically, into the `rotation` field of the nearest enclosing `Transform` node. This,
however, need not be the case. Entire groups of objects may be rotated independently of each other using this node, and complex scenes, such as the
solar system, where each planet orbits the sun, but also spins around its own
axis, can be modelled with relative ease.

A short example demonstrating the use of the `OrientationInterpolator`
node is as follows.

```
#VRML V2.0 utf8
#
# Rotates a cube a bit
DEF TRANSFORM Transform {
  children [
    Shape {
      geometry Box {
      }
      appearance Appearance {
        material Material {
          diffuseColor 1 1 1
```

```
            }
          }
        }
      DEF OINTERP OrientationInterpolator {
        key [ 0.0, 0.33, 0.66, 1.0 ]
        keyValue [ 0 0 1 0, 1 0 0 3.14, 0 1 0 5.14, 0 0 1 3.14 ]
      }
      DEF CLOCK TimeSensor {
        cycleInterval 5.0
        stopTime 0
        startTime 1
        loop TRUE
      }
    ]
  }
  ROUTE CLOCK.fraction_changed TO OINTERP.set_fraction
  ROUTE OINTERP.value_changed TO TRANSFORM.set_rotation
```

In this example, the cube will rotate along each axis, one after the other. Again, notice the smooth rotation between the axes.

A more exciting example that we can use to illustrate the power of OrientationInterpolator nodes in conjunction with nested transformations in the scene graph, and mobile PointLight nodes is as follows, where we have our henge scene from Chapter 4, illuminated by the sun, which revolves around the world.

```
#VRML V2.0 utf8
#
# Simple orbiting demonstration
EXTERNPROTO trilithon [ field SFFloat height ] "trilithon.wrl"

Viewpoint {
    position 0 0 30
  }

Transform {
    children [
        ### The orbiting objects.....
```

```
DEF ORBIT Transform {
    children [
        Transform {
            translation 0 0 -30
            children [
                ### The yellow Sphere representing
                ### the Sun
                Shape {
                    geometry Sphere {
                        radius 4
                        }
                    appearance Appearance {
                        material Material {
                            diffuseColor 1 1 0
                            }
                        }
                    }

                ### A yellow point light
                PointLight {
                    location 0 0 -30
                    color 1 1 0
                    intensity 10
                    radius 100
                    }
                ]
            }
        ]
    }

### A flattened Sphere upon which the trilithons sit
Transform {
    scale 1 0.1 1
    translation 0 -1 0
    children [
        Shape {
            geometry Sphere {
                radius 15
                }
            appearance Appearance {
```

```
                        material Material {
                            diffuseColor 0 1 1
                            specularColor 1 1 1
                            shininess 10
                        }
                    }
                }
            ]
        }

### The four trilithons in the henge
Transform {
    translation 10 0 0
    rotation 0 1 0 1.57
    children trilithon {}
}
Transform {
    translation 0 0 10
    children trilithon {}
}
Transform {
    translation -10 0 0
    rotation 0 1 0 -1.57
    children trilithon {}
}
Transform {
    translation 0 0 -10
    children trilithon {}
}

### The Clock
DEF CLOCK TimeSensor {
    cycleInterval 50
    stopTime 0
    startTime 1
    loop TRUE
}

DEF OINTERP OrientationInterpolator {
    key [ 0, 0.20, 0.40, 0.60, 0.80, 1.0 ]
```

```
                keyValue [ 0 1 0 0.0, 0 1 0 1.25, 0 1 0 2.5,
                          0 1 0 3.75, 0 1 0 5, 0 1 0 6.25 ]
              }
          ]
      }


      ROUTE CLOCK.fraction_changed TO OINTERP.set_fraction
      ROUTE OINTERP.value_changed TO ORBIT.set_rotation
```

In this example, the `TimeSensor` drives the `OrientationInterpolator` which is ROUTEd into a `Transform` node that rotates both the `Sphere` representing the sun and the `PointLight` node co-located with the `Sphere`.

PositionInterpolator

The `PositionInterpolator` node is primarily used for smoothly moving objects around the three-dimensional space the world defines. The `value_changed` eventOut is usually ROUTEd to the `translation` field of an enclosing `Transform` node. As with the `OrientationInterpolator` node, this makes for powerful repositioning capabilities.

A short example that moves a cone around a scene follows.

```
#VRML V2.0 utf8
#
# Moves a cone around a scene
Viewpoint {
  position 0 7 12
  orientation 1 0 0 -0.5
 }

DEF TRANSFORM Transform {
  children [
    # A local co-ordinate system for the cone
    DEF CONETRANSFORM Transform {
      children [
        Shape {
          geometry Cone {
           }
          appearance Appearance {
            material Material {
```

```
                    diffuseColor 1 0 0
                  }
                }
              }
            ]
          }
        # The floor
        Shape {
          geometry Box {
            size 10 0.1 10
          }
          appearance Appearance {
            material Material {
              diffuseColor 0 1 1
            }
          }
        }
        DEF PINTERP PositionInterpolator {
          key [ 0.0, 0.18, 0.36, 0.5, 0.68, 0.86, 1.0 ]
          keyValue [ 0 1 0, 0 1 -1, 1 1 -2, 0 2 -5, 0 5 -3,
                     0 6 -2, 0 1 0 ]
        }
        DEF CLOCK TimeSensor {
          cycleInterval 5.0
          stopTime 0
          startTime 1
          loop TRUE
        }
      ]
    }
    ROUTE CLOCK.fraction_changed TO PINTERP.set_fraction
    ROUTE PINTERP.value_changed TO CONETRANSFORM.set_translation
```

In this example, we have demonstrated the capability of moving a local object around the scene. However, if we change the ROUTE statement that ROUTEs the eventOut of the interpolator node to the exposedField of the Transform node, from

```
    ROUTE PINTERP.value_changed TO CONETRANSFORM.set_translation
```

to:

```
ROUTE PINTERP.value_changed TO TRANSFORM.set_translation
```

we'll get the quite funky effect of both the floor and the cone moving around!
That's the power of the coupling of interpolator nodes and local co-ordinate
system in action!

ScalarInterpolator

The final interpolator that is specified in the *VRML97 Specification* is the
ScalarInterpolator. This node is used to interpolate scalar values from
an input value, the resulting **eventOut** containing an **SFFloat** value. There
are many possibilities with this node, one of the most interesting being the
ability to alter the visibility limit of **Fog** causing a "descending mist" effect.
You could also use this effect with a background colour of black, and a fog
colour of black to give a "nightfall" effect, if you so desired.

```
#VRML V2.0 utf8
#
# Makes Fog nearer and further away using a ScalarInterpolator
Viewpoint {
    position 0 5 30
  }

DEF FOG Fog {
    visibilityRange 100
    color 1 1 1
    fogType "LINEAR"
  }

Transform {
    children [
        Shape {
            geometry IndexedFaceSet {
                coord Coordinate {
                    point [ -20 0 20,
                            -20 0 -20,
                             20 0 -20,
                             20 0 20 ]
                }
                coordIndex [ 0, 1, 2, 3, -1 ]
                solid FALSE
```

```
                        }
                    appearance Appearance {
                        material Material {
                            diffuseColor 0 0 0
                        }
                    }
                }
            DEF SINTERP ScalarInterpolator {
                key [ 0.0, 0.1, 0.2, 0.3, 0.4, 0.5,
                      0.6, 0.7, 0.8, 0.9, 1.0 ]
                keyValue [ 70, 60, 50, 40, 30, 20,
                           30, 40, 50, 60, 70 ]
            }

            DEF CLOCK TimeSensor {
                cycleInterval 15.0
                loop TRUE
                stopTime 0
            }
        ]
    }


    ROUTE CLOCK.fraction_changed TO SINTERP.set_fraction
    ROUTE SINTERP.value_changed TO FOG.set_visibilityRange
```

Collision Detection

Finally, in the remit of covering the basic behavioural and interaction features of VRML2.0, we must look at the topic of *collision detection*. This is possibly the most important part of producing a realistic effect within a three-dimensional world. The ability to act as if you were *real*, or, at least, less ethereal!

Collision detection provides realism through solidity to the user navigating a three-dimensional world. For example, if I am navigating through the passageway in Skara Brae in real life, I would possibly be brushing against or bumping into the walls of narrow sinuous passageway. In a three-dimensional world with no collision detection, I would simply *pass through* the walls, as if a ghost. With collision detection, it is noted by the browser that I have "hit" something, and it will stop me from passing through that piece of geometry. This is more *real* to the average user than being able to float through walls. Admittedly, there are good occasions when floating through walls is the desired behaviour, but in most cases collision detection is a desired feature.

VRML2.0 implements a simple model for collision detection, in that even though *all* objects in the world are collidable by default, the only collisions tested are those between the user's avatar and other objects in the scene. In the case of two objects colliding, this is *not* calculated by the browser. To clarify this point, since it is an important one, we shall look at some examples.

The stone-carver one evening decides to go for a walk along the shoreline. He gets up in the dark and stumbles around his house bumping into objects. The objects move away from him when he hits them. A pot falls to the floor and disappears through it. He then bumps into the door, pushing it outwards into the passageway. It tips over, disappearing through the floor of the passageway never to be seen again! After much crashing and banging, the stone-carver makes it to the shoreline and watches a gull drop oysters onto a rock from a height. The oysters continue their travels through the rock and disappear. The gull swoops down, picks up another oyster and drops it on the stone-carver's head. He dies instantly.

There are obviously many words of wisdom in this tale. Most of all, don't stand under gulls when you have collision detection enabled. It can be quite distressing.[5]

But digressions aside, the fact that objects other than the avatar do not interact with each other is quite a collosal limitation in the usefulness of the `Collision` node. However, we shall now take a look at the `Collision` node itself and discuss some of the possibilities we have open to us.

The `Collision` node is a grouping node in the scene graph, akin to `Transform`, `Group`, `Anchor` and `Billboard`. Therefore, the collision detection parameters specified in a `Collision` node will affect all the nodes specified in the `children` field. This is syntactically equivalent to using a `Transform` node, for example.

---

[5]You will be happy to know that the gull in question did in fact manage to break the oyster open on the stone-carver's head, and had a perfectly enjoyable dinner.

Since all nodes in a scene are collidable by default, you may disable collision detection for all children of a given `Collision` node by setting the field `collide` to FALSE. For example, to make the scene have no collision detection at all, we could write a small VRML file:

```
#VRML V2.0 utf8
#
Collision {
  collide FALSE
  children [
    Transform {
      children [
        Shape {
          geometry Box {}
          appearance Appearance {
            material Material {
              diffuseColor 1 1 1
            }
          }
        }
      ]
    }
  ]
}
```

i.e., the `Collision` node specifying no collision detection encapsulates the entire scene graph.

As with the other grouping nodes, the `Collision` node has fields specifying the size and location in three-dimensional space of the centre of a bounding box that encompasses all children of that `Collision` node. This allows the browser to test collision detection is a finely granulated way.

Collision detection is a fairly computationally intensive operation requiring the bounding box surrounding the user's avatar to be tested for intersections against all the other bounding boxes of all the nodes within the scene, as shown in Figure 7.8. In this instance, we would be testing against seven separate bounding boxes, each with six planes of intersection to test against.

A simple speed-up would be to only test against the bounding boxes of the

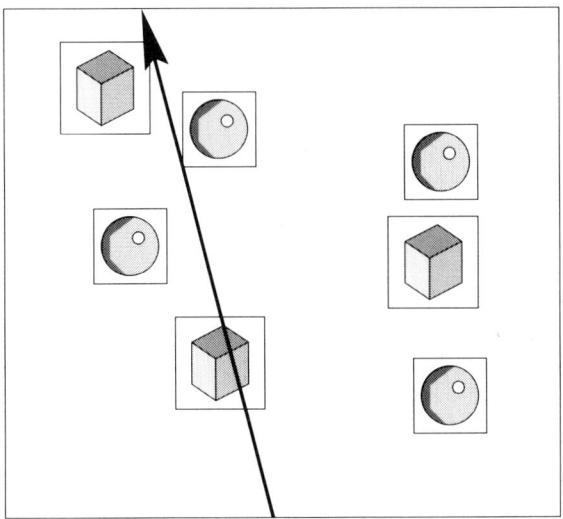

Figure 7.8: Object-Level Bounding Boxes In A Scene

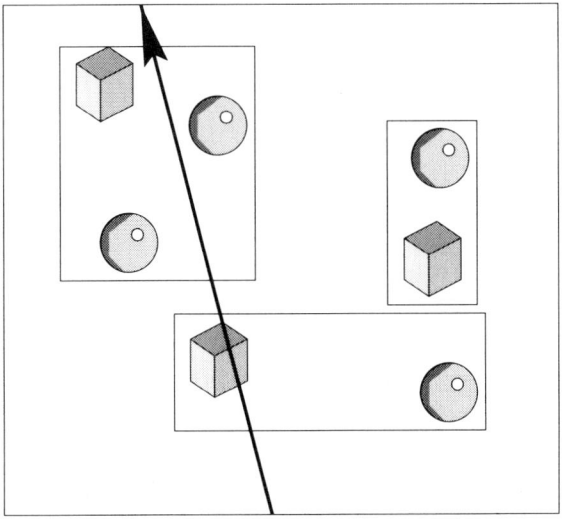

Figure 7.9: Grouping-Node-Level Bounding Boxes In A Scene

grouping nodes in the scene, since we may make the assumption that if we have not intersected with the bounding box of the grouping node, we cannot possibly have intersected with the bounding box of any of its children, as seen in Figure 7.9. Now, in this case, we need to make three bounding box tests for collision, which returns that we have collided with two out of three. We would then need to test each individual bounding box within the target grouping nodes. This is actually slightly worse than before! However, as discussed in Chapter 3, careful bounding box construction is the key here. In Figure 7.10, we have arranged the bounding boxes more intelligently, which saves us an object-level bounding box test. Of course, this example is fairly pathological, since we will be passing through the densest area of the world, but hopefully the principle is clear.

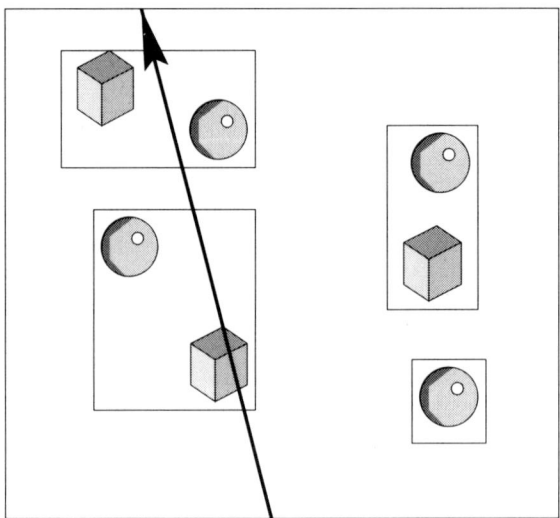

Figure 7.10: A Better Grouping Of Grouping-Node-Level Bounding Boxes

Finally, Figure 7.11 illustrates the principle working at its best. In this case, we are moving through a more sparsely populated area of the scene. Using an object-level collision-detection algorithm, we would make seven tests. Using bounding box tests, we make four bounding box tests, and a single object-level test. Multiply the number of objects in the scene, and you will find that the number of tests required increases dramatically and the value of the

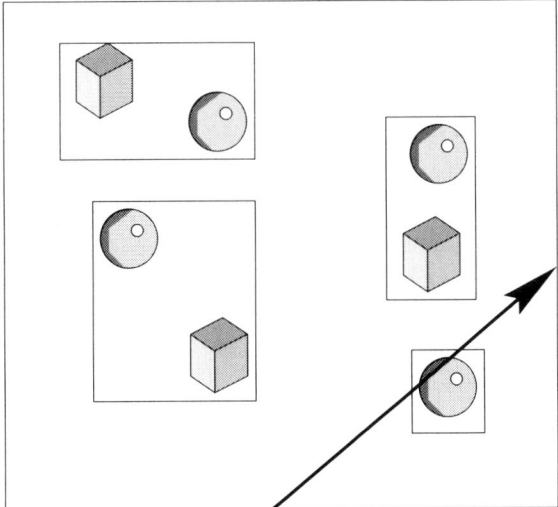

Figure 7.11: Taking A Less Dense Path Through The Scene

bounding-box-level test becomes more readily apparent.

A further optimization would be to attempt to calculate collision detection on bounding *spheres* instead of bounding *boxes*. To explain this seemingly bizarre statement, we have to realize that with a sphere there is only one distance from the centre of the sphere to any point on the "skin" of it, and that is the *radius*. If we simply test the distance from the centre of the sphere to the nearest edge of a bounding box,[6] we can tell immediately if it intersects. We do not need to test any other parts of the bounding box. This is shown in Figure 7.12.

In the case of testing a bounding box against another bounding volume, we have to test each *plane* of the bounding box, which requires possibly up to six tests per object. Of course, testing by bounding sphere is not necessarily as accurate as testing against a bounding box, as seen in Figure 7.13. To the left and right of the object, there is quite a lot of space which will be considered to have intersected with the object when it in actual fact nowhere near.

---

[6]Or better still, another bounding sphere.

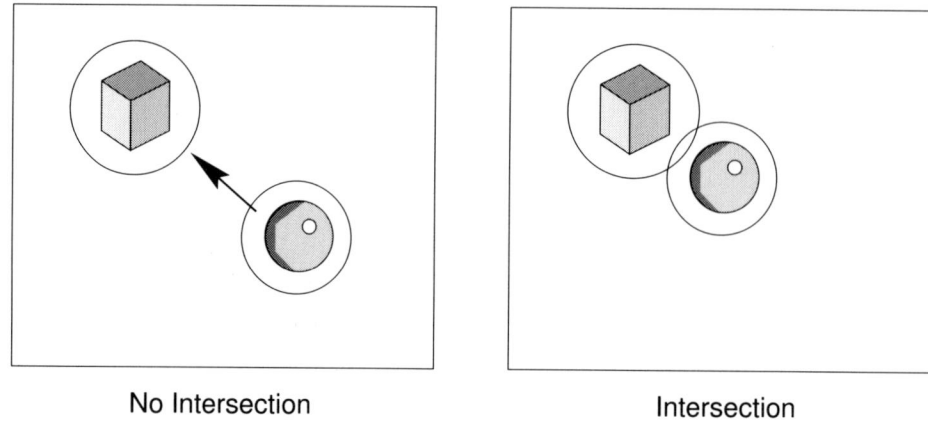

No Intersection   Intersection

Figure 7.12: Spherical Bounding Boxes

Cuboid bounded by spherical bounding volume

Figure 7.13: An Over-Enthusiastic Spherical Bounding Box

This facility of specifying another bounding volume is supported by the `Collision` node in the form of the `proxy` field. This field contains a standard geometry node, *e.g.* a sphere, which will be used in place of the calculated bounding box of the `Collision` node. However, note carefully that the *size* of the proxy bounding volume is *not* calculated for you! For example:

```
#VRML V2.0 utf8
#

Transform {
  children [
    Collision {
      collide TRUE
      proxy {
        Shape {
          geometry Sphere {
            radius 5
          }
        }
      }

      children [
        Transform {
          translation 0 3 0
          children [
            Shape {
              geometry Cube {}
              appearance Appearance {
                material Material {
                  diffuseColor 1 1 1
                }
              }
            }
          ]
        }

        Shape {
          geometry Cone {}
```

```
          appearance Appearance {
            material Material {
              diffuseColor 1 0 0
            }
          }
        }
      ]
    }
  ]
}
```

So, the moral of this story is to be very careful about using the `proxy` field! You can do faster collision detection, thereby making your worlds both more pleasurable to interact with and realistically 'solid', but at the expense of occasionally over-enthusiastic collisions with objects in the scene.

A pertinent question is: "How do we know we've collided with something?". The answer is perfectly straightforward. The `Collision` node contains an `eventOut` called `collideTime`, which is of type `SFTime`. This `eventOut` is generated upon detection of a collision between the avatar and any collidable object in the scene. We then **ROUTE** this value elsewhere. For example, if the stone-carver walks into a door, he might well cry out in pain, and the door will topple inwards. We can simulate these events using a combination of the techniques we have been discussing, and present the example code below.

```
#VRML V2.0 utf8
#
# Small scene in which the avatar walks into a door,
# which causes him to cry out in pain, then the door
# topples away from him.

Transform {
    children [

        ### The door with a Collision node
        DEF DOORCOLLIDE Collision {
            children [
                DEF DOOR Transform {
                    children [
                        Shape {
                            geometry Box {
```

```
                          }
                      appearance Appearance {
                         material Material {
                            diffuseColor 1 1 1
                         }
                      }
                  }
              ]
          }
      ]
  }


    ### An AudioClip containing the word "Ouch!"
    DEF OUCH AudioClip {
       url "ouch.wav"
    }


    ### A TimeSensor used to animate the door falling
    DEF CLOCK TimeSensor {
       cycleInterval 5.0
       loop FALSE
    }


    ### An Orientation Interpolator to move the door
    DEF OINTERP OrientationInterpolator {
       key [ 0.0, 0.25, 0.5, 0.75, 1.0 ]
       keyValue [ 1 0 0 0.62,
                  1 0 0 1.25,
                  1 0 0 1.88,
                  1 0 0 2.51,
                  1 0 0 3.14 ]
    }
  ]
}


ROUTE DOORCOLLIDE.collideTime TO OUCH.startTime
```

```
ROUTE DOORCOLLIDE.collideTime TO CLOCK.startTime


ROUTE CLOCK.fraction_changed TO OINTERP.set_fraction
ROUTE OINTERP.value_changed TO DOOR.set_rotation
```

Chapter 8

Script Nodes

As we discussed in the previous chapter, VRML has many powerful and useful animation, behaviour and interactivity extensions, but what if we want to do something more complicated, or something not quite covered by these extensions, or something that doesn't quite fit into the event model?

That is where the usefulness of the `Script` node comes into play. This node allows you to set up your own definition, involving `field`, `exposedField`, `eventIn` and `eventOut` fields. The `Script` node also has several fields included in it by default, which we shall look at in more detail. The full capability of the `Script` node is rounded out by the association of a piece of arbitrary code, written in either Java, JavaScript or VRMLScript, which contains the logic desired by the content creator.

Anatomy Of A `Script` Node

The `Script` node, as we noted above, is somewhat unusual when compared to the other nodes in the *VRML97 Specification*, in that it allows the content creators to create their own custom node definition and associate a short program with that node as specified in the `url` field. A sample `Script` node definition may look like this:

```
DEF GRAPHSCRIPT Script {
    url "http://some.url.com/scriptBody.class"
    eventIn SFTime startTime
```

197

```
        eventIn SFFloat variance
        field SFInt32 xDimension 10
        field SFInt32 yDimension 10
        eventOut MFFloat pointHeight
}
```

which would be useful for building a three-dimensional graph, by passing in various parameters, such as the x and y dimensions of the graph, and a variance value used to perturb the output values. The actual Java code that will be used to calculate the graph functions is located at the URL specified in the url field.

The Script node also has three standard fields that are implicitly defined in your Script nodes, namely:

```
    exposedField MFString url          []
    field        SFBool   directOutput FALSE
    field        SFBool   mustEvaluate FALSE
```

These fields have the following definition:

url contains a list of URLs at which the code containing the logic of the Script node can be located. Each URL is tried until one successfully provides the code logic.

The contents of the url field allow for a varied mixture of information regarding the actual code logic used to drive the Script node.

- *Java*
  Java classes may be referred to by a legal URL in compiled bytecode format (the .class file). You may not refer to Java source code[1] in the url field.

- *Inlined Java bytecode*
  Java bytecode may be *inlined* in the url field of a Script node. This is accomplished by converting the binary .class file generated by the Java compiler into *BASE64* encoding, which is an ASCII encoding. The BASE64 encoded bytecode is what is included in the url field. We also need to supply a hint to the

---

[1]At least, not at the moment, although I would imagine at some point in the future, some browsers may well feature built-in Java compilers.

browser to let it know it should parse the `url` field as BASE64 encoded bytecode instead of as a legal URL that points at Java bytecode external to the `Script`. This is done by specifying the first few characters in the `url` field as `javabc:`—for example:

```
DEF INLINESCRIPT Script {
    url "javabc:
        AAVDFEFJAJSJDJJX88345jJSJK8234234jJSKDF
        SDFKLJWER*(&RWEJLKJ#KJLKJLKJDSF&&(S*&GA
      "
}
```

At parse-time, the contents of the `url` field are decoded and a new Java class instantiated. Further internal copies of that Java class may now be made without further need to decode.

We should also note that the VRML browser that you are using needs to support this method of decoding inline Java bytecode for this technique to work.

- *JavaScript*
  JavaScript source code may be included in the `url` field of a `Script` node. This is primarily due to the fact that JavaScript cannot actually be compiled into Java bytecode, and therefore requires that the source code be included, or referenced to.

  For direct inclusion in the `url` field of a `Script` node, the first few characters of the `url` field must be `javascript:`. For example:

```
DEF JAVASCRIPT Script {
    url "javascript:
        function setToFalse() {
            value = FALSE;
          }
        function switchValues() {
            value =
                ( value == FALSE ) ?
                    value = TRUE : value = FALSE;
          }
```

```
                "
        }
```

The JavaScript code is parsed once at parse-time for the VRML world, and an execution tree is built which is duplicated as required, *e.g.*, if the `Script` node is instantiated multiple times in the VRML world.

It should be noted that it is required for this style of scripting that the browser that you are using supports JavaScript internal scripting.

- *VRMLScript*
  VRMLScript is a small, compact Java-based language designed and implemented by Silicon Graphics to allow small, yet powerful, internal scripting capabilities to VRML2.0.

  As with JavaScript, there are no VRMLScript compilers currently available, so the logic of the `Script` node as implemented in VRMLScript must be included as source code, or the source code be referenced by a legal URL. The `url` field again supplies a hint to the VRML parser as to the contents of the `url` field. If the first few characters of the `url` field are `vrmlscript:`, then the remainder of the contents of the `url` field should be parsed as inlined VRMLScript source code. For example:

```
DEF VRMLSCRIPT Script {
    url "vrmlscript:
        function setFalse() {
            value = FALSE;
          }
        function setTrue() {
            value = TRUE;
          }
          "
    }
```

VRMLScript-based `Script` nodes are parsed once at parse-time for the VRML world, and the resulting execution tree is merely duplicated in the case of multiple instantiations of the `Script` node.

Again, it should be noted that the browser needs to have implemented a VRMLScript parser for any sort of VRMLScript-based `Script` nodes to successfully parse and run.

`directOutput` allows the `Script` node to issue events directly to any node to which it has access, *e.g.*, a node passed into the `Script` node, either as an `exposedField` or an `eventIn` field of type `SFNode`. This node may also dynamically establish or break `ROUTE`s at will.

This behaviour will occur when `directOutput` is set to `TRUE`. With the default setting of `FALSE`, the `Script` node may only affect the rest of the world via events sent through its `eventOut` fields.

`mustEvaluate` allows the browser to delay sending input events to the `Script` node until the values used in the defined `eventOut` fields are required by the browser. This is the default behaviour of this field, *i.e.*, `mustEvaluate` is set to `FALSE`. When `mustEvaluate` is set to `TRUE`, the browser should send input events to the `Script` node as soon as possible.

The `Script` node, as mentioned above, allows the content creator to define as many new custom fields as desired in the `Script` node. These can be of three assorted field types:

1. `field`
2. `eventIn`
3. `eventOut`

and can have a data type of any of the legal VRML datatypes as discussed in Chapter 7. Sharp-eyed readers will no doubt notice that `exposedField` field types are not allowed within `Script` nodes.

The fields defined by the content creator are subject to the same syntactic rules as other predefined fields within the standard set of nodes, *e.g.*, you may use `DEF` / `USE` or `IS`, in the case of the `Script` node being embedded in a `PROTO` node. To elaborate on this topic further, we shall now present a short example of a `Script` node driven by a Java class. This example takes an `ElevationGrid` node and perturbs the vertices in that node, by randomly altering their heights over time. This behaviour produces a wave effect that can be reused time and time again.

```
#VRML V2.0 utf8
#
# Random wave effect

PROTO wave [ field SFFloat choppiness 0.25
             field SFInt32 xDimen 10
             field SFInt32 zDimen 10
             field SFFloat xSpace 2
             field SFFloat zSpace 2 ] {
```

Firstly, we declare the code as being a `PROTO` called "wave". We also define several arguments which the content creator may pass into the `PROTO` which alters the appearance and behaviour of the node, namely:

choppiness regulates the maximum and minimum heights allowed by the wave generation code. Higher values of this parameter provide for extremely choppy water, whereas lower values generate more smooth rippling effects.

xDimen, zDimen specify the size in units of the `ElevationGrid` that we are using as the base geometry producer for the wave node. These values correspond to the `xDimension` and `zDimension` fields of the `ElevationGrid` node.

xSpace, zSpace specify the size in units of each cell of the `ElevationGrid`. These values correspond to the `xSpacing` and `zSpacing` fields of the `ElevationGrid` node.

```
Transform {
    children [
        Shape {
            geometry DEF EGRID ElevationGrid {
                xSpacing IS xSpace
                zSpacing IS zSpace
                xDimension IS xDimen
                zDimension IS zDimen
                solid FALSE
                creaseAngle 1.05
            }
            appearance Appearance {
                material Material {
```

```
                    diffuseColor 0 0 1
                }
                texture ImageTexture {
                    url "water.gif"
                }
            }
        }
    ]
}
```

This section defines the geometry for the scene, being a single ElevationGrid node, with the appearance of a texture map of water mapped on to it.

The interesting points to note in this section are the use of the IS keyword which maps the parameters specified above onto the appropriate fields of the ElevationGrid node, allowing the content creator to alter the dimensions and properties of the underlying geometry. We also choose to name the ElevationGrid node, which will allow us to make reference to it later on.

```
DEF CLOCK TimeSensor {
    cycleInterval 1.0
    loop TRUE
    stopTime 0
    startTime 1
}

DEF SCRIPT Script {
    url "wave.class"
    eventIn SFTime cycleTime
    eventIn SFFloat time_changed
    field SFFloat choppiness_ IS choppiness
    field SFInt32 xDimension IS xDimen
    field SFInt32 zDimension IS zDimen
    eventOut MFFloat height
}

ROUTE CLOCK.cycleTime TO SCRIPT.cycleTime
ROUTE SCRIPT.height TO EGRID.set_height
}
```

This final section details the Script node and the TimeSensor node that drives the scene, as well as the ROUTEing required to pass events between nodes.

As can be seen from the example code, we have placed our compiled Java bytecode that contains the logic to generate random waves in the file called `wave.class`. We have also defined several custom fields for handling input, output and parameters to the Java code, which are:

cycleTime, time_changed are used to take values constantly from the Time-Sensor node, which causes the Script node to be driven constantly. We shall discuss this topic in more detail below.

choppiness is aliased, using the IS keyword, to the value we passed into the PROTO. This allows the Java code to use the parameter directly to affect the generation of waves.

xDimension, zDimension are aliased, using the IS keyword, to the values passed into the PROTO. This allows the Java code to ensure that the amount of data being generated by the wave generator (in terms of geometry) matches the dimensions of the ElevationGrid node whose geometry will be affected by the Script node.

height will contain a two-dimensional array of floating-point numbers, representing the new heights of all the vertices in the ElevationGrid node.

Finally, we define the ROUTEs that will pass the data between the Script node and the ElevationGrid node, and also the data from the TimeSensor node used to continuously drive the Script node. The first sends any cycleTime events to the Script node, *e.g.*, a cycleTime event will be generated every cycleInterval seconds, which, in the case of the VRML world listed above, would be every second. The second assigns to the height field of the ElevationGrid called EGRID in the VRML world the floating-point values contained in the two-dimensional array that is created and populated by the Java code referred to in the Script node.

Therefore, the flow of the entire VRML world over time can be illustrated in Figure 8.1. As you can clearly see, the TimeSensor node will issue a cycleTime event each second, with the knock-on effect that the Script node will then be driven to produce a two-dimensional array of floating-point values, which is then used to set the ElevationGrid node's height field.

Now that we are aware of the VRML side of the Script node syntax, we shall take a look at an actual scripting API (application programming interface) itself, namely, the Java Scripting API.

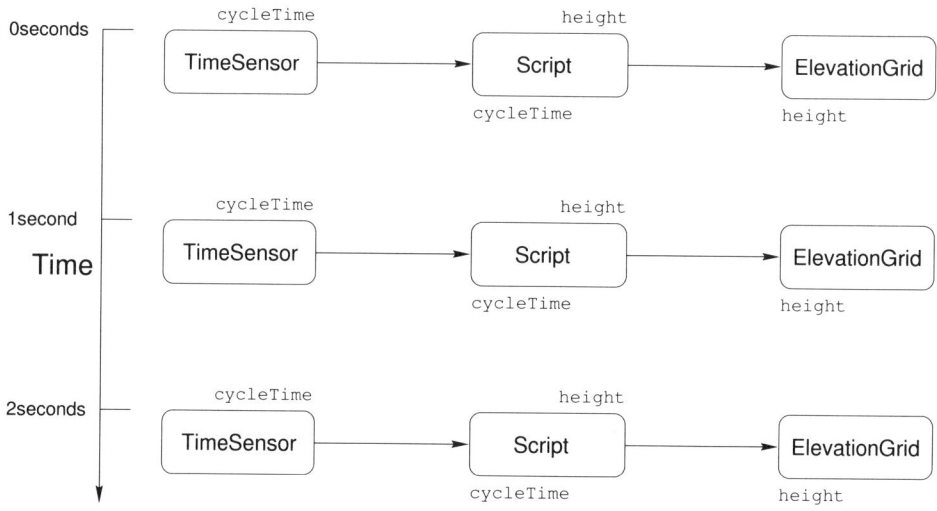

Figure 8.1: Flow Of The "Wave" `PROTO`

The Java Scripting API

The Java Scripting API Specification can be found in Appendix C of the *VRML97 Specification.* This appendix details the numerous classes and methods that comprise this scripting interface, and should be consulted often.

However, in this section of the book, we shall attempt to elucidate and explain some of the more common parts of functionality within this specification, and demonstrate some example uses of it. We shall also discuss some of the potential problems that may be associated with this scripting interface.

The `vrml.*` Hierarchy

Firstly, we shall take a look at the Java class hierarchy **vrml.***, which contains implementations of the classes and methods defined in the Java Scripting API

Specification. These classes are regarded as being browser-independent, and provide a single unified Java API for VRML scripting.

vrml.node.Script and Basic Methods

All Java classes that are implemented as being the logic behind a Script node must be a subclass of **vrml.node.Script**, which is the class that implements the basic methods that a Script node may use. These basic methods are:

initialize() which is called upon instantiation of the Java class associated with a Script node. This is called exactly once per Script node, and is called *before* any events are passed into or out of the Script node. Its default behaviour is to have no operation. The prototype of this method is:

```
public void initialize();
```

The initialize() method is usually used to create **private** variables corresponding to the **eventIn**, **eventOut** and **field** fields defined by the content creator in the Script node that the Java code is likely to use. This reduces processing overhead in the long run, as we shall demonstrate below.

shutdown() which is called upon destruction of the Script node with which the current Java code is associated. This method is called exactly once. Its default behaviour is no operation, and the prototype of this method is:

```
public void shutdown();
```

The shutdown() method is extremely useful for freeing resources used within the Java code associated with a Script node, and should be used on all occasions.

processEvent() which is called upon reception of *any* event from the corresponding Script node with which the current Java code is associated. This method is generally used to drive any behaviour within the Script node, and usually will generate any **eventOut**s that are required. The default behaviour of this method is to have no operation, and its prototype is defined as:

```
public void processEvent( Event event );
```

The **Event** mentioned in the argument list is of class `vrml.Event`, which we shall be examining in more detail below.

`processEvents()` which is called when an array of events with identical timestamps is received by the `Script` node, *e.g.*,

```
Transform {
  children [
    DEF TS TouchSensor {}
      Shape {
        geometry Box {
        }
      }
    ]
  }
DEF SCRIPT Script {
  url "someclass.class"
  eventIn SFBool isActive
  eventIn SFTime touchTime
}
ROUTE TS.isActive TO SCRIPT.isActive
ROUTE TS.touchTime TO SCRIPT.touchTime
```

This piece of VRML would, when the user clicked on the box, emit two **eventOut**s with identical timestamps. When the `Script` node receives these events, it will use the `processEvents()` method, instead of the `processEvent()` method.

However, the default behaviour of `processEvents()` is to merely iterate over each event, invoking `processEvent()` on each one, as is shown in the following fragment of code:

```
public void processEvents( int numEvents,
                           Event events[] ) {
   for ( int i = 0 ; i < numEvents ; i++ ) {
      processEvent( events[i] );
   }
}
```

It is more usual for the content creator to override the `processEvent()` method as opposed to `processEvents()`.

`eventsProcessed()` which allows the content creator to have more control over the generation of `eventOuts` from the `Script` node. In the cases where `mustEvaluate` is TRUE, this method is of most use, in that the `Script` node does not generate `eventOuts` whenever an `eventIn` is received. `eventsProcessed()` is called after every invocation of `processEvents()`. The prototype for this method is:

```
public void eventsProcessed();
```

and its default behaviour is no operation.

Now that we have discussed the basic methods that we may override in the `vrml.node.Script` class, we will take a look at our "wave" example code, that we will be using to implement the `Script` node.

The basic skeleton of the Java code will look like the following. At the moment, we haven't implemented any new information in any of the methods, but it will demonstrate how we implement the basic functionality.

```
/** We import the vrml.* hierarchy here */
import vrml.*;
import vrml.node.*;
import vrml.field.*;

public class wave extends Script {

   /**
    * This is called exactly once upon
    * instantiation of this Java class
    * when the Script node is created in
    * the VRML world.
    */
   public void initialize() {
      System.err.println( "initialize()" );
    }

   /**
    * This is called every time that an eventIn
```

```
    * is received by the Script node.
    */
   public void processEvent( Event e ) {
       System.err.println( "processEvent()" );
     }

   /**
    * This is called exactly once when the
    * corresponding Script node is deleted from
    * the VRML world.
    */
   public void shutdown() {
       System.err.println( "shutdown()" );
     }
 }
```

Loading the "wave" VRML world that we listed above, will load the compiled Java bytecode representing the code above, and you should see output similar to the following:

```
   initialize()
   processEvent()
   processEvent()
   processEvent()
```

and, if we load another scene, or kill the browser, the message:

```
   shutdown()
```

should be displayed on the screen, which should illustrate the points in a Script node's life cycle in which each method is typically called.

We have now sketched out the framework within which Java-enhanced Script nodes operate, but there isn't currently a tremendous amount we can do with this framework. We cannot, for example, emit an eventOut, nor can we read the value of any eventIns being ROUTEd into the Script node. For this, we must look at how we can access fields and events.

Fields and Events

In this section, we shall be looking at various ways in which we can manipulate the data that is being ROUTEd into our Script node, or emitted out *via* the defined `eventIn` and `eventOut` fields.

Firstly, we shall take a look at some methods defined in the `vrml.node.Script` class for referencing any fields, `eventIn`s or `eventOut`s that a given `Script` node may have defined. For the purposes of explaining the following methods, we shall reference a small VRML file as follows:

```
#VRML V2.0 utf8
Transform {
    children [
        DEF TS TimeSensor {
            cycleInterval 1.0
        }
        DEF SCRIPT Script {
            eventIn SFTime cycleTime
            field SFFloat someFloat
            eventOut SFInt32 someEventOut
        }
    ]
}
```

`getField()` which will return the reference to the `Script` node's field member whose name is given as the argument to the method. The prototype
for this method is:

```
Field getField( String fieldName );
```

For example, the method invocation of:

```
SFFloat someFloat =
    (SFFloat)getField( "someFloat" );
```

would create a new Java object of type `SFFloat`[2] and assign to it the value of the field `someFloat` in the `Script` node. It is quite important to remember that the method above is *within the Java class associated with the* `Script` *node*, and that the variable `someFloat` is *not* the field `someFloat` *in the VRML* `Script` *node*. Using this method, we take a copy of the current value in the `Script` node, but, if we alter our local variable, it does *not* alter the value in the `Script` node. Not, at least, until we tell it to! However, more on that later.

---

[2] Actually of class `vrml.field.SFFloat`.

getEventIn() which will return a reference to the Script node's eventOut member whose name is given as the argument to the method. The prototype for this method is given as:

```
Field getEventIn( String eventName );
```

Thus, if we wanted to get the value of the cycleTime eventIn in our VRML Script node, we would use a method invocation of:

```
SFTime cycleTime =
    (SFTime)getEventIn( "cycleTime" );
```

The points we made in the getField() explanation above equally apply in the getEventIn() method.

getEventOut() which will return a reference to the Script node's eventOut member whose name is given as the argument to the method. The prototype for this method is given as:

```
Field getEventOut( String eventName );
```

So, if we wished to get a reference to the someEventOut eventOut in our VRML Script node listed above, we would invoke this method in the following way:

```
SFInt32 someEventOut =
    (SFInt32)getEventOut( "someEventOut" );
```

Generally speaking it is advisable to use the three methods listed above in the initialize() method once and once only. This minimizes method overhead when referring to the variables. To illustrate the point, here's our small example class that we outlined above, with some field and event handling code added into initialize().

```
/** We import the vrml.* hierarchy here */
import vrml.*;
import vrml.node.*;
import vrml.field.*;

public class wave extends Script {
```

```
private SFTime cycleTime = null;
private SFFloat someFloat = null;
private SFInt32 someEventOut = null;

/**
 * This is called exactly once upon
 * instantiation of this Java class
 * when the Script node is created in
 * the VRML world.
 */
public void initialize() {
    System.err.println( "initialize()" );

    /** Fetch references to all our fields */
    cycleTime = (SFTime)getEventIn( "cycleTime" );
    someFloat = (SFFloat)getField( "someFloat" );
    someEventOut =
        (SFInt32)getEventOut( "someEventOut" );
  }

/**
 * This is called every time that an eventIn
 * is received by the Script node.
 */
public void processEvent( Event e ) {
    System.err.println( "processEvent()" );

    /** #!#!#!#! Manipulate our SFFloat */
    if ( someFloat < 10 ) {
       someFloat += 10;
     }
  }

/**
 * This is called exactly once when the
 * corresponding Script node is deleted from
 * the VRML world.
 */
public void shutdown() {
    System.err.println( "shutdown()" );
```

```
        }
    }
```

If you look at the two lines after that marked with `#!#!#!#!`, you will see that we are using our floating-point number as extracted from the VRML file. Or are we?

Actually, no, we're not. And to understand why, we need to examine the classes defined in the `vrml.field.*` hierarchy, before we can start effectively using the data we now have at our fingertips.

Accessing Field Information

As we have seen in the section above, we can now get a reference to the fields defined within our VRML `Script` node, but we cannot obtain the actual value of these fields from the encapsulating classes, *e.g.*, the `SFFloat` class.

Each VRML datatype, as listed in Chapter 7, has a corresponding Java class within the `vrml.field.*` hierarchy, *e.g.*, an `SFFloat` will use the class `vrml.field.SFFloat` and so on. Upon closer inspection, there are actually two classes with `SFFloat` in the name:

1. `vrml.field.SFFloat`

2. `vrml.field.ConstSFFloat`

The difference between these lies in usage of the data. The classes prefixed with `Const` are *read-only* classes, *i.e.*, you may read the value from them, but not alter it at any time. Classes *without* the `Const` prefix are both *readable* and *writable*, *i.e.*, you can both *get* and *set* the value of that variable.

All of the datatype classes are subclasses of the `vrml.Field` class, and they each define two base methods for either getting or setting the values of `vrml.field.*` objects:

`getValue()` which returns the underlying value of object, *e.g.*:

```
        SFFloat someFloat =
            (SFFloat)getField( "someFloat" );
        float actualFloatValue = someFloat.getValue();
```

VRML Datatype	Java Datatype	VRML Datatype	Java Datatype
SFBool	boolean		
SFColor	float[]†	MFColor	float[][]†
SFFloat	float	MFFloat	float[]†
SFImage	byte[]†		
SFInt32	int	MFInt32	int[]†
SFNode	vrml.Node	MFNode	vrml.Node[]†
SFRotation	float[]†	MFRotation	float[][]†
SFString	String	MFString	String[]†
SFTime	double	MFTime	double[]†
SFVec2f	float[]†	MFVec2f	float[]†
SFVec3f	float[]†	MFVec3f	float[]†

Entries marked with † require the content creator to allocate the storage for the return values in advance.

Table 8.1: VRML And Java Datatypes

Each datatype within `vrml.field` returns a different type of variable which can be seen in Table 8.1. As you can no doubt see from Table 8.1, the `getValue()` method is not at all orthogonal. Some datatypes, typically the `MF*` types, require that you pass a pre-allocated array. This array is populated within the `getValue()` method. For example, if we wished to get the actual values contained within an `SFColor` field, we would need to use code similar to the following:

```
SFColor someColor =
    (SFColor)getField( "someColor" );
float[] colorValues = new float[3];
someColor.getValue( colorValues );
```

`setValue()` which allows the content creator to set a given reference to a given value, which is propagated back into the VRML `Script` node. For example,

```
SFInt32 someEventOut =
    (SFInt32)getEventOut( "someEventOut" );
someEventOut.setValue( 666.66 );
```

As with the `getValue()` method, `setValue()` is not orthogonal.

In addition to this, MF* datatypes, such as MFFloat, have additional default methods associated with them, which are listed below.

getSize() which returns the number of elements in a multiple-value datatype field.

get1Value() which returns a single value, of appropriate datatype as shown in Table 8.1, at the given index in the multiple value datatype field. The index of the first element in any multiple value field is 0. Attempts to reference an index greater than the size of the array will result in an exception being thrown.

set1Value() which is the corollary function of get1Value(). This method sets the single-value element at the given index in the multiple-value field to the given value.

addValue() which will extend the length of the multiple-value field by 1, and insert the given value at the end of the array.

insertValue() which will insert a new value at the given array element. The array elements are numbered sequentially from 0 upwards, and attempts to insert a value at an index of less than 0 or greater than the size of the array will result in an exception being thrown.

However, if you weren't confused enough already with the various different return types or whether or not array pre-allocation is required, each type *may* have additional methods for extracting data from the encapsulating class, *e.g.*, in the case of SFColor, there additional methods of:

1. float getRed()

2. float getGreen()

3. float getBlue()

defined for our convenience. We recommend keeping a copy of the *Class Definitions* as defined in Appendix C, Section 8 of the *VRML97 Specification* close to hand!

Finally, before we go crashing off into adding all sorts of data handling code into our "wave" example, we should examine the vrml.Event class, which will allow us to put precise event handling into the processEvent() method.

Events Unravelled

As we have seen above, upon reception of any event, the `processEvent()` method is invoked. However, what happens if we have two distinct `eventIns` on one node, each of which produces an entirely different response? How can we differentiate between the incoming events?

The answer lies in the `vrml.Event` class, and the methods defined therein. The `vrml.Event` class has four core methods associated with it, the three of most interest to us being:

`getName()` which returns a new Java `String` object containing the name of the `eventIn` that generated this `Event`.

`getTimeStamp()` which returns a `double` containing the time, in seconds, since 00:00:00 GMT on 1st January 1970, that the current `Event` was generated at.

`getValue()` which returns the value contained within the current `Event`. However, this returns a `vrml.field.*` object, which must be manipulated as described above, with the `getValue()` method.

Thus, we can flesh out a `processEvent()` method to look something like the following:

```
public void processEvent( Event inEvent ) {
    if ( inEvent.getName().equals( "someIntegerEvent" ) ) {
        int someInteger =
            (SFInt32)(inEvent.getValue()).getValue();
    } else {
        if ( inEvent.getName().equals( "someFloatEvent" ) ) {
            float someFloat =
                (SFFloat)(inEvent.getValue()).getValue();
        }
    }
}
```

which, as we can see, performs different operations on the incoming event information depending on what `eventIn` it happens to be currently processing. This system allows us to perform very fine operations on many, possibly simultaneous, `eventIns` without fear of performing a wrong operation on an `eventIn`.

We shall finish off our "wave" demonstration, now that we have enough knowledge of event handling and variable operations to allow us to manipulate data correctly and with ease.

Flying The Flag On Open Seas

We shall build a small demonstration world that creates some rippling water using our "wave" PROTO node. The full listing of the Java Script code is given below:

```
import vrml.*;
import vrml.node.*;
import vrml.field.*;

public class wave extends Script {

  private int WIDTH = 0;
  private int DEPTH = 0;

  private SFInt32 width;
  private SFInt32 depth;

  private MFFloat height;
  float[] heightFields = null;

  private SFFloat choppiness_;

  public void initialize() {
      /** Initialize the fields and events */
      height = (MFFloat)getEventOut( "height" );
      choppiness_ = (SFFloat)getField( "choppiness_" );
      width = (SFInt32)getField( "xDimension" );
      depth = (SFInt32)getField( "zDimension" );

      /**
       * Create a couple of handy Java variables to
       * save us having to call getValue() over and
       * over again.
       */
      WIDTH = width.getValue();
```

```
        DEPTH = depth.getValue();

        /**
         * Create a new array to store the perturbed
         * height values in and initialize them to
         * 0, i.e., the surface to ripple is stilled.
         */
        heightFields = new float[ WIDTH * DEPTH ];
        for ( int blah = 0 ; blah < WIDTH * DEPTH ; blah++ ) {
            heightFields[blah] = 0;
        }
    }

    public void processEvent( Event e ) {
        /**
         * Check to see if the event being processed
         * is the one that we want.
         */
      if ( e.getName().equals( "cycleTime" ) ) {
        /**
         * If it is the correct one, then process it
         * by looping through the number of cells
         * in the ElevationGrid node and create new
         * height values for each one.
         */
        for ( int x = 0 ; x < WIDTH ; x++ ) {
          for ( int z = 0 ; z < DEPTH ; z++ ) {
            heightFields[(z * WIDTH) + x] =
                (float)( Math.random() * choppiness_.getValue() );
          }
        }
        height.setValue( heightFields );
      }
    }

    public void shutdown() {
      heightFields = null;
      width = null;
      depth = null;
      height = null;
```

```
        }
    }
```

If we now apply this `Script` node in a scene, we can create a nice rippling
water effect. A sample `PROTO` for creating a patch of water is as follows:

```
#VRML V2.0 utf8
#
# $Id$
#
# Random wave effect
#
PROTO wave [ field SFFloat choppiness 0.25
             field SFInt32 xDimen 10
             field SFInt32 zDimen 10
             field SFFloat xSpace 2
             field SFFloat zSpace 2
             field SFString texurl "water.gif" ] {
    Transform {
        children [
            Shape {
                geometry DEF EGRID ElevationGrid {
                    xSpacing IS xSpace
                    zSpacing IS zSpace
                    xDimension IS xDimen
                    zDimension IS zDimen
                    solid FALSE
                    creaseAngle 1.05
                }
                appearance Appearance {
                    material Material {
                        diffuseColor 0 0 1
                    }
                    texture ImageTexture {
                        url IS texurl
                    }
                }
            }
        ]
    }
```

```
    DEF CLOCK TimeSensor {
        cycleInterval 1.0
        loop TRUE
        stopTime 0
        startTime 1
      }

    DEF SCRIPT Script {
        url "wave.class"
        eventIn SFTime cycleTime
        field SFFloat choppiness_ IS choppiness
        field SFInt32 xDimension IS xDimen
        field SFInt32 zDimension IS zDimen
        eventOut MFFloat height
      }

    ROUTE CLOCK.cycleTime TO SCRIPT.cycleTime
    ROUTE SCRIPT.height TO EGRID.set_height
}
```

Since we have wrapped both the geometry and **Script** nodes into our "wave"
prototype, we can now build powerful scenes from it. A more complex scene
could involve a small island in rippling water, with a flag flapping in the
breeze. We can simply reuse the **Script** node to simulate that effect as well.
The following code will create a scene with a small island in the midst of a
sea with a flagpole on it replete with flapping flag!

```
#VRML V2.0 utf8
#
# Desert island
EXTERNPROTO wave [ field SFFloat choppiness
                   field SFInt32 zDimen
                   field SFFloat xSpace
                   field SFFloat zSpace
                   field MFString texurl ] "wave.wrl"
Viewpoint {
    position 5 0 25
  }

Transform {
    rotation 1 0 0 0.78
```

```
children [
    ### The sea
    DEF WATER Transform {
        children [
            wave {
                choppiness 0.75
            }
        ]
    }

    ### The island in the sea
    DEF ISLAND Transform {
        translation 10 0.5 10
        scale 1 0.1 1
        children [
            Shape {
                geometry Sphere {
                    radius 3
                }
                appearance Appearance {
                    material Material {
                        diffuseColor 1 1 1
                    }
                    texture ImageTexture {
                        url "sand01.jpg"
                    }
                }
            }
        ]
    }

    ### The flagpole on the island
    DEF FLAGPOLE Transform {
        translation 11 2 9
        children [
            Shape {
                geometry Cylinder {
                    height 2
                    radius 0.1
                }
```

```
                          appearance Appearance {
                             material Material {
                                diffuseColor 0.644 0.164 0.164
                             }
                          }
                       }
                    ]
                 }

         ### The flapping flag on the flagpole
         DEF FLAG Transform {
             translation 11 2 9
             rotation 1 0 0 -1.57
             children [
                 wave {
                     choppiness 0.05
                     texurl "hermlogo.gif"
                     xDimen 15
                     zDimen 10
                     xSpace 0.1
                     zSpace 0.1
                 }
             ]
         }
      ]
   }
```

Directly Interfacing Java and VRML

In this section, we shall discuss the possibilities that Java `Script` nodes offer us, by merging some of the more powerful features of Java into VRML.

Since `Script` nodes may be written in Java, we can actually use the full range of Java functionality in our `Script` nodes; for example, we could create a `Frame` object that contains AWT `Component`s that can manipulate the contents of a scene directly. A short example of this follows, in which a scene containing a `Cone` can be manipulated via the buttons in the additional `Frame` that pops up. By clicking on any of the buttons, the `Cone` will change to that colour.

Here's the VRML that creates the scene and establishes ROUTEs.

```
#VRML V2.0 utf8
#
# Edit an object!
#
Transform {
    children [
        Shape {
            geometry DEF CONE Cone {
                }
            appearance Appearance {
                material DEF MATERIAL Material {
                    diffuseColor 0 0 1
                    }
                }
            }

        DEF SCRIPT Script {
            url "edit.class"
            eventOut SFColor colour
            }
        ]
    }


ROUTE SCRIPT.colour TO MATERIAL.set_diffuseColor
```

The `Script` node implementation is fairly short and to the point, in that it simply grabs the `eventOut` and creates the `Frame` in which we choose the object's colour.

```
/**
 * Object editor
 */

import vrml.*;
import vrml.node.*;
import vrml.field.*;

import java.awt.*;
```

```
public class edit extends Script {

    /**
     * The eventOut that carries the colour
     * to the cone's material node
     */
    private SFColor colour;

    /** The Frame in which we click buttons */
    private editFrame f = null;

    public void initialize() {

        /** Get the eventOut reference */
        colour = (SFColor)getEventOut( "colour" );

        /** Create a new Frame */
        f = new editFrame( colour );
    }
}
```

The final piece of the jigsaw is the code that will create the **Frame** and handle any AWT events, such as button clicks.

```
/**
 */

import vrml.*;
import vrml.field.*;
import vrml.node.*;

import java.awt.*;

public class editFrame extends Frame {

    /** The VRML EventOut we wish to set */
    private SFColor colour = null;

    /** Constructor */
    public editFrame( SFColor colour ) {
        this.colour = colour;
```

```java
    setLayout( new FlowLayout() );
    add( new Button( "Blue" ) );
    add( new Button( "Red" ) );
    add( new Button( "Green" ) );
    add( new Button( "Magenta" ) );
    add( new Button( "Yellow" ) );
    add( new Button( "Cyan" ) );

    pack();
    show();
    resize( 200, 200 );
  }

public boolean handleEvent( java.awt.Event evt ) {
    try {
        switch ( evt.id ) {
            case java.awt.Event.ACTION_EVENT: {
                if ( evt.arg.toString().equals( "Blue" ) ) {
                    colour.setValue( 0.0f, 0.0f, 1.0f );
                    return true;
                  }
                if ( evt.arg.toString().equals( "Red" ) ) {
                    colour.setValue( 1.0f, 0.0f, 0.0f );
                    return true;
                  }
                if ( evt.arg.toString().equals( "Green" ) ) {
                    colour.setValue( 0.0f, 1.0f, 0.0f );
                    return true;
                  }
                if ( evt.arg.toString().equals( "Magenta" ) ) {
                    colour.setValue( 1.0f, 0.0f, 1.0f );
                    return true;
                  }
                if ( evt.arg.toString().equals( "Yellow" ) ) {
                    colour.setValue( 1.0f, 1.0f, 0.0f );
                    return true;
                  }
                if ( evt.arg.toString().equals( "Cyan" ) ) {
                    colour.setValue( 0.0f, 1.0f, 1.0f );
```

```
                        return true;
                    }
                }
            }
        } catch ( NullPointerException e ) {
            System.err.println( "Blah" );
        }
        return false;
    }
}
```

vrml.Browser

The above methods are generally used to manipulate values that are being ROUTEd to and from the scene via Java, but there is another way in which we can manipulate the scene, and that is *via* the vrml.Browser class, which is a Java encapsulation of the current VRML browser.

The vrml.Browser class contains several methods that can be used to query information about the current browser implementation, and, more interestingly to the content creator, some methods that allow you to create scene information from data sources, or even replace the world entirely. We shall look at these methods in reverse order.

Creating VRML From Thin Air

Another interesting facet of Java Script nodes is that we can create arbitrary VRML from them, then insert those nodes directly into the scene graph. To perform this activity, we can use the methods called createVrmlFromString(), which creates VRML nodes from VRML stored in a String, or createVrml-FromURL(), which has the same functionality but loads the VRML from a given URL.

For example, to create a simple Cone within a Java Script node, we could write the following code.

```
/**
 * Creates a Cone within the VRML scene
 */
```

```
import vrml.*;
import vrml.node.*;
import vrml.field.*;

public class createCone extends Script {

  /** The String containing VRML */
  private String cone =
    new String( "Transform {\
                  children [\
                    Shape {\
                      geometry Cone {}\
                      appearance Appearance {\
                        material Material {\
                          diffuseColor 0 0 1\
                        }\
                      }\
                    }\
                  ]\
                }" );

  private MFNode addChildren = null;
  private Node rootNode = null;
  private SFTime cycleTime = null;

  /** The number of cones we've created so far */
  private int currentCone = 0;

  public void initialize() {

    rootNode =
      (Node)( (SFNode)getField( "rootNode" ) ).getValue();

    addChildren =
      (MFNode)rootNode.getEventIn( "addChildren" );

    cycleTime =
      (SFTime)getEventIn( "cycleTime" );
  }
```

```
    public void processEvent( Event evt ) {
      if ( currentCone < 10 ) {
        if ( evt.getName().equals( "cycleTime" ) ) {
          createCone();
        }
      }
    }

    /** Creates a cone and adds it to the scene */
    public void createCone() {

      /** Create a new cone */
      try {
        BaseNode nodes[] =
          this.getBrowser().createVrmlFromString( cone );
        if ( nodes[0].getType().equals( "Transform" ) ) {
          SFVec3f translation =
            (SFVec3f)( ((Node)nodes[0]).getExposedField(
                                      "translation" ) );
          translation.setValue( currentCone * 3, 0, 0 );
        }

        /** Add the cone into the scene */
        addChildren.setValue( nodes );

        /** Increment the number of cones in the scene */
        currentCone++;
      } catch ( InvalidVRMLSyntaxException e ) {
        System.err.println( "Cannot create VRML from String: " +
                            e.toString() );
      }
    }
  }
```

The `createVrmlFromString()` method returns an array of Nodes which can be further manipulated directly without having to ROUTE the node information from the scene back into the Script node.

`createVrmlFromURL()` operates in a similar way, except that we tell this method which node in the scene we wish to act as the root node that the nodes about to be loaded are to become children of. We may also specify an event which can be used to trigger some additional behaviour in the `Script` node, for example, start a behaviour running, or perform some sort of notification operation. This event should be handled in `processEvent()` or `processEvents()` as per usual.

Another useful method defined in the `vrml.Browser` class is `replaceWorld()`, which will completely replace the existing scene with nodes in a `Node[]` array, as is returned from `createVrmlFromString()`, instead of merging the new nodes into an existing scene. This method may be used to implement some forms of the `Anchor` node, in that clicking upon an object in the world may cause a brand new scene to be loaded from somewhere, completely replacing the original.

`loadURL()` is another method that could be used to perform this task. This differs slightly from `replaceWorld()` in that you specify the URL from which the new world should be loaded, as well as an array of additional parameters that are to be handled by the browser. This functionality allows you to load new scenes into additional frames within a browser, for example, specifying the frame `TARGET` as a parameter.

There are three final methods that can be used to manipulate the scene directly from the browser, being `addRoute()`, `deleteRoute()` and `setDescription()`.

`setDescription` simply sets some verbose comments concerning the world, usually specified in the `WorldInfo` node.

`addRoute()` and `deleteRoute()` are slightly more interesting in that they allow the content creator to directly manipulate the `ROUTE`s within a scene. This can be extremely useful in cases where we create a new node which is required to behave in sync with already existing nodes in the scene. For example, we might have a `TimeSensor` being used to drive animation in the scene, and after loading some new objects from another source, these objects must also be driven by the same `TimeSensor`. This is where `addRoute()` is invaluable. By the same token, `deleteRoute()` allows us to remove `ROUTE`s to objects that have been dynamically removed from the scene by a `Script` node using the `removeChildren eventIn` present in grouping nodes. This cuts down on the amount of information being `ROUTE`d to non-existent nodes.

Querying the Browser

The other methods that we have available to us in the `vrml.Browser` class pertain to querying the browser for information. The methods currently defined in the *Java Scripting Interface* are:

`getName()` This method returns the name of the browser which you are currently using. For example, Liquid Reality will return "Liquid Reality Browser".

`getVersion()` This method returns the version number of the browser. The versioning used by companies in their browsers can vary dramatically.

`getCurrentSpeed()` This method returns the current speed of the avatar within the scene. This should correspond to the `speed` field in a `NavigationInfo` node in the current world, which, if not specified, should be `1.0`.

`getCurrentFrameRate()` This method returns the current number of *frames per second* (fps) that the rendering engine of the browser is currently producing. This value will vary depending on the speed of your machine, and the size and complexity of the current world. Factors such as the rendering engine's power itself will also affect this figure. Frame rates of around 6 fps give an acceptable feeling of responsiveness in a world; anything less than that will give the user the feeling of jerky motion or moving through treacle. Very high frame rates can also render a world unnavigable since you will tend to slew around wildly at the slightest motion of the mouse.

`getWorldURL()` This method returns the URL of the current world.

Chapter 9

Interlude

When we first started developing a distributed multi-user virtual reality system we wanted to create a system that did more than play games or demonstrate *gee-whiz!* graphics that were exciting to people who like *gee-whiz!* graphics but leave the remaining 99.99% of the population wondering what the point was and why people get paid for wasting their time on this sort of thing.

So we picked on a model that could be easily incorporated into systems that had very different potential markets.

Orkney—a group of more than seventy[1] islands 10 miles off the north-east coast of mainland Scotland—is beautiful, sparsely populated and, perhaps, not an obvious choice for a model of a virtual reality world. But that is the point—there is much more to virtual reality than the science-fiction/fantasy clichés.

- Tourists can view places that they might be interested in visiting in a new way; not as a replacement for descriptions and photographs, but as an additional resource.

- Rock-climbers (there are stunning high cliffs and sea-stacs around the coasts of the islands) can make judgements on where they want to visit, based on their climbing ability and the difficulty of the routes, by looking

---

[1]How many islands actually make up Orkney depends on how you choose to count them.

at representations of the actual climbing areas. Possible routes can be shown on the rock faces for the aid of those who need assistance.

- Archaeologists and historians can view reconstructions of monuments. Orkney has such a profusion of historical and archaeological monuments, buildings, settlements, and so on that it is difficult to walk more than twenty yards without tripping over something of great historical or archaeological significance. There are settlements which pre-date the pyramids in Egypt; houses with intact furniture from 5000 years ago; tombs which contained bones from hundreds of human bodies; standing stones, stone circles and henges; Iron Age circular coastal defensive structures called brochs; subterranean *earth-houses*; Pictish, early Christian and Viking settlements; palaces of wicked medieval rulers. There is much that can be done with reconstruction for the academic visitor. But there is also much potential for the amateur and tourist visitor with reconstructions showing the landscape and structures at different times, virtual information boards giving detailed descriptions of what is being seen, and guided tours presented by virtual guides.

- Of course, there are also the science-fiction/fantasy clichés—prehistoric landscapes are just the thing for sword and sorcery type role-playing games. If you want prehistoric landscapes, Orkney is the place for you!

In the chapters that follow, examples are often based around the village of Skara Brae, with excursions into the areas around the Ring of Brodgar, the Stones of Stenness and the tomb of Maes Howe.

Sometime around 1850, a great storm battered the west coast of the main island (called Mainland) of Orkney, tearing away much of the coastal sand and turf. After the storm had abated, it became clear that the ground covered the structures of a number of ancient buildings. In 1928 the village of Skara Brae was excavated by Professor Gordon Childe from the University of Edinburgh, and further excavations were performed in the 1970s by David Clarke.

There are at least eight well-preserved houses that date from the last occupation of the settlement, about 2500 BC, and below these are remains from earlier occupations going back perhaps another 500 or 600 years. What remains is not only the structure of the houses, but also the furniture. Wood on Orkney is a very scarce resource, and the furnishings in Skara Brae are made from stone. Some of the houses are obviously dwelling places, whilst others seem to be part of the "industrial quarter" as they lack the domestic furnishings and there is much debris from the working of stone.

Between the lochs of Harray and Stenness, also on Mainland, is a major ceremonial area and this includes the stone circle and henge monuments of the vast Ring of Brodgar and the Stones of Stenness, as well as the Maes Howe tomb. The Stones of Stenness were certainly in existence by 3000 BC, and the other two monuments were probably constructed sometime in the following five hundred years. Maes Howe is such a huge tomb that it can be easily mistaken for a small round hill. The main chamber is awe-inspiring in the precision of its construction, and there is a wonderfully constructed entrance passage; the passage is precisely oriented such that light from the mid-winter setting sun shines through to illuminate the back wall of the main chamber. The tomb was ransacked by Vikings during the twelfth century AD and they left behind them graffiti in Runic script.

If this book fails to stimulate your interest in building virtual reality systems, we hope that it will at least spark an interest in the beautiful and fascinating Orkney Islands.

Chapter 10

Virtual Reality Servers

Why More Servers?

At present, most VRML worlds are delivered to a VRML browser by way of HTTP (i.e. from links on Web pages) or by directly copying a VRML file to the machine that the browser is being executed on and viewing the world model locally. That's fine for a lot of simple applications of virtual reality, where all you want to do is view a simple model; and it is fine for the early days of the evolution of "virtual reality for the people" where much of the excitement is creating models—and seeing models that others have created— that previously could only be produced by experts in their ivory towers.

But when use of virtual reality progresses beyond the realms of "exciting new technology" into the area of "everyday mundane use", this method of distributing worlds will start to show its limitations. Two such limitations are the following:

- Multi-user applications—if I want to interact not just with the world model, but also with other people who are simultaneously interacting with the same world model (or, in English, if I walk into a shopping mall I don't expect to be the only person there: I expect to see all the other shoppers; I expect to be able to talk to the other shoppers; I expect to be able to talk to the shop assistants; I expect to be able to be able to hold a piece of virtual jewellery up in front of a shop assistant's face and say "You want me to pay *how much*?") then something more than

235

a file of VRML definitions is needed. I need my browser to be able to tell a server that I am talking to Sam, that I am moving across the room, that I am tripping over a trailing wire. And I need the server to tell my browser that Chris is shouting to me, that someone has locked the door that I just walked through. If I am putting money into virtual reality on the Internet by buying space in a virtual shopping mall then I need the server to tell me that someone is holding a piece of virtual jewellery up in front of my face in the virtual shop that I have opened and saying to me "You want me to pay *how much?*"

- Distributability and scalability—to reach beyond the domain of the academic and the hobbyist it will have to be possible for virtual worlds to expand in small chunks: I might be willing to try setting up a virtual jewellery shop for my Orkney jewellery where potential buyers can pick up and examine pieces of my art. If successful I might be able to persuade my friend, who sells Orkney cheese and Orkney biscuits, to invest in some shop space which can be added to the existing world. This might spark an interest from the Cheesemakers' Guild world-wide. But if the visitor cannot wander from cheese-shop to cheese-shop in the International Cheese Mall, most of the world's cheesemakers are likely to get no visitors at all. OK, maybe cheese-selling[1] isn't likely to be the first big success of distributed virtual reality, but the principle is the same. When small shops cluster together, they tend to get more visitors than if they are miles apart and don't acknowledge each other's existence. Shopping centres, whether you love them or hate them, attract shoppers. If virtual reality servers allow for distribution of virtual worlds, then virtual shops on opposite sides of the world can be placed next to each other—whilst this doesn't give any of the virtual shops any guarantee of success, it at least gives them all an additional *chance* at success.

The following chapters take a look at aspects which relate to providing virtual reality servers:

---

[1]There are quite a lot of Web sites on the Internet which relate to cheesemaking—if you look carefully you can find quite a few mentions of Orkney cheese. But if you were to stumble across one of these sites, the chances are that you will not get to see any other cheesemaking sites. At the time of writing, I could find no cheesemaking sites with links to other cheese-making sites. And the world of cheesemaking is probably all the poorer for that. I think we should have a moment's silence and reflect on the poor electronic state of the cheesemaking world...

- an introduction to some of the technical aspects of networking;

- an explanation of multi-threading in Java—multi-threading allows many aspects of server creation to be simplified;

- a guide to many of the aspects of virtual reality which need to be addressed to provide a useful virtual reality server;

- an introduction to the techniques which can be used to provide distributed virtual reality servers.

Chapter 11

Multi-Threading for a
Java-Based Server

In order to write an effective server, life really is made much easier if we are able to write a multi-threaded program. Multi-threading is one of those topics which many people find a bit scary, and which other people like to pretend is difficult (perhaps to defend their reputation as experts).

Multi-threaded programming is not hard. But it does provide some new ways to get things wrong. Don't let the fact that things in multi-threaded programs are *different* lead you into thinking that they are *difficult*. This chapter aims to dispel that myth and make you into someone who realizes that threads are your friends. You will then be able to impress people at parties and will have an extra skill that is worth noting on your *curriculum vitae*—at least until everyone else realizes how straightforward multi-threading can be.

Why Multi-Thread?

Multi-tasking is generally agreed to be a Good Thing. It allows your computer to run more than one program at a time. Whilst a machine with only one processor can strictly only be running one program at any one moment, the whole throughput of the system may increase as, say, a mathematics program can be doing some intensive numerical processing whilst a word-processor program is waiting for keyboard input and a database client is waiting for some data to be returned over a network.

The advantages of multi-threading, where a single program can be doing more than one thing at once—that is, a single program can have more than one *thread of execution*—are very similar. If a server is looking after many client connections at the same time then a lot of time can be wasted by having to check whether any of those clients have sent any messages to the server. This time might otherwise be spent on more useful tasks. If each of the clients is handled in its own thread then any individual thread need not necessarily be too concerned about what the rest of the threads of execution in the program are doing at any point. If thread A is waiting for input from user Fred then it need not be concerned about whether user Katrina is being properly looked after... that's the concern of thread B.

And should the multi-threaded program run on a machine with more than one processor, the program may be able to take advantage and have different threads on different processors and the program will literally be able to do more than one thing at a time.

An obvious question here is: "How is this different from ordinary multi-tasking?".

A very good question. I'm glad you asked.

When multiple programs wish to share data, there are assorted hoops that must be jumped through. Some operating systems allow you to set up areas of memory which can be shared between programs. Otherwise, some form of communication channel must be set up between the programs and the data transmitted from one to another.

Multiple threads of execution within a single program automatically share resources and global data areas. The only complication is some kind of synchronization control to prevent a thread from modifying a shared resource whilst it is also being used by another thread. Of course, this is not a complication that is *added* by multi-threading; it is just a complication which is not removed. When multiple separate programs are sharing memory and resources, it is a brave[1] programmer who doesn't provide some form of syn-

---

[1] Read "foolish"!

chronization using semaphores or lock files or the like!

Thread Class Or Runnable Interface?

There are two different ways to create a thread—you can create a class which implements the **Runnable** interface, or you can subclass the **Thread** class. There are differences between two methods, but these differences are not *usually* relevant. Implementing the **Runnable** interface can be somewhat more flexible (and can be used under conditions where you cannot subclass the **Thread** class), and you may be interested to note that the **Thread** class itself implements the **Runnable** interface—although that shouldn't surprise you when you are familiar with threads. However, you should use whichever method you find suits your own style. Indeed, it might be might be fairer to say that there are two ways to create the **run** method for a Java thread; whichever you use, you end up with an instance of the **Thread** class (or an instance of a subclass of the **Thread** class).

As I say, implementing the **Runnable** interface is more flexible, but it is undoubtably best to be familiar with both methods and make use of whichever seems most appropriate for the class you are creating.

Using the Runnable Interface

The **Runnable** interface is about as simple as things can get. A class which implements it must provide an implementation of the **run()** method, which is defined by the interface as:

```
public abstract void run();
```

A **Thread** object can then be instantiated with the **Runnable** object provided as a parameter. The new thread will start the **run()** method of the provided object and execute until the **run()** method exits, in much the same way as a single-threaded Java program will execute the **main()** method of the program and execute until the **main()** method exits. This is demonstrated in the following (very) simple threaded program.

```
/*********************************
**
** thr1
**    a simple class which creates and runs a thread
```

```
**
*/

import java.*;

public class thr1 implements Runnable
{
    // the 'main' method - it is invoked when the
    // program starts
    public static void main( String[] args )
    {
        new Thread( new thr1() ).start();
    }

    // the 'run' method, which is effectively the
    // 'main' method of a thread - it is invoked
    // by the 'start' method of the thread
    public void run()
    {
        System.out.println("Threaded Hello World");
    }
}
```

The start() method of the Thread class invokes the run() method. A thread does not start running until the start() method is invoked, so it is quite possible to create a thread at one point in a program and not have that thread start executing until another, later, point in the program. To make this explicit, consider a minor variation on our simple example:

```
/*********************************
**
** thr2
**   a simple class which creates a thread and some
**   time later runs the thread
**
*/

import java.*;
```

```
public class thr2 implements Runnable
{

    public static void main( String[] args )
    {
        // create a new thread, but don't yet
        // start the execution of that thread
        Thread myThread = new Thread( new thr2() );

        // now start the execution of the thread -
        // the 'start' method will invoke the 'run'
        // method
        myThread.start();
    }

    public void run()
    {
        System.out.println("Threaded Hello World");
    }
}
```

There are a couple of things that are worth noting here as differences between instances of the **Thread** class and instances of other classes which you can write which implement the **Runnable** interface. A **Thread** object runs until the thread's **run()** method exits, and then the thread is "dead". However, an instance of the **thr2** class which we defined above is not necessarily "dead" just because its **run()** method is no longer active. This might seem counter-intuitive if you have not grasped the distinction between a thread created by creating an instance of the **Thread** class and a thread created by a class which implements the **Runnable** interface.

As an analogy, to make this clearer, consider the need for a "class" that will send written messages across dangerous countryside. Creating an instance of the **Thread** class is like hiring a messenger to whom you give the message. The messenger sets off running and if he gets eaten by a werehamster then that is that—he's dead. Creating an instance of another class which implements the **Runnable** interface allows you to implement a higher-level messenger. This is like hiring someone who owns a hut full of carrier pigeons: the creation of the instance of this class doesn't actually start any threads running; but the messenger that we have created can make a copy of the message, attach it to a carrier pigeon (thread) and send the pigeon out (start the thread running). If the pigeon is eaten by a sparrow-hawk, the messenger class is still there and he can choose to release another pigeon (start another thread).

To demonstrate the fact that the class with the `Runnable` interface effectively "contains" the thread rather than "is" the thread, consider the following variation on our above class:

```
/*********************************
**
** thr3
**   more complex example which starts multiple
**   threads
**
*/

import java.*;

public class thr3 implements Runnable
{

    Thread myThread;

    public static void main( String[] args )
    {
        // create a new thread, but don't yet
        // start the execution of that thread
        myThread = new Thread( new thr3() );

        // now start the execution of the thread
        myThread.start();
        // sleep for half a second
        try {
            Thread.currentThread().sleep( 500 );
        }
        catch ( InterruptedException e ) { }
```

```
        // stop the thread
        myThread.stop();
        // wait for the thread to die
        try {
            myThread.join();
        }
        catch ( InterruptedException e ) { }

        // sleep for another half-second
        try {
            Thread.currentThread().sleep( 500 );
        }
        catch ( InterruptedException e ) { }

        // and do it all one more time
        myThread = new Thread( new thr3() );
        myThread.start();
        try {
            Thread.currentThread().sleep( 500 );
        }
        catch ( InterruptedException e ) { }
        myThread.stop();
        try {
            myThread.join();
        }
        catch ( InterruptedException e ) { }
    }

    public void run()
    {
        // loop forever
        while ( true ) {
            System.out.println("Threaded Hello World");
        }
    }
}
```

This will spend half a second in a loop printing the string `Threaded Hello World`, then will pause for half a second, and then will spend another half a second printing the same string before exiting.

This program introduces a number of new features. Firstly, every Java program contains at least one thread; even when you aren't writing programs which contain instances of the `Thread` class or classes which implement the `Runnable` interface, the program is a thread. Indeed there will usually be several threads: the Java garbage collector will generally be running as a low-priority thread whenever a Java program is running. Every thread has a thread identifier and the thread ID of the current thread can be obtained by using the method `Thread.currentThread()`. Useful methods of the `Thread` class include `sleep()`, which will cause the current thread to sleep (that is, pause in its execution) for a given number of milliseconds. You may like to note that you can instruct a thread to sleep for a specified number of nanoseconds, too, by giving a second argument to `sleep()`. For example, `Thread.currentThread().sleep( 0, 125 )` would cause the current thread to sleep for 0 milliseconds + 125 nanoseconds. But remember that there are *one thousand million* nanoseconds in a single second—you will rarely want to specify things to that level of precision. And even when you do *want* to, you will probably find that your system cannot provide that level of precision and it will round up the requested value to the nearest value that it really can cope with. On some systems this "granularity" of precision may be as large as one second!

Secondly, a thread can be told to stop by invoking its `stop()` method. However, due to the nature of scheduling multiple threads of execution, a thread that has been told to `stop()` is not necessarily dead just yet. To wait until the thread is definitively dead, you must invoke that thread's `join()` method.

Finally, if you were to compile and run the above class, you might find that it does nothing like what I have described: it may just sit in an infinite loop printing `Threaded Hello World` until the cows come home. This is due to the way that threads are scheduled.

Scheduling Threads

Java, of course, has been implemented on various kinds of system and will doubtless be implemented on many more. Some of these systems will have very good built-in support for multi-threaded languages and other systems may find that multi-threading doesn't fit in quite so easily. For example, UNIX has long been able to do several tasks at the same time (and many UNIX and UNIX-like systems have support for multi-threading straight out of the box), whereas MS-DOS was written with the expectation that it would only ever want to do one thing at a time.

At a different level, Microsoft-Windows (before the advent of Windows NT and Windows 95) was designed to be able run several programs at the same time but the system would generally need some help from the running programs to tell it when was a good time to switch from that program to another one.

The system that is running a Java program can have a big influence on the way that a multi-threaded program will run. If there are aspects of a Java program which must be consistent across disparate systems then you may need to help the operating system from inside your program, telling the operating system: "Now is a good time to switch to another thread, if there is one waiting to run".

Figure 11.1 shows how multiple threads could run on a system that contains several processors and has good support for multi-threading. Thread 1 is the "main" thread which creates all the others. As each thread is created it is run on a separate processor and all the threads execute at the same time. Generally speaking, this is the ideal way to run a multi-threaded program. And for the immediate future and for the average person, it is the least common way to run a multi-threaded program.

Figure 11.2 shows a much more common situation: the same multi-threaded program is running on a system with only one processor, therefore only a single thread can execute at any one time. (The thread that is executing is shown with a solid line). The system here has good support for multiple threads and ensures that each thread gets an opportunity to run at regular intervals. Or, more accurately, the system ensures that the thread which is

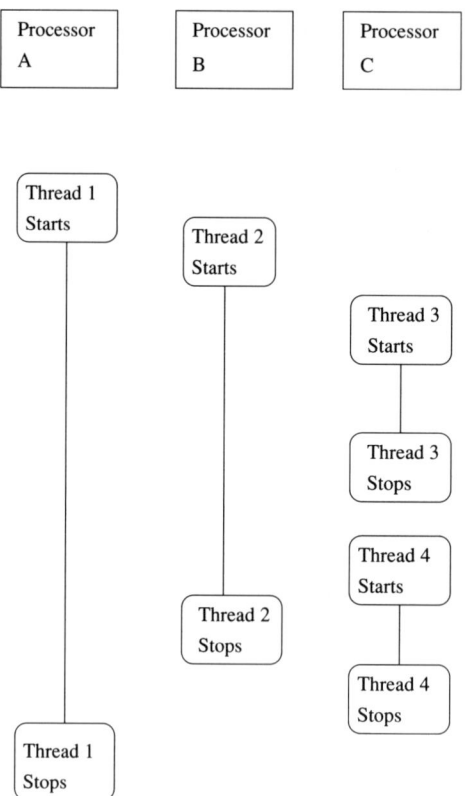

Figure 11.1: Multiple Threads Running On Multiple Processors

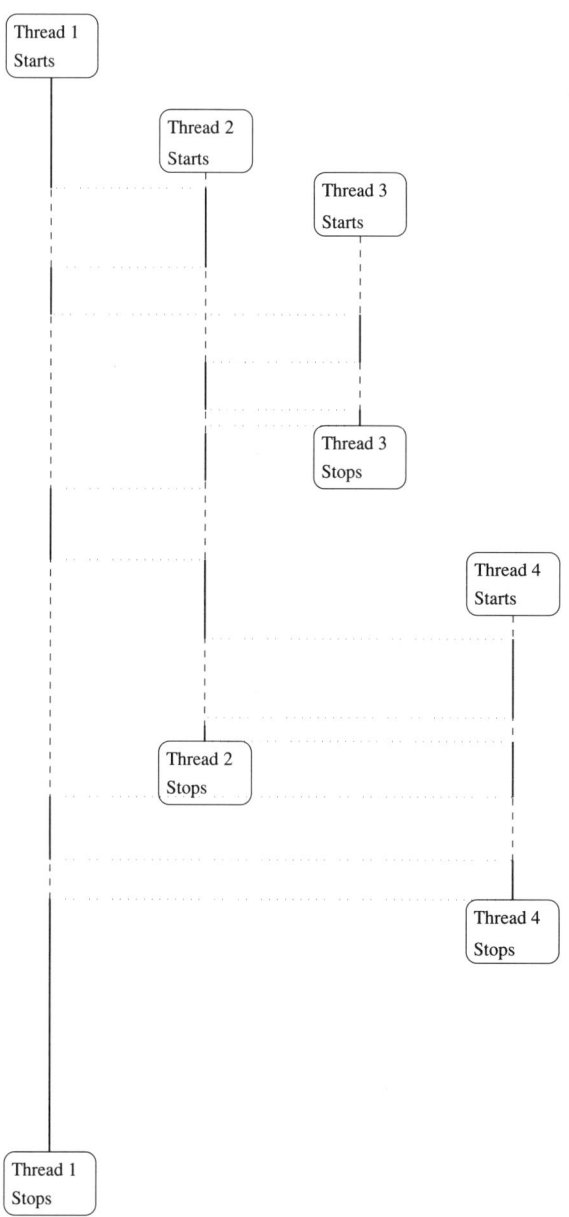

Figure 11.2: Multiple Threads On A Single Processor With Good Scheduling

currently running will be stopped at regular intervals in order to give another thread the opportunity to run. Note that when a thread "starts" it is created and ready to run. It doesn't necessarily get any processor time to begin executing at the time it is created.

On a system where there is not good support for multi-threading, as is the situation in Figure 11.3, the threads may run very unevenly, with one thread hogging the processor for long periods of time. Clearly this could result in a program which behaves somewhat differently, and perhaps unacceptably, on different systems.

The Java language provides methods which can go some way to helping improve this situation. These methods allow the program to tell the system that "now is a good time to stop the current thread and switch to another thread". Of course, it is only possible for the running thread to say to the system: "now is a good time for me to stop running". It is not possible for a thread which is not running to say to the system: "now is a good time for me to start running"![2]

In our earlier example, where a thread sat in a loop printing the string `Threaded Hello World`, it may have been helpful to give another thread the opportunity to run at the end of each iteration of the loop. This can be done by means of the method `yield()`, which is part of the `Thread` class and tells the system that this thread is willing to give up (or yield) the remainder of its time-slice. And so the `run()` method could be rewritten as:

```
public void run()
{
    // loop forever
    while ( true ) {
        System.out.println("Threaded Hello World");
        Thread.currentThread().yield();
    }
}
```

As has already been suggested, whether or not this is a helpful thing to do

---

[2]This is one of those things which a novice multi-threading programmer often wants to do. The problem is, if a thread is not running then it can't do *anything*—including sending messages to the system.

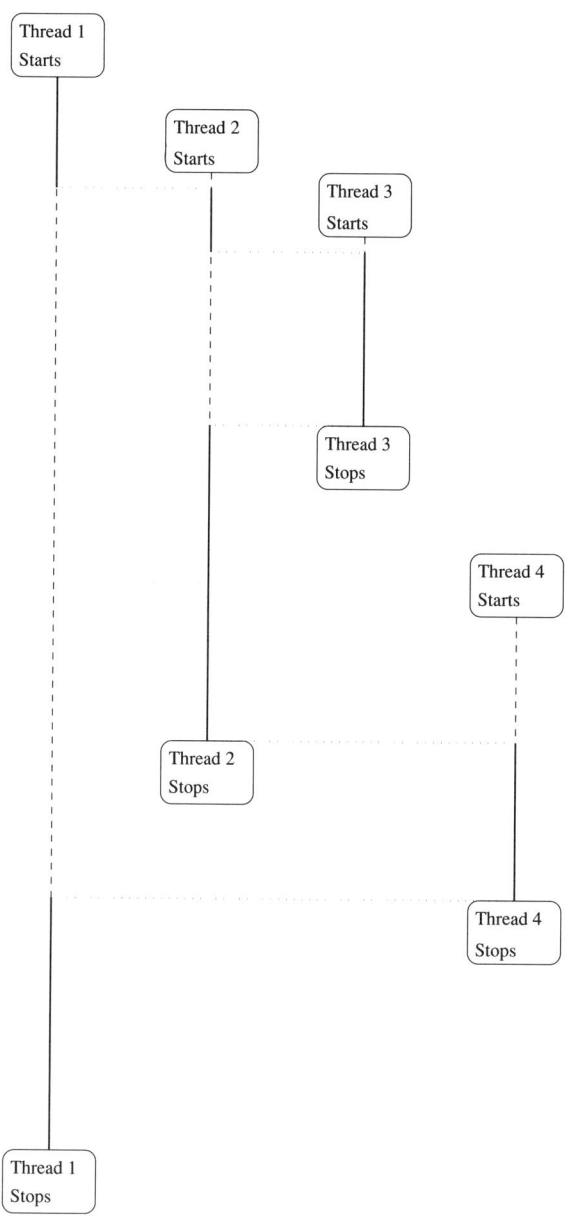

Figure 11.3: Multiple Threads On A Single Processor With Poor Scheduling

depends on the nature of the system on which Java is running. On some systems it is necessary, on others it is unnecessary.

Scheduling Threads Your Way

The Java scheduler will generally try to give each of your threads a fair share of processor time, and it will usually do a pretty good job of it. But there will always be occasions when you have a thread which needs to have a higher priority than other threads, or less important threads which can be allowed to run less frequently (or get less time on the occasions when they do run)—see Chapter 13 for examples of this within a virtual reality server.

The `Thread` class allows the priority at which any given thread will run to be specified. Higher-priority threads will be given larger time-slices by the scheduler than will lower-priority threads. The `Thread` class defines two public variables which specify the range of allowable values for thread priorities. These are `MIN_PRIORITY`, which represents the priority of threads which will get the least amount of processor time, and `MAX_PRIORITY`, which represents the priority of threads which will get the greatest amount of processor time. High priority should be given only to threads which absolutely must finish quickly; having high-priority threads can have a detrimental effect on the running of other threads within the application. A third public variable is defined, `NORMAL_PRIORITY`, which represents the default priority which is given to a thread. You will not usually need to change a thread's priority from this.

If you have to change the priority at which a thread runs, the `setPriority()` method is available. For example, if we wanted to change our earlier class to run its thread at a reduced priority:

```
/********************************
**
** thr4
**    threaded program which runs a thread at
**    reduced priority
**
*/

import java.*;
```

```java
public class thr4 implements Runnable
{

    public static void main( String[] args )
    {
        // create a new thread, but don't yet
        // start the execution of that thread
        Thread myThread = new Thread( new thr4() );

        // set the thread priority to be slightly less
        // than the default
        try {
            myThread.setPriority( Thread.NORMAL_PRIORITY-1 );
        }
        catch ( IllegalArgumentException e ) {
            // the value that we tried was out of range, so
            // use the guaranteed minimum value
            try {
                myThread.setPriority( Thread.MIN_PRIORITY );
            }
            // This exception cannot occur!
            catch ( IllegalArgumentException e2 ) {
                System.out.println( e2.getMessage() );
            }
        }
        // now start the execution of the thread
        myThread.start();
    }

    public void run()
    {
        System.out.println("Threaded Hello World");
    }
}
```

This will attempt to set the priority of the thread to one less than the default value NORMAL_PRIORITY. If the argument of the method setPriority() is not within the range MIN_PRIORITY to MAX_PRIORITY then an IllegalArgu-

`mentException` is thrown. When that exception is caught (that is, if the default priority is the same as the minimum priority—this is not normally the case) the priority of the thread will instead be set to the lowest valid priority.

Should you ever need to retrieve the priority of a thread, the `getPriority()` method is available.

Synchronizing Threads

If you are familiar with threads from the POSIX universe you may be a bit discouraged, not to say mightily alarmed, to discover that Java threads do not have such things as mutexes and condition variables.[3] Don't panic! All is not lost!

Later, in Chapter 13, we will see that a server will want to keep note of all clients which are connecting to it. That's not a problem in itself. Also, the server will be allowing new clients to connect at any time. Again, not a problem. The difficulty arises when you consider the implications of the fact that both of these operations could be (and possibly should be) handled by different threads. As a result, one thread could be removing details from a "connection table" (that is, a table containing details of all the clients which are currently connected) whilst another thread is adding details to the same connection table. To see how this can be a problem, take a look at Figure 11.4.

In state A there are two clients connected to the server. Their details are shown in the connection table as:

- the connection number (unique for each connected client);

- the username of the connected client;

- the hostname of the machine from which the client is connecting.

Of course, this is rather simplified for our example. As you will see in Chapter 13, there are plenty of other details that need to be stored in the connection

---

[3]If you aren't familiar with threads from the POSIX universe, this might look like gobbledegook Don't worry. It probably *is* gobbledegook!

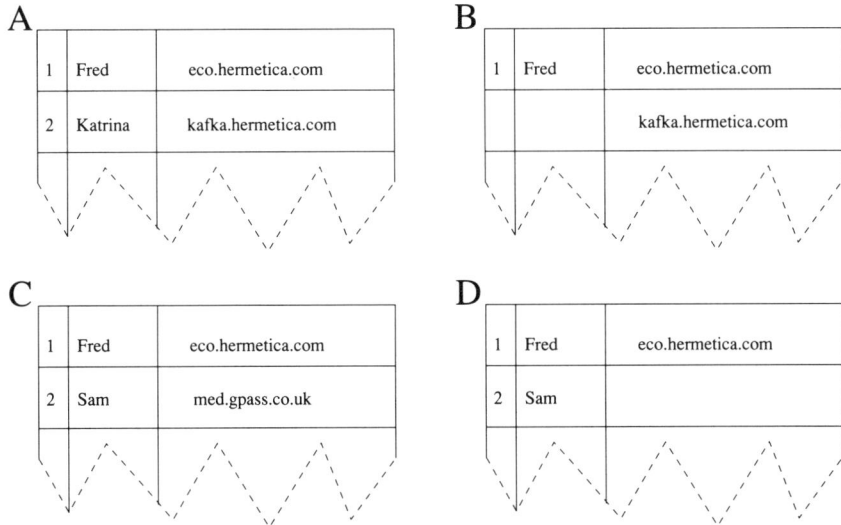

Figure 11.4: Interference Between Threads

table, but this is quite an adequate subset to demonstrate the potential problems when multiple threads need to access the same data areas.

Remember that there are two or more threads that are going to be accessing this table: one that is adding an entry to the table when a new client connects and one which is removing an entry from the table when that thread's client disconnects or when the link to the client goes "dead". The "connecting" thread fills in the next empty slot in the table, which it defines as one that does not contain a valid connection number. The "disconnecting" thread shows that a client is no longer connected by removing the client details from the table.

Now Katrina decides that she has something better to do and disconnects from the server. The thread that is dedicated to watching Katrina's connection notices that Katrina has gone and starts to remove her details from the connection table, as shown in state B, where the connection number and the username have been cleared out. Before it has completed removing all the details—the hostname of the client's machine is still to be blanked out—the scheduler performs a context switch and gives control to the "master" thread, just as Sam connects to the server. The "master" thread sees Sam connecting and dedicates a new thread to Sam's connection. This thread looks for the first free slot—that is, one without a connection number. And the one that it finds is the one that our "Katrina" thread has been working on. Oblivious to this, the "Sam" thread fills in the table with all of Sam's details, leaving us in state C.

The scheduler again performs a context switch, and the "Katrina" thread carries on from where it left off. It was just about to finish clearing out the table entry for Katrina, and it does so—not aware that it has actually cleared out some of the details for the still-connected Sam. That leaves us in state D where there are two clients connected but one of them—the connection details for Sam—has corrupted data. This is *not* a Good Thing.

The solution is to make use of the `synchronized` modifier and the `wait()` and `notify()` methods. The `synchronized` modifier can be applied to methods or blocks of code. Use of the `synchronized` modifier tells the scheduler that it *must not* perform a context switch which will pass control from one piece of synchronized code within an object to another within the same object. To put it more simply, having more than one piece of synchronized code within an object prevents those pieces of code from executing at the same time. So in our example above, if we synchronized both the code where the "connection" thread adds a client's details to the connection table and the code where the "disconnection" thread removes a client's details from the connection table, then there would never be an occasion where one thread was adding details to the table whilst the other thread was removing details.

So within each thread that is controlling a connection, we would have a piece of code that updates the connection table when that thread first starts, which would be something like:

```
    ...
    synchronized {
        connectionTable.add( myConnectionsDetails );
    }
    ...
```

and we know that the `synchronized` modifier prevents more than one thread performing an update at any one time.

Similarly, when the thread receives a command from the client to close the connection (more on this in the server chapters when we discuss protocols) we can safely remove details from the connection table using something like:

```
   ...
   synchronized {
      connectionTable.remove( myConnectionDetails );
   }
   ...
```

A complete example of how to synchronize threads within a server is given in Chapter 13.

The Need For Inhibitions

What is really happening when we state that a method or a code block is synchronized? How does the system know when it can switch context between two threads and when it can't?

There may also be occasions when we don't want the system to be completely held up by a synchronized section of code. Consider the case where a client has started to make a connection to the server. The server has some of the details from the client (such as who it claims to be and which machine it is coming from) but it wants to confirm the details before it commits to writing them all into the connection table. However, the network connection between the server machine and the client machine may be very slow, or the client machine may even have died before completing the connection negotiation. Whilst the server is sitting waiting for confirmation details to come back from the client machine, no other client can be added to the connection table, nor can "expired" clients be removed. Even when this delay is as short as a few seconds, it can be very noticeable and irritating to someone who thought that they were making a real-time connection. Of course, there are ways around these problems—otherwise it would have been something of a waste of time writing this section!

Monitors

Every object within your Java program is associated with a monitor. When a synchronized piece of code starts running it grabs the monitor and doesn't release it until it has completed executing. If another piece of synchronized code within the same object wishes to start running, it cannot because it cannot acquire the monitor.

The way to persuade two pieces of synchronized code within the same object to run simultaneously[4] is for one of the pieces of code to (temporarily) give up the monitor and to inform any other pieces of code that are waiting for the monitor that it is now available for acquisition. This operation is done using the methods `notify()` and `wait()`. Note that `notify()` and `wait()`, although used for thread synchronization, are methods of the `Object` class and so can be used to synchronize any class (as all classes are derivatives of the `Object` class) between threads.

The `wait()` method causes an object to go to sleep (and in going to sleep it gives up its monitor if it is currently holding it). There are a number of forms of the `wait()` method:

- `wait()` will sleep indefinitely;

- `wait( long` *time_ms* `)` will sleep until *time_ms* milliseconds have elapsed;

- `wait( long` *time_ms,* `int` *time_ns* `)` will sleep until *time_ms* milliseconds plus *time_ns* nanoseconds have elapsed.

The `wait()` method will cause the calling thread to sleep until:

- the specified timeout period has elapsed;

- another thread calls the waiting object's `notify()` method;

- an exception is thrown (the possible exceptions that could be thrown being `InterruptedException` and `IllegalMonitorStateException`).

When the waiting thread is reawakened, it automatically reacquires the monitor which it relinquished and so again another thread of the same object cannot take control.

As a general rule, you need not perform any specific processing for when one of the possible exceptions is thrown—if you are doing some processing which

---

[4]Well... simultaneously-ish. On a single processor, only one piece of code will be actually running at any one time, but there may be any number in a running *state*.

needs to specifically do something as a result of an `InterruptedException` being thrown then you probably already know about it! An `IllegalMonitorStateException` is thrown as a result of bad code—for example, invoking an object's `wait()` or `notify()` from code which is not within a synchronized method, or from a thread which does not currently own the object's monitor.

An `InterruptedException` would generally be handled by a piece of code that checks to see if what was being waited upon had really completed. For example:

```
public class AClass {

    boolean Complete = false;

    public synchronized aMethod() {
        while ( !Complete ) {
            try {
                wait();
            }
            catch (InterruptedException e) { }
        }
    }

    public synchronized anotherMethod() {
        .
        .
        .
        Complete = true;
        notify();
    }
        .
        .
        .

}
```

So when `aMethod()` goes to sleep, it not only waits to be notified that another thread has completed before continuing, but also checks that the other thread has claimed that it has completed what it is doing by setting the `Complete` variable to `true`. If the `wait()` was interrupted then there is no specific processing that is performed, but the `Complete` variable will still be set to false and the method will know that it wasn't an "official" wake-up call—it will simply go back to sleep.

Now if you are already familiar with multi-threading from a system other than Java, you may be worrying about some things here and thinking that it is not all that sophisticated. Sadly, you would be right to think this.

First, if you are using one of the `wait()` methods that takes a timeout, the system does not provide you with any convenient method to determine if your thread has woken up because the timeout timed out, or if another thread invoked your `notify()` method. An obvious simple solution to this problem is to have a variable which is set before `notify()` is invoked, something like in this example:

```
public class AnotherClass {

    boolean Notified = false;

    public synchronized aMethod() {
        try {
            wait( 1000 );
            if ( Notified == false ) {
                // we weren't notified, so we must have timed out
            } else {
                // notify() must have been invoked
            }
        }
        catch (InterruptedException e) { }
    }

    public synchronized anotherMethod() {
        .

        .

        .

                // label 1
        Notified = true;
                // label 2
        notify();
    }
}
```

```
        .
        .
        .
}
```

Nice and straightforward; before invoking `notify()` we set a variable to indicate that we are sending a notification. Whether or not that variable is set determines what happened during the `wait( 1000 )`.

If only life were that easy. Suppose that 999 milliseconds have elapsed when the program reaches the line commented with `label 1`, and suppose that 1000 milliseconds have elapsed immediately after the `Notified` variable has been set to `true` but before `notify()` is invoked. At that point, the `wait()` method might time out, but the variable says that it did not time out. This is not likely to happen very often and your application may not suffer too much from a wrong interpretation like this. Or it may suffer a lot. Certainly, if you're happy with this and you're writing flight-control software for a fly-by-wire plane then I'd like to know so that I can pick which airline I fly with.

The correct solution would be for the Java designers to change the implementation of `wait()` so that it throws some kind of exception if it times out. In the meantime, use the `wait()` method with a timeout with caution.

So how is this of use to us in a virtual reality server? As has already been seen, clients can be connecting and disconnecting to the server all the time and the connection table is updated accordingly. But we have assumed until now that the client will actually tell the server that it wishes to disconnect. That will not always be true. Either because the client has been badly implemented, or because of circumstances beyond the client's control—for example, if your main power fuses blow and your computer goes dead. If only those clients which disconnect politely are dealt with, the connection table will slowly (or even rapidly) fill up with lots of details of unconnected machines. What we can do is set up a watcher thread which spots any client threads which have exited. The watcher thread can then clean up the connection table for that thread. There are some new concepts that we need to introduce here. We only want the watcher thread to look at threads within the server that are supposed to be talking to clients—any other threads which might be running to perform other tasks within the server should be outside the watcher's scope of interest. Java allows us to gather sets of threads together into `ThreadGroup`s.

Every thread that is ever created is a member of a `ThreadGroup`. By default a new thread is added to the same group as the thread which creates it, but it is possible to create and name a `ThreadGroup` and add a thread to that group. The `Thread` class constructor has an optional first parameter which specifies the `ThreadGroup` to which the new thread should be added. For example:

```
...
public class ThreadedServer extends Thread
{
    ...
    ThreadGroup clientGroup = new ThreadGroup(
        "Client Connection Threads" );
    ...
    ClientConnection conn = new ClientConnection( clientGroup );
    ...
}

class ClientConnection extends Thread
{
    static int threadID = 0;
    ...
    public ClientConnection( ThreadGroup clientGroup )
    {
        // add this thread to the clientGroup ThreadGroup
        // and give the thread a unique identifier
        super( clientGroup, Integer.toString( threadID++ ) );
        ...
    }
}
...
```

This creates a new `ThreadGroup` called "Client Connection Threads". When a new `ClientConnection` is created, it invokes its superclass constructor (i.e. the `Thread` constructor) to set that thread's `ThreadGroup` to be "Client Connection Threads".

Summary

In this chapter we have looked at Java's relatively simplistic multi-threading facilities and how they can be applied to construction of a server. Whilst not so sophisticated as other multi-threading schemes, and certainly with their fair share of problems and pitfalls to catch the unwary programmer, they are well worth the trouble of getting to know.

With just a little practice, you should be happy with the concept of a program which can do more than one thing at a time and have a new tool to improve the efficiency and structure of your Java programs.

Chapter 12

Superstrings

"It's an energy field created by all living things. It surrounds us and penetrates us. It binds the galaxy together."

Obi-Wan Kenobi[1]

Virtual reality, if it wishes to truly represent reality, needs to include the ability for people to communicate with other people in virtual space. For us to accomplish this, we need to discuss some basic issues regarding the subject of networking.

In this chapter, we shall be focusing primarily on using TCP/IP as the protocol over which we shall be transmitting and receiving data. However, we shall also take a look at *IPng*[2] and *multicasting* as alternative data transportation protocols.

---

[1] *Star Wars: A New Hope*, ©LucasFilm Ltd.

[2] Packets of data that are sent over the Internet are transmitted using a protocol known, not surprisingly, as the Internet Protocol. The Internet as a whole currently uses version four of this protocol. It is known as IPv4 or, more usually, simply IP. To overcome certain limitations, groups are working on an updated version of the protocol known as version 6 (IPv6—no, don't ask what happened to v5!) or "next generation" (IPng).

String, Sellotape and Blu-Tack

. . . are the three main components of any good network!

We make this observation only half-jokingly, since the state of evolution of the largest network on the planet, the Internet, does not seem to have adhered to any particular plan or design.

This only serves to illustrate the diversity of building networks, and highlights some of the obstacles and problems we are likely to hit on our way to designing an efficient networking protocol for realistic virtual reality.

A "network" can be defined as being a logical connection of two or more computers, or devices, joined together via some physical medium.

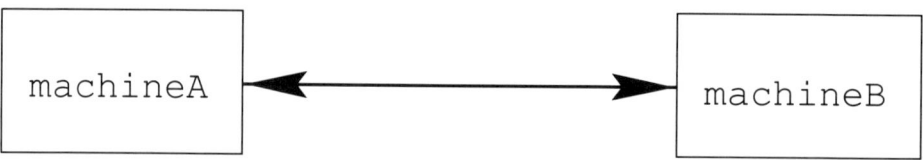

Figure 12.1: A Basic Network

The network shown in Figure 12.1 is about as simple as a network is likely to get, and, for the purposes of this discussion, is highly unlikely to crop up. However, a core principle of network design is that no matter how complex the network, essentially it all boils down to this type of connection which could be described as either *point-to-point* [3] or *peering*.

This network, albeit small, would let at least two people use a multi-user networked virtual reality system, very probably at high speeds. However, suppose the owners of this network, company A, decided they wanted their business partners, company B, to participate in their virtual reality system (see Figure 12.2). What now?

---

[3]Don't confuse a "point-to-point" network connection, with the Point-to-Point Protocol, or PPP. They are quite different (for the current purpose, at least!).

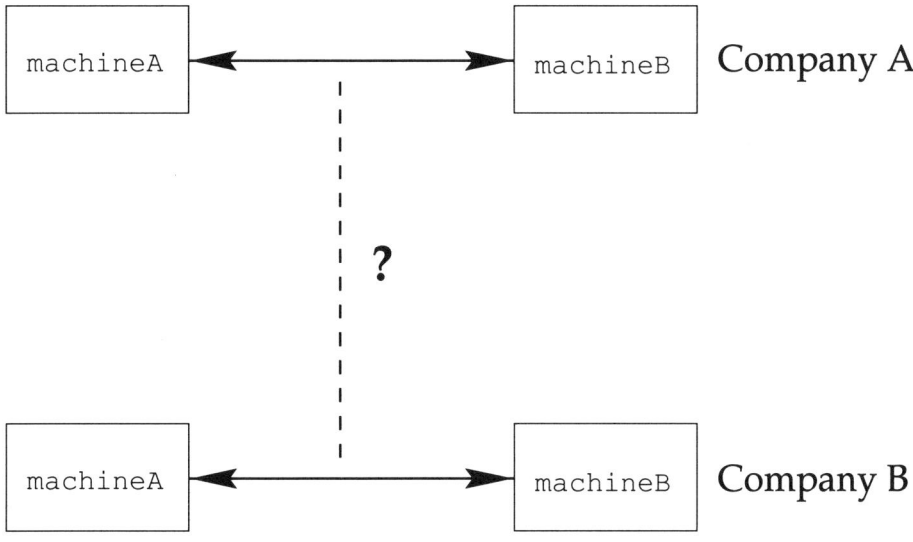

Figure 12.2: Two Basic Networks

Assuming company B aren't in the vicinity, and thus, can't be physically connected to company A's machines, we need to look at different ways of connecting these two networks together.

Physical Networks

The physical aspects of networking computers together are quite simple. You wire two network devices together. Couldn't be easier... However, there are a multiplicity of ways in which these devices can be joined together, the wires are different colours and thicknesses, and the network devices can be half a world apart.

Telephone Line, ISDN

Network connections running over telephone lines (ISDN—Integrated Services Digital Network—is basically digital telephony) are possibly the most common form of connectivity in the Internet today. They provide a low-bandwidth way of extending networks to, for example, the home, the laptop and the PDA (Personal Digital Assistant). They are the most *portable* form of networking, especially in today's age of radio modems and GSM (Global System for Mobile Telecommunications) connections where you can use your cellular phone as a network device!

Developments of networking over phone lines using TCP/IP have been quite recent, by computing standards. There have been two separate attempts to define a protocol that would run effectively over telephone lines, the first being SL/IP, the *Serial Line Internet Protocol*, followed soon after by PPP, the *Point-to-Point Protocol*, which was far more sophisticated and remarkably easy to use compared to SL/IP, which was once remarked to have been "designed by a grad student after drinking too much one night". We shall discuss these protocols later on.

Logical Networks

Assuming we've now got a fine lattice of wires trailing about the room, under the floorboards, round the air-conditioner, out of the building and into someone else's offices, we can take a look at what we can now *do* with all this wire.

A network is not a tremendous amount of use for computing without an agreed protocol between the network devices that are attached to the network. For example, in Figure 12.1, the two network devices would only be aware that each end of the network was attached to something, due to the electrical characteristics across the wire, or perhaps how far along the wire the other device was. Without an agreed protocol for sharing information between them, they wouldn't be able to communicate at all.

In 1969, the Defense Advanced Research Projects Agency (DARPA) funded research to create an experimental packet switching network. This network was called the ARPANET, and in 1975 it became fully operational. Shortly afterwards, the development of a set of protocols known as TCP/IP[4] began.

In 1983, the TCP/IP protocols were adopted as standards, and all network devices connected to the ARPANET were required to convert to use them. Since then, the rise of TCP/IP has been meteoric, due in part to the following factors:

---

[4]Transmission Control Protocol / Internet Protocol, if you must know.

- Open protocol standards. The source code for TCP/IP is generally freely available for porting to new operating systems and network devices.

- TCP/IP is independent of the wiring or physical network layer that propagates the information.

- Its robust addressing scheme for uniquely identifying network devices.

There are other non-TCP/IP protocols in existence such as Appletalk, Novell's IPX,[5] Microsoft's Windows for Workgroups networking layer and so on, but we shall concentrate on the more ubiquitous and widespread TCP/IP.

TCP/IP is an incredibly flexible network protocol and can be encapsulated across any number of different protocols, *e.g.*, if you wished to run the Point-to-Point Protocol over telephone lines, you would be able to use any TCP/IP service across that link since TCP/IP is encapsulated over PPP.[6] We shall now examine the architecture of TCP/IP more closely.

TCP/IP can be defined in many ways with reference to the OSI Network Reference Model, but a comfortable way of doing it is to use a four-level structure, instead of the seven layers used by the OSI model. These layers can be divided as shown in Figure 12.3.

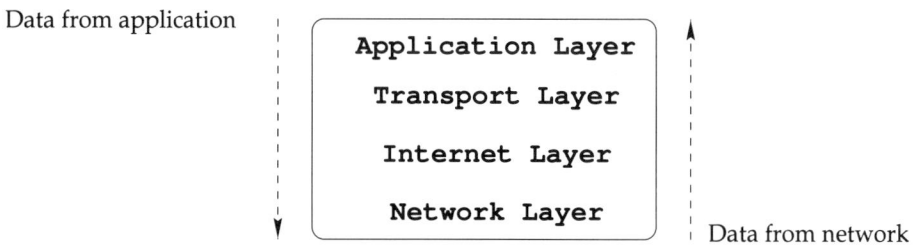

Data from application

Application Layer

Transport Layer

Internet Layer

Network Layer

Data from network

Figure 12.3: TCP/IP Architecture

The flow of data through this model is sequential, *i.e.*, data must pass from

---

[5]This is based on TCP/IP.

[6]The same theory holds for SL/IP, which is an older and less robust dial-up TCP/IP protocol.

the top to the bottom, and back again, or from the bottom to the top and back again. There are no jump-off or jump-on points in the middle of the stack, nor can data "skip" a layer. On the way down through the stack, each layer prepends a piece of control information, known as the *header*, to the data passed down by the layer above. This is to ensure correct delivery from layer to layer. On the way back up through the stack, each header is stripped off and the raw data is eventually popped off the top of the stack. The format of the data at each layer varies, as, unfortunately, do the terms used to describe these data structures.

We'll now take a closer look at each layer of the TCP/IP protocol.

Network Access Layer

The *Network Access Layer* is the lowest-level layer of the TCP/IP architecture. The protocols that this layer provides allow the physical network device components to talk to the network itself, and to deliver the packets from the applications across that network.

The primary functions of the Network Access Layer are to convert, or encapsulate, IP datagrams from the Internet Layer into *frames* used by the underlying physical network segment; and to map IP addresses to the physical addresses used by the network.

The Network Access Layer differs from the other three TCP/IP layers, in that it needs to know the exact details of the underlying network to which it is attached. The other three layers work on an abstract concept of what the network is. Therefore, the Network Access Layer, even though never used directly by the average user or programmer, is the most complex to maintain, since a *device driver* for each network standard must be written, *e.g.*, X.25, 10-Base-T or Frame Relay.

Internet Layer

The *Internet Layer* is the second lowest layer of the TCP/IP architecture. The Internet Layer, or *Internet Protocol*, is the core of TCP/IP and the most important aspect of the TCP/IP architecture. This layer is defined in RFC

791 - `Internet Protocol`[7] which was compiled from multiple versions of the *ARPA Internet Protocol Specification*.

The Internet Layer is itself primarily composed of two different protocols, *IP*, the *Internet Protocol*, and *ICMP*, the *Internet Control Message Protocol*. However, ICMP itself uses part of the basic major functionality of IP.

IP is the core of TCP/IP and handles several extremely important functions, chiefly:

- definition of the building block of TCP/IP, the *datagram*;

- definition of a cohesive addressing scheme for all network devices;

- transmission of datagrams from the Transport Layer to the Network Access Layer and *vice versa*;

- procedures for *fragmenting* and *reassembling* datagrams being transmitted between hosts.

IP is limited in scope to providing the necessary functions to transmit datagrams over interconnected networks from a given source to a given destination. IP, in itself, has no provision for error detection or correction, no flow control and therefore, as a logical consequence, no built-in *reliability*.

Because of these "limitations", IP is regarded as being a *connectionless protocol*, *i.e.*, it does not check to see if the remote end of the connection is ready to receive data before the source sends it. IP therefore relies heavily on other protocols such as TCP to provide facilities such as error detection and correction. IP is also regarded as being a *unreliable protocol* since it does not provide error detection and correction. This is an unfair term, since IP will *always* deliver the data to the host network device. However, it does not check whether or not the host network device received the data correctly.

---

[7] An RFC is a "Request For Comments". It's usually a paper written to express a coalescing of ideas on a certain topic, which is then published to a wider audience for discussion. The RFC process is one of the core institutions of the Internet at large. For an index of all available RFCs, see `ftp://rs.internic.net/rfc`.

Datagrams

The datagram was designed to travel over the existing framework laid down in the ARPANET, which was a *packet switching* network. Packet switching networks are networks where the packets, or datagrams, contain the information required to transmit them from host to host, rather like an envelope, to draw an analogy with the standard postal service. In the case of the datagram, both the *source address* and *destination address* are written into a *header block* that is prepended to each datagram. This allows IP to examine the destination address to work out what to do with the packet, which, if the destination address is on the local network, will result in IP delivering the packet, or, if the destination address is not on the local network, delivering the packet to the nearest gateway for further transmission.

The *header* of a datagram is a block of data, usually five or six 32-bit *words* long.[8] The layout of the datagram header block is shown in Figure 12.4

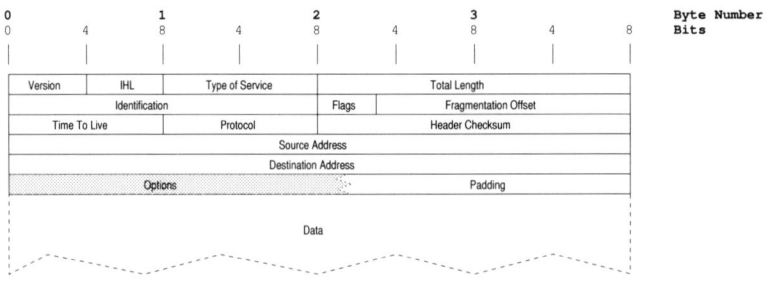

Figure 12.4: IP Datagram Header Block

As we mentioned above, a core function of IP is to fragment and reassemble datagrams. Why do we want to do that?

To answer this question, we must take a step backwards and recall from a previous section the dissimilarity of physical networking possibilities, *i.e.*, connections may range from 1 Mbit/second serial lines to 14.4 Kbits/second telephone lines using modems. Because of this vast range of bandwidth that must be seamlessly navigated by packets, networks have a metric associated

---

[8]The actual length of the header is contained in the field tagged IHL, or *Internet Header Length*, in the header block.

with them, known as the *maximum transmission unit*, or *MTU*. This metric quantifies the maximum size of a packet that can be transmitted over that particular network. For example, a packets being transmitted from an Ethernet network to a host over a PPP link would go from a relatively large MTU, possibly around 3500, to quite a small one, possibly 576. The variability in MTUs requires IP to split larger datagrams into a number of smaller datagrams that will "fit" into the new MTU. This process is known as *fragmentation*.

The corollary of fragmentation is obviously *reassembly*, in that once our host receives the datagrams it must reassemble them into a single datagram for further handling. For this process to work satisfactorially, IP must be aware of the order in which the packets were split up, and therefore the sequence in which they should be re-assembled. The IP datagram header block contains the information necessary for this function in the `Identification`, `Fragmentation Offset` and `Flags` fields. The `Identification` field contains an identifier of the original packet that this fragment belongs to and is used to group fragments together. The `Fragmentation Offset` field informs IP which position in the original packet this fragment is at, and the `Flags` field may contain a bit that informs IP whether or not all fragments of the original datagram have been re-assembled.

ICMP

The other core protocol of the Internet Layer is the Internet Control Message Protocol.[9]. ICMP is designed to act as a sentinel for IP, in that it oversees the flow of datagrams between sources and destinations and transmits informational datagrams to the appropriate hosts as required. Some of these informational datagrams are as follows:

ICMP Source Quench This message is transmitted by ICMP to the source address in cases when packets from the source are arriving too quickly for the current host to process. This message instructs the source to temporarily stop sending datagrams.

Network is Unreachable This message is transmitted by ICMP to the source address when it is detected by a host that it cannot make a

---

[9]This protocol is defined in `RFC 792`.

connection to either the destination address or the nearest gateway.

ICMP Redirect This message is generated when there are two or more gateways that the current host can possibly send a datagram to for further transmission and one gateway instructs ICMP to use the other gateway, perhaps if the first choice gateway is overloaded and the second is not. In this case, ICMP will redirect the datagram to the second gateway. Both gateways must be on the same network as the source host for ICMP Redirects to occur.

ICMP Echo This message is used to detect whether or not a remote host's Internet Layer is running and functional. When a remote host receives an ICMP Echo message, it simply returns the message to the source host.[10]

Transport Layer

The *Transport Layer* is an important one, since it is at this level that the protocols for providing higher-level access to datagram delivery are defined. The two main protocols for doing this are *TCP* and *UDP*. Both protocols deliver data between the Application Layer and the Internet Layer, but there the similarities stop. UDP is the simpler of the two protocols providing an unreliable, connectionless delivery mechanism which incurs low overhead due to a reduced packet size, whereas TCP provides reliable and connection-orientated packet delivery with error detection and correction. TCP packets are much larger than UDP packets as a result of these additional delivery safeguards.

UDP

UDP, or the *User Datagram Protocol*, allows programmers direct access to a datagram delivery service, which allows them to transmit and receive packets over the network incurring extremely low overhead. This is possible due to the extremely simple nature of UDP itself,[11] which is the minimum gloss added to raw IP to make it usable by entities other than IP itself!

UDP is an unreliable datagram protocol, which, as we noted before, merely means that it is guaranteed to deliver packets, but will not bother checking

---

[10]The UNIX `ping` utility uses ICMP Echo messages.

[11]UDP is defined in `RFC 768`.

that the destination address received them correctly. This, if you are planning to write an extremely fast networking protocol of your own, is not necessarily a bad thing.

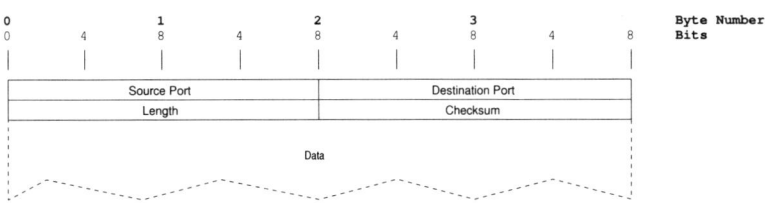

Figure 12.5: UDP Packet Header Block

The format of a UDP packet is extremely simple and is shown in Figure 12.5. As you can see, the bare minimum has been included in this packet, which makes it extremely compact. This very compactness is an alluring attribute for programmers, since, if the data being transferred is small, for example, a positional update of 10 bytes, then the overhead of 24 bytes per TCP header (see below) is collosal compared to the size of the packet. The overhead of UDP, eight bytes, is far more acceptable and far more efficient.

TCP

The TCP protocol is the more readily recognized Transport Layer protocol, partly because it's mentioned in TCP/IP, but more likely because it provides a reliable, connection-orientated datagram delivery service, complete with error detection and correction capabilities. TCP, therefore, is 100% rock-solid in terms of data delivery since, unlike UDP, it checks to ensure that the destination address received the data correctly.

A disadvantage of TCP is obviously that the packet size that needs to be used to provide this functionality is much larger than that of UDP, 24 bytes compared to the eight of UDP. The TCP packet header block can be seen in Figure 12.6.

TCP uses a system of *positive acknowledgement* to provide the layer of error detection and correction that makes it a reliable protocol. This system relies on the simple principle that each packet sent to its destination address should

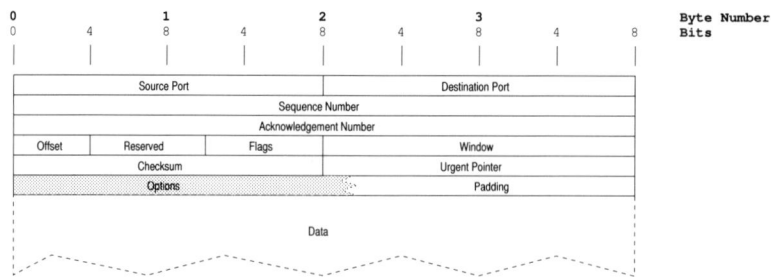

Figure 12.6: TCP Packet Header Block

be *acknowledged*, or `ACK`'d. If the source address doesn't receive an `ACK` to a packet within a certain time, the packet is retransmitted. Furthermore, each packet contains a `Checksum` field which is used to to verify that the packet was received undamaged. If the packet is damaged, the destination address will reject the packet and wait until the source address resends it after the period it has been waiting for an `ACK` elapses.

Application Layer

The *Application Layer* is the layer which the programmer tends to be most interested in. This layer is the one at which all the *services* that run over a network exist, for example, TELNET, FTP, SMTP, NNTP and, last but certainly not least, our own virtual reality system.

These applications use the lower-level messaging protocols to handle data transmission, but they themselves define the protocol that data is to be transmitted and received in. Therefore, in the case of a multi-user server, the server will transmit and receive data using either TCP or UDP. However, the protocol the server talks—an example of a very simple protocol definition could be: the four bytes "`USER`" mean that someone is attempting to logon to the server—is defined completely at the Application Layer.

A more complete, but over-simplified, overview of the entire TCP/IP architecture in action, showing the interaction between the various layers and protocols that make up the architecture, is given in Figure 12.7. It is fairly obvious that our networking design must flow through the Internet Layer by default, but we have a choice of Transport Layer to use to transmit and

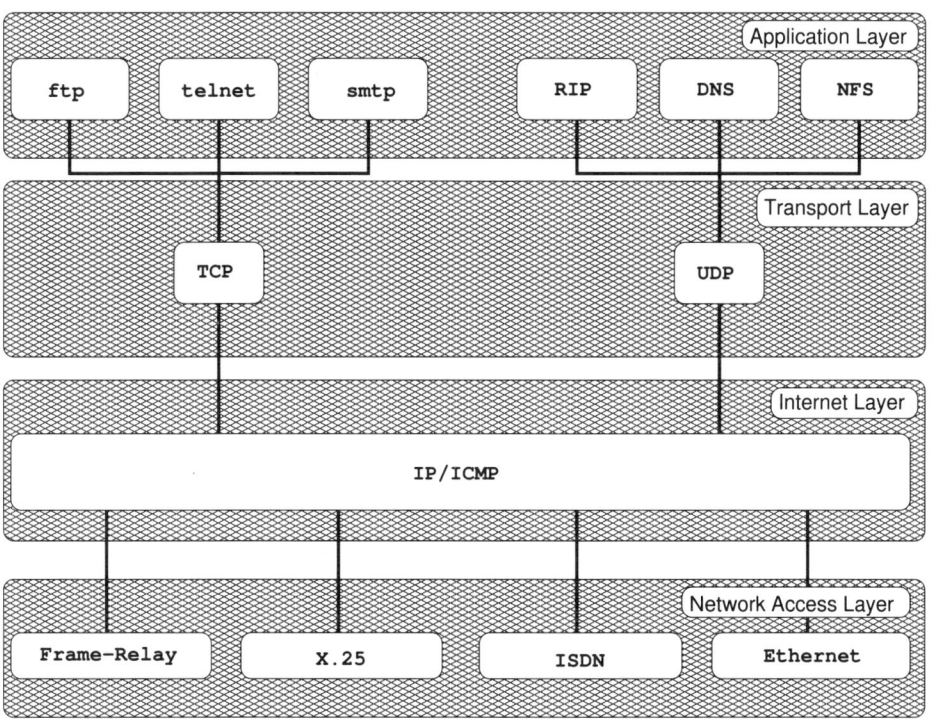

Figure 12.7: TCP/IP Architecture Overview

receive data.

Name That Machine In One!

As we discussed in the section above on the Internet Layer, all network-connected devices have a unique identification number, called an *IP address*. This number tells the Network Access Layer where to send packets to and where they have come from.

An IP address is in the form of a "dotted quad", or:

a.b.c.d

The number is read from left to right in order of network refinement. Each part of the IP address is composed of eight bits, hence a full IP address is 32 bits, or four bytes. The address can be described using the following rules:

- If the first bit *only* of an IP address is 0, then the address is known as a *Class A* address. The next seven bits identify the network, the final 24 bits identify the host. This can be seen in Figure 12.8. From examining the fact that the first bit out of eight is not used in the network number, we can see that there can only be a maximum of 127 Class A networks in the IP address space. This may not seem a lot, but there can theoretically be 2^{24} individual network devices within each Class A address.

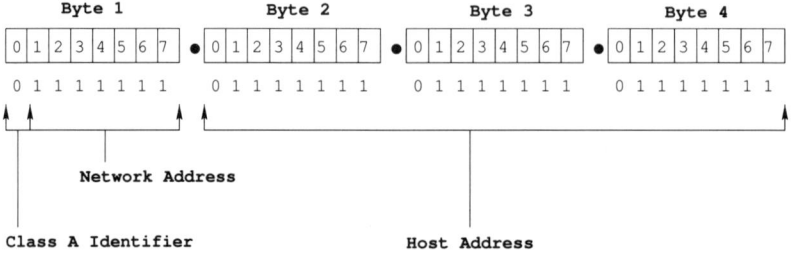

Figure 12.8: Class A Network IP Address

- If the first *two* bits of an IP address are 1 0, then the address is known as a *Class B* address. The next 14 bits identify the network and the final 16 bits identify the host. This can be seen in Figure 12.9. Since the first two bits of 16 are taken as the Class B network identifier from the network number, we are restricted to only having 2^{14} Class B networks.[12] Each Class B address, however, theoretically has space for 2^{16} uniquely identified network devices.

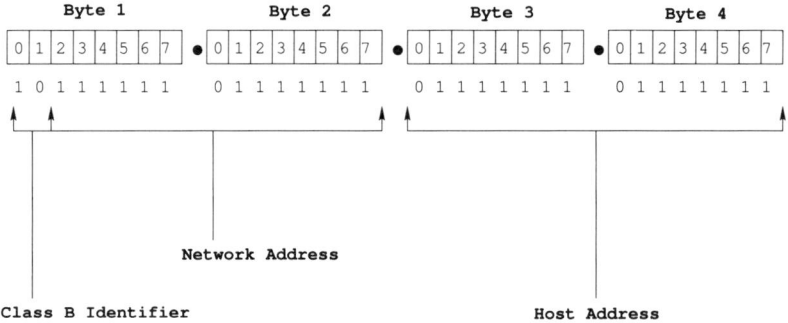

Figure 12.9: Class B Network IP Address

- If the first *three* bits of an IP address are 1 1 0, then the address is known as a *Class C* address. The next 21 bits identify the network and the final eight bits identify the host. This can be seen in Figure 12.10. Since the Class C has so many bits to identify its network number, it isn't surprising that there are around $2^{21} - 1$ valid Class C addresses available for us.[13] Each Class C address can theoretically address up to 256 hosts.

- If the first *three* bits of an IP address are 1 1 1, then the address is known as a *Class D* address. IP addresses in this network range do not really belong to specific networks, but are currently assigned to *multicast* addresses, which we shall discuss below.

As you may have noticed from the rules of IP address structure, we used the word "theoretically" quite often. "Why's this?!", you cry, agitatedly.

---

[12] If restricted is the word here!

[13] It's probably more surprising that these are now almost completely used up! The Internet has very little free address space.

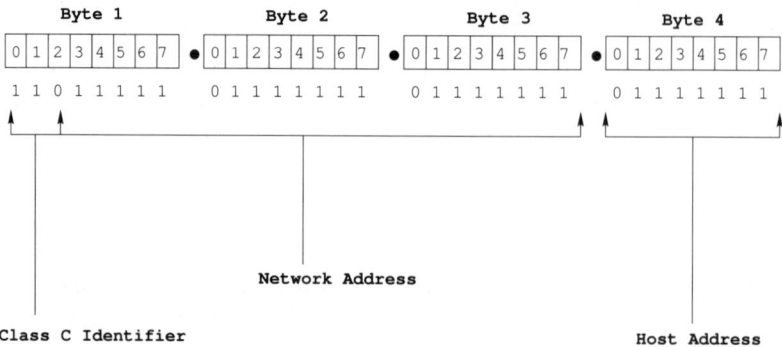

Figure 12.10: Class C Network IP Address

Well, quite simply, not all network or host addresses are available for use. If we look more closely at the way that the network identifiers are partitioned in the rules above, what we see is this:

Class	Class identifier	Bits in 'a' number	'a' range
A	0	1111111	0–127
B	10	111111 11111111	128–191
C	110	11111 11111111 11111111	192–223
D	111	11111 11111111 11111111	224–255

However, as we stated before, Class D networks are off-limits at the moment, which means that the network number range can only go from 0 to 223. Furthermore, the Class A network with network number 0 is reserved for *default routing* and the Class A network with network number 127 is reserved for the *loopback* address, which is used for configuring the machine and checking the network interfaces are functional.

Furthermore, in all network classes, the host numbers 0 and 255 are reserved for identifying the network itself and the *broadcast address*, respectively. The former is used in routing tables, which we shall explain below. Broadcast addresses are used to address *all* network devices on the given network simultaneously.

A final thought on IP addressing strategies covers the topic of *subnetting*.

Subnetting is a technique used to logically subdivide networks up into less standard sections—that is, into ranges that do not fall into the Class A, B or C ranges. For example, if company A has a Class C network assigned to it, and it acquires company B which hasn't addressed its computers yet, then company A's network administrator could logically partition or subdivide company A's Class C into two portions, one for company A, the other for company B.

A subnet is defined by an IP address known as the *subnet mask*, which is a bit-mask that is applied with a *bitwise AND*[14] onto the IP address itself. For example, if we have a Class C network:

$$193.130.62.0$$

then the standard subnet mask for this network would be:

$$255.255.255.0$$

i.e., 193 ANDed with 255 returns 193. The last digit calculates as 0 AND 0 which equals 0, which lets the TCP/IP software know that the last digit is *not* part of the network number, *i.e.*, it's a host. What subnetting does is quite simple... it changes the size of the network number in bits to create more "logical" networks. These subnets are only required on the network in which the subnetting is active, since TCP/IP will pass data to the entire (non-subnetted) network which will then work out what to do with it.

For example, if we wish to split our Class C network 193.130.62.0 into two new subnets, we should alter the subnet mask of all hosts on that network from 255.255.255.0 to 255.255.255.128. This will create two subnets.[15] Now, the IP address for the machines on these two subnets may also require alteration because we *increased* the number of bits in the network number, so

---

[14]

	0	1
0	0	0
1	0	1

[15]Actually it will create $2^{newnetworkbits}$ subnets (where *newnetworkbits* is the number of bits by which the the network number has been increased).

there are fewer *hosts* per subnet (or network) now. So the IP address allocation in the first subnet can range from 193.130.62.1 to 193.130.62.127, and the addresses in the second subnet can range from 193.130.62.128 to 193.130.62.254. IP addresses that are in the wrong subnet will probably not get data sent to them!

As you'll hopefully have worked out, the subnet mask is applicable to any bits in the entire IP address space, so you could feasibly alter the subnet on a Class A network which would create thousands (if not millions) of extra "logical" networks. However, most network administrators tend to stick to using byte-aligned subnet masks, since they are the default on most operating system implementations of TCP/IP, and more importantly, a lot easier to maintain and administrate![16]

Packet Roulette

In the previous sections, we explored the architecture that underlies the TCP/IP protocol, and the physical media we can use to transmit and receive data over wide area networks. We are now going to apply these principles to allow the network to send data between interconnected networks.[17]

Routing

Routing is one of the core methods of passing data from network to network. Nowadays, dedicated machines called *routers* handle all tasks related to routing, but software-based routing on workstations and desktop computers is also heavily used for inter-network routing.

Historically, the Internet was comprised of a *core* of networks and routers

---

[16]However, since the IP address space is running out rapidly, the address delegation bodies are now asking for network diagrams of companies' networks prior to address space allocation. The use of subnets is generally a much better solution than assigning valuable address space willy-nilly. In our experience, most companies don't seem to use subnetting at all! A rise in the "wastage" of address space is due to "virtual" WWW servers. These can be run on subnetted networks without address space wastage just as easily as on wasted address space.

[17]Or internets. Note, lower-case 'i'. Capital 'I' refers to The Internet, that large network people keep raving about as being the saviour of the human race. An internet (lower-case 'i'), is an interconnected collection of networks. Of course, the Internet is an internet, but more hyped. Network engineers now find it difficult to discuss inter-networking without people enquiring what "cool Web sites are" – We don't care.

which used a protocol called GGP or *Gateway to Gateway Protocol* for disseminating routing information[18] to all the connected networks. This system was akin to the way hostname information was disseminated prior to the introduction of DNS or *Domain Name Service*, in that there was a central point of contact through which all information *had* to flow. In the case of routing, all routes in the Internet had to be processed by the gateways in the Internet core. As the number of networks outside the core increased,[19] the load that was being pushed into the core began to raise serious performance degradation issues.

Therefore, a more elegant solution was required to propagate routing information around the Internet core. The protocol known as the *Exterior Gateway Protocol* (EGP) was introduced to allow autonomous systems to share *reachability information* between themselves, independently of the Internet core. In addition to this, the *Border Gateway Protocol* (BGP) was introduced to create the concept of *routing domains*, or, collections of autonomous systems. These routing domains maintain tables of interconnectivity between other routing domains, which drastically reduces the size of *routing tables* and distributes the load of routing updates much more evenly.

Routing domains are a far more elegant way of maintaining routing information, in that, as an autonomous system, you need not worry about propagation of routing information. The routing domain takes care of this and ensures routing across the Internet core, and between other routing domains, is taken care of.

Of course, this still doesn't imply that our example network is going to be routing information yet! We still have to take a look at how packets are sent about, and for that, we need to examine the concept of the routing table.

A routing table is a list maintained by a router, be it hardware- or software-based, that tells the Internet Layer where to send packets destined for various networks. For most network devices, the routing information is quite simple:

- If the packet is for a host on the local network, then deliver the packet straight to that host.

---

[18] A router used to be, and occasionally still is, referred to as a "gateway".

[19] These are known as "autonomous systems".

- If the packet is for a host outwith the local network, forward the packet onto the local router or gateway for further processing.

Therefore, in most cases, the routing table will comprise two entries, one for local network delivery, the other a "catch-all" route that forwards all unknown traffic somewhere else.

Obviously, for this system to work, the local gateway that's getting forwarded all these packets must know some more information about where to send the packets to. This router may have an ISDN line attached to it on another physical interface through which all unknown packets are forwarded again onto the Internet. At this point, the next router "upstream" of our local gateway will perform exactly the same action until a gateway somewhere down the line can connect to the network which contains the host for which the packet is destined, at which point it forwards the packet to that gateway.

Routing tables can be extraordinarily complex once you get closer to "backbone" gateways, usually comprising part of the Internet core. The current routing tables for core routers are approximately 20,000 networks long.

Two Tins And A Bit Of String

We have discussed, in the earlier parts of this chapter, how data can be sent across wires, converted into packets, routed about the logical networks and eventually delivered at the correct network device, but (and it's quite a big but!), how does the network device know which *process* to deliver the data to?

For example, we have a computer running UNIX with 200 users. Each user has used the `telnet` program to log into another UNIX machine. That's 200 network connections running simultaneously. A packet of data gets delivered to the machine in response to one of the users typing something into `telnet`. How does it know which user typed the command and is waiting on the response?

The simple answer is that IP uses a *protocol number* to identify which IP protocol should handle the incoming data. In addition to this, each network connection uses an outgoing *port number* to identify itself uniquely.

For example, a user is using the `telnet` program. `telnet` connects to port

23 of the remote host. However, the port number assigned to the local end of the connection could be 61432, for example. Thus, this network connection can be uniquely identified by the following information:

Local information	Remote information
193.130.62.160:61432	193.130.61.231:23

The local port number is assigned in a way that guarantees uniqueness,[20] and the remote port number may be what is called a *well-known service* or port, in that you can almost guarantee which service is running on that port.

As we mentioned before, port 23 is a well-known service corresponding to the `telnet` service. Some other well-known services are:

Port Number	Service
7	echo
20 21	ftp
23	telnet
25	sendmail (SMTP)
70	gopher
80	http (WWW)

For a more complete list of assigned well-known services, check a file called `/etc/services` on your machine. If you look at `/etc/services`, you will notice that the port numbers listed against the services have some characters after them, *e.g.*, `/udp` or `/tcp`. This denotes the *protocol* that that service uses to communicate. For a more complete list of the protocols your machine can understand, take a look at the file `/etc/protocols`. There should be corresponding entries for each of the protocols listed in `/etc/services`.

Splatterfest

The concept of *multicasting* is quite an established one. As far back as 1989, the RFC describing the *Host Extensions of IP Multicasting* (RFC 1112) was

---

[20]Although once that particular connection has closed, the local port will be reused by another connection after a period of time.

published for discussion. However, due to the nature of multicasting, it is only relatively recently that this form of networking has started to take off outwith the research sector.

Multicasting is a protocol that distributes packets simultaneously all across a *multicast backbone* network, known more usually as the *MBone*. The MBone is a *virtual network, i.e.,* it is encapsulated over the existing Internet connections and protocols.[21] The multicasting of the packets is handled by *multicast routers*, or `mrouters`. These `mrouters` are usually computers with kernel modifications and special software; however, more IP router hardware manufacturers are incorporating multicast protocol handling extensions into their hardware. A further technique of multicasting can be achieved by a technique known as *tunnelling* which encapsulates multicast packets inside standard IP packets, which are routed according to normal IP rules. Upon arrival at a multicast-aware network, the packet will be converted back into a multicast packet for further propagation.

This network of software routing, multicast packet encapsulation and hardware routing is still in an early experimental stage, although the applications and capabilities of multicasting are extremely encouraging.

Bandwidth and Saturation

One of the major issues and potential problem areas with the MBone, and the concept of multicasting in general, is bandwidth. We are, after all (you will say), propagating packets to *all* hosts on a virtual network, and that virtual network may span the Internet in distribution.

"Very true," I reply. "However, the packets are only distributed once and all hosts connected to the MBone will *simultaneously* receive the transmitted packets. If we were using IP, then each packet would have to be sent once to *each host* desiring the packet."

---

[21] A full discussion of the MBone is outwith the scope of this book; however, the file `pub/mbone/faq.txt` available via anonymous FTP from the host `venera.isi.edu` contains a number of frequently asked question (and their answers) on the topic and may be a good starting point.

And therein lies the difference. Of course, this is an over-simplification of the worst kind. And wrong, at least, from a certain point of view.

If we implemented multicasting in the way described above, the MBone *would* flood, and, due to the nature of multicasting, it would flood at an astonishing rate since each packet being released onto the MBone would be replicated to *all* the `mrouter`s for further multicasting! This would be disastrous as packets "fan" out from the initial multicast host as can be seen in Figure 12.11.

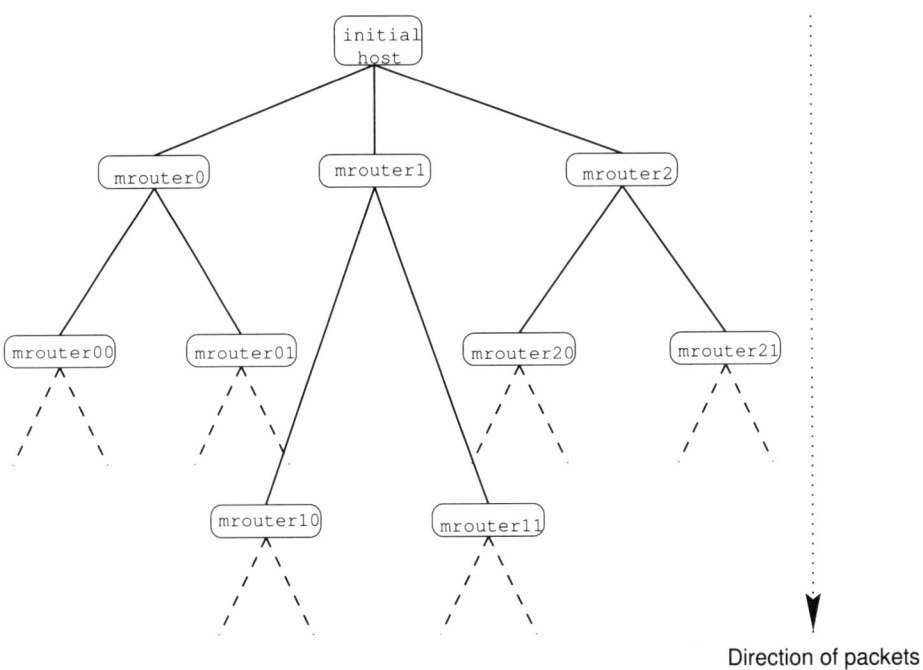

Figure 12.11: Multicast "Storm"

Therefore, we need to control what gets sent, what can send and where it can send to.

To do this, multicasting uses the *time-to-live* concept from the IP packet definition as a baseline.[22] In the specific case of multicasting, each packet has a time-to-live that can be tuned depending on the desired propagation *distance* since the time-to-live field's behaviour has been altered from being a time-based function, *i.e.*, decremented by at least 1 second per module processing the packet, to a distance-based function, *i.e.*, decremented by 1 per `mrouter` that propagates the packet.

Using this baseline technique, we can restrict multicast packets to various networks or subnets by correctly tuning the time-to-live field of the multicast packets being distributed by our local `mrouter`s. For example, in Figure 12.12, we could restrict propagation of packets outwith our local area network to the Internet by setting the time-to-live to 2. However, if we were to connect the two routers marked as `mrouter10` and `mrouter11`, multicast packets *would* be propagated onto the Internet since there is only *one* `mrouter` between the initial host and the MBone itself. Of course, by the time the rogue packets hit the MBone, the time-to-live would be 1, which will have dramatically reduced its capacity to flood networks!

 Other techniques under discussion and development involve intelligent *pruning* and *grafting* of multicast packets' transmission routes using a complex hybrid of IP routing and existing multicast routing.

But Why?!

Why are we interested in multicasting in virtual reality?

This will become much clearer in Chapter 14 where we discuss distributed servers—that is, servers where the virtual world and/or the multitude of clients that are connected to the virtual world are hosted on multiple (potentially very many) machines.

When a change to the world is made on one of the machines which make up the distributed server, and if that change is something that all the servers need to know about (such as a change of weather, or nightfall—if it is raining in one part of town then it is probably raining or about to start raining in another part of town; if the sun has set, then it should have set or be setting for many miles around) then the machine that is controlling the event

---

[22]It should be noted that Steve Deering, the designer of multicasting, calls this method "a hack"!

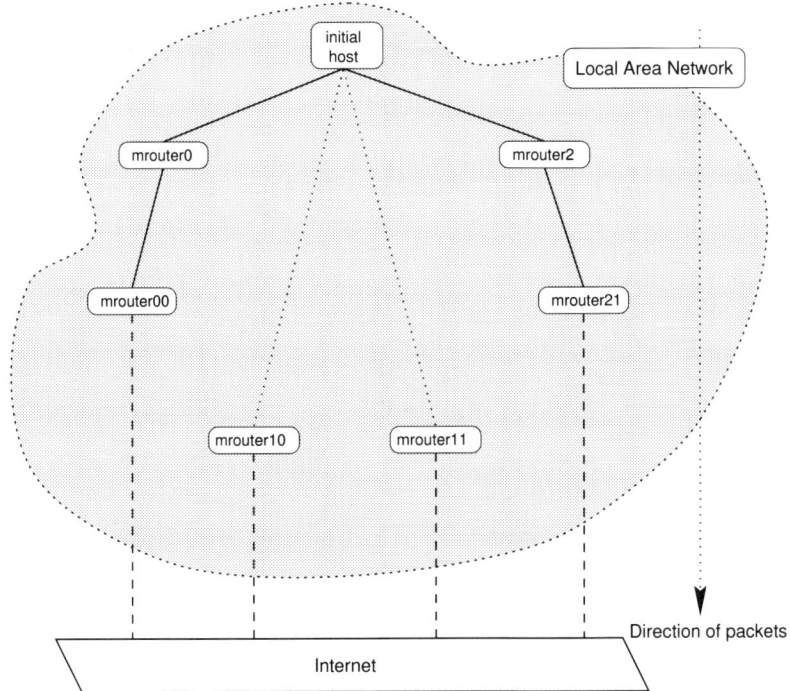

Figure 12.12: Multicast And "Time-To-Live"

must tell all the other machines that the change has occurred. To do this the machine must know all the other machines that make up the server, or there must be a master machine which knows about all the other machines and the master machine must be told so that it can pass the information on to all the other nodes in the distributed server. Or the information could be multicast or broadcast. In this latter method, of course, there is much greater flexibility as new machines can be added to (or existing machines removed from) the existing distributed server without the system having to be reconfigured—in more rigid configurations it may even have been necessary to restart the entire distributed server when a component machine is added or removed.

Summary

This chapter has presented many of the basic concepts in networking—in particular using TCP/IP. You should now be sufficiently familiar with the important aspects of networking to understand (and solve) many of the problems that appear when considering creation of a virtual reality server.

Chapter 13

Conferring Favours

We should render a service to a friend to bind him closer to us,
and to an enemy in order to make a friend of him.

CLEOBULUS (6th Century BC)

Providing Worlds To The World

A server which provides world descriptions to remote (or local, for that matter) users for viewing generally has its performance constrained by a number
of things. These include:

- the number of clients connected to the server at any one time;

- the bandwidth of the connection between the server and the network
  backbone;

- the amount of data which must be exchanged between the server and
  the client (which can depend upon the size of the world which the server
  knows about, the number of objects in the world that are not static, and
  even which direction the client is currently "facing").

This chapter and the next will look at some of the particular problems of
a server which provides a world to which multiple clients may connect and
through which they may interact. How the performance may be improved,

and how the size and content of the world may be scaled up to practically infinite size and complexity, are considered with a look at distributed servers.

Concepts are illustrated with examples from a multi-user server implemented using Java.

Server Basics

There are a small number of things that a server must be able to do in order to provide a useful service for a multi-user virtual reality system that can represent something more useful than a simple static world where nothing happens:

- Perhaps most obviously, the server must be able to accept connections from clients so that the clients may view, and interact with, the world. This might involve some kind of user-authentication procedure so that the server knows *who* has connected.

- Obviously, again, the server must be able to take a world description and present the information about where in space all the objects are and what are the various attributes of their appearance (such as colour, transparency, texture) to the client in a form that the client understands. This *could* involve taking a world which is defined using VRML and presenting it to the client as VRML; or the world might be defined using some other language, the server translating the world definition into VRML;[1] or some completely different language may be used at both server and client.

- The server must be able to provide some representation of each user who has a client connected (or *avatar*) so that connected users may see each other.

- It must be able to inform the client when something in the world has changed. For example, a world which consists of a blue sphere and a purple cube is simple to the server, and simple for the server to describe to the client. If the world definition states that the blue sphere melts

---

[1]Or creates some VRML which provides a *close enough* approximation of what the world definition contains, if the world definition language can provide features which are beyond VRML's feature set and capabilities.

into a blue puddle[2] whenever the purple cube is touched, all the clients must be informed when one of the clients touches the cube.

- It must be able to prioritize messages which indicate that something in the world has changed. To continue with the example of the melting blue sphere, if the fact that the sphere has melted is no more important than other events that can happen in the world then the message(s) from server to client containing details of the melting sphere can just be added to the tail of a queue of messages that can be sent to the clients in turn, and the clients can process those messages in turn. However, if all the clients are represented as orange beasties which live on the surface of the blue sphere then it is probably important for all the clients to know *right now* that the sphere has melted, no matter what else the server needs to tell the client, and no matter what else the client happens to be doing. At the other extreme, there may be much less important data that the client will find useful, but which it doesn't actually need in order to adequately represent the world. It must be possible for the server to supply this data to the client without wasting communication resources.

- One of the must useful aspects of virtual reality in a multi-user environment is the ability for clients to communicate with each other. Or, avoiding the technospeak, you should be able to chat with your pals.

There are a host of related issues here—the server must also be able to converse with the client in some agreed protocol. That is to say, there must be some agreed way whereby the client can say to the server: "Hello there, I'm user 'Fred' and my password is 'toothpick' " or "Tell me how many objects there are in this world". Similarly, the server may want to initiate conversations with messages like: "User 'Ingrid' says 'Would you like to go for a virtual coffee?' ".

Unless there is an agreed way in which the clients and the servers will talk to each other then the clients and the servers may as well be opposing political

---

[2]Observant readers may notice that a *puddle* is not a simple Platonic shape and has various *liquid* attributes that the server must be able to explain to the client. Not to mention the difficulty of how to describe the act of melting, when the blue object is neither a sphere nor a puddle, and yet has attributes of both of these. This is a complication that is best passed over at this stage. We hope that the reader will no longer see this as a difficult problem by the time the chapters on servers have been digested.

parties—lots of words get exchanged, but there is little effective communication.

Other features which, whilst not essential, are extremely useful to many multi-user worlds are considered:

- The ability for the server to provide *pseudousers* which can communicate with real users and may even be indistinguishable from real users.[3] These pseudousers can be useful in assorted ways. For example:

  - in multi-user games the pseudousers can operate as computer-controlled opponents, or act as dungeon-masters;

  - in a shopping-mall world the pseudousers could act as sales assistants, offering advice to browsers[4] and perhaps using artificial intelligence techniques to answer simple questions about products or getting the help of a real person to answer more complex questions;

  - in a shopping-mall again, a shop might "employ" pseudousers to wander in and out of the shop to make it appear to the casual passer-by that the shop is worth investigating;

  - in an archaeological reconstruction a pseudouser could act as a guide, leading interested visitors around exhibits and providing an "information board" commentary;

  - returning to our village of Skara Brae... when a visitor wanders into the workshop of the stone carver in house 7, he might stop chipping away for a few moments to explain what he is doing.[5]

- The ability for the server to accept "plug-in" modules which change the behaviour of the server. These can provide new functionality to the server (such as defining the behaviour of pseudouser avatars and what messages they will respond to and how), can change the behaviour of the server (objects in the world may change their appearance depending on values stored in a database rather than have fixed attributes), or

---

[3]Of course, they aren't really indistinguishable from real users—pseudousers will generally talk less nonsense.

[4]Browsers in the sense of people who wander around shops looking at things, not browsers in the sense of programs which display World Wide Web pages or virtual worlds!

[5]Or, in a less friendly (and therefore probably more realistic) reconstruction he might tell you to get lost and stop disturbing him because he is far too busy.

may even limit or remove features of the server (perhaps to provide for applications which require higher levels of security).

- The ability for the server to keep a note of the speed of the network connection between the server and the client and adjust the amount and type of information that it provides to the client, accordingly. Likewise, "net death" (when communication with a remote machine is no longer viable because there is severe network congestion, or an intermediate machine may no longer be available, or the remote machine may no longer be available) can be spotted and dealt with, to avoid cluttering up the server internals with details of "dead" clients and to avoid littering the world with "dead" avatars. This is good for all the "live" clients still connected, as the server can now dedicate resources to them which might otherwise have been needed to watch the "dead" connection. It is good for unconnected clients who wish to connect—if a server can handle 200 connected clients and there are 200 "dead" clients connected then the server may as well not be there. It can also be good for the users of the "dead" clients—for example, if you were playing a multi-user dungeon game and suffered link-death but the server left you connected, how would you defend yourself against the slavering three-headed beastie which is currently chewing on your head?

All these aspects of a server will be considered in a non-distributed system[6] in this chapter. The next chapter will look at the joys and heartaches involved in spreading a server or a world over more than one machine.

Let Me In, Let Me In!

For clients to be able to connect to your server, your server must be somewhere that a client can expect to find it. Plainly the client must know the internet address of the server's machine (either as a recognized name, or as the four-byte numerical address), but it must also know the *port number* for the socket on which your server will accept connections. A thread[7] within the

---

[6]Here, "distributed" and "non-distributed" are referring to the components of the server; the system is still "distributed" in the sense that the clients could potentially be in any part of the world.

[7]See Chapter 11 for an introduction to multi-threaded programming in Java. S.Kleiman, D.Shah, B.Smaalders, *Programming With Threads*, Prentice Hall, 1996, is a good guide to POSIX multi-threaded programming.

server must keep watch on this port for new incoming connections. When a new connection is seen, the server can negotiate with the client to make sure that they both wish to talk to each other and that the client is authorized to use this server.

Let's start with a very simple server which we can quickly build up into something considerably meatier.

A Simple Server

The Absolute Basics

This simple server will do very little. The server will listen on port 5000 for a connection from a client and then communicate with the client using a trivial protocol: when the connection is successfully made, the server will send the message "200 HELLO <clientname>" to the client. If an input line from the client starts with the text "quit" then the server will send the message "500 BYE <clientname>" to the client and close the connection. Any other text from the client will be prepended with the message "299 ECHO " and sent back to the client.

```
// Very basic server

import java.lang.System;
import java.net.*;
import java.io.*;

public class Server1
{

    public static final int LISTENING_PORT = 5000;

    public static void main( String args[])
    {
        try{
            ServerSocket svsock = new ServerSocket(
                    LISTENING_PORT );
            int localPort = svsock.getLocalPort();
```

```
            System.out.println( "Listening on port " +
                               localPort + "." );
        do {
            Socket client = svsock.accept();

            DataInputStream in = new DataInputStream(
                           client.getInputStream() );
            PrintStream out = new PrintStream(
                           client.getOutputStream() );

            String clientName = client.getInetAddress(
                                      ).getHostName();

            out.println( "200 HELLO " + clientName );

            boolean waitingForHellToFreezeOver = true;

            do {
                String lineIn = in.readLine();
                if ( lineIn.equalsIgnoreCase( "quit" ) ) {
                    out.println( "500 BYE " + clientName );
                    waitingForHellToFreezeOver = false;
                } else {
                    out.println( "299 ECHO " + lineIn );
                }
            } while ( waitingForHellToFreezeOver );

            in.close();
            out.close();
            client.close();
        } while( true );
    } catch ( IOException e ) {
        System.out.println( "Caught an IOException" );
    }
    }
}
```

This very simple server allows us to have the following basic conversation:

```
kafka:~$ telnet eco 5000
Trying 192.168.2.1...
Connected to eco.marty.house.
Escape character is '^]'.
200 HELLO kafka.marty.house
Hello eco
299 ECHO Hello eco
This is Fred.  Talk to me.
299 ECHO This is Fred.  Talk to me.
You're no fun.
299 ECHO You're no fun.
quit
500 BYE kafka.marty.house
Connection closed by foreign host.
kafka:~$
```

This server has very major limitations, not least of which is the fact that it can only accept a single client connection at one time.

The First Glimpse of a Real Server

Let's improve matters by starting a new thread of execution for each client. We'll also make some trivial improvements such as allowing the default port to be overridden on the command line.[8]

```
// Very basic multi-threaded server

import java.lang.System;
import java.net.*;
import java.io.*;

public class Server2 extends Thread
{
```

---

[8]If you have ever worked in a team where there is one person trying to develop and test a new version of the client using a stable version of the server, and at the same time there is another person needing to develop and test a new version of the server using a stable version of the client, and all this on the same machine, then you will immediately see the benefits of simple improvements like this!

```java
public static final int LISTENING_PORT = 5000;
int port;
ServerSocket svsock;

public static void main( String args[])
{
    int port = LISTENING_PORT;

    if ( args.length == 1 ) {
        try {
            port = Integer.parseInt( args[0] );
        } catch ( NumberFormatException e ) {
            port = LISTENING_PORT;
        }
    }

    new Server2( port );
}

public Server2( int port )
{
    this.port = port;
    try{
        svsock = new ServerSocket( port );
    } catch ( IOException e ) {
        System.err.println( "Can't create server" +
                            " socket:" + e );
        System.exit( 1 );
    }

    this.start();
}

public void run()
{
    int localPort = svsock.getLocalPort();
    System.out.println( "Listening on port " +
                        localPort + "." );
    try {
```

```
            while( true ) {
                Socket client = svsock.accept();
                ClientTalk ct = new ClientTalk( client );
            }
        } catch ( IOException e ) {
            System.err.println( "Error whilst accepting" +
                                connections: " + e  );
            System.exit( 1 );
        }
    }
}


class ClientTalk extends Thread
{

    Socket client;
    DataInputStream in;
    PrintStream out;

    public ClientTalk( Socket c )
    {
        client = c;

        try {
            in = new DataInputStream( client.getInputStream() );
            out = new PrintStream( client.getOutputStream() );
        } catch ( IOException e ) {
            System.err.println( "Can't open client streams: " +
                                                e );
            try {
                client.close();
            } catch ( IOException e2 ) {
                System.err.println( "Can't close client: " + e2 );
            }
            return;
        }

        this.start();
    }
```

```
public void run()
{
    String clientName = client.getInetAddress().getHostName();

    out.println( "200 HELLO " + clientName );

    boolean waitingForHellToFreezeOver = true;

    try {
        do {
            String lineIn = in.readLine();
            if ( lineIn.equalsIgnoreCase( "quit" ) ) {
                out.println( "500 BYE " + clientName );
                waitingForHellToFreezeOver = false;
             } else {
                out.println( "299 ECHO " + lineIn );
            }
        } while ( waitingForHellToFreezeOver );
    } catch ( IOException e ) {
        System.out.println( "Caught an IOException: " + e );
    }

    try {
        in.close();
        out.close();
        client.close();
    } catch ( IOException e ) {
        System.err.println( "Can't close client: " + e );
    }
}
}
```

This improved server makes use of Java's multi-threading capability.

Simple Protocol

Before we take this server any further, we really should define a protocol that is going to be understood by the server and by any clients which will want to

Command	Action
quit	close the connection

Table 13.1: Simple Protocol: Commands From the Client

Response	Meaning
200 HELLO	confirmation of connection
299 ECHO	input accepted and echoed
900 BYE	quit command recognized, connection closing

Table 13.2: Simple Protocol: Commands From the Server

talk to it.

The protocol as it is currently defined recognizes commands from the client as listed in Table 13.1 and recognizes the replies from the server listed in Table 13.2.

There is a lot to be said for simplicity, but this really is taking things to extremes!

The protocol that we want to implement (and which we will want to extend later on) is as in Table 13.3 and we need to provide a lot more information from the server to the client as shown in Tables 13.4–13.7. This is still an extremely simple protocol, but it at least will give us a server that can provide a useful service (effectively a "chat" room) that can be used in a multi-user virtual reality environment. More importantly, it provides a fairly solid base onto which extensions to this protocol can be easily added.

```
// Basic multi-threaded server
// Handles a simple protocol which allows messaging

import java.lang.System;
import java.net.*;
```

Command	Action
user	client's username
pass	client's password
who	request a list of users currently connected to this server
msg	send a message to another user connected to this server
loc	set my location within the world
quit	close the connection

Table 13.3: Useful Protocol: Client to Server

Response	Meaning
100 HELLO	confirmation of connection
900 BYE	quit command recognized, connection closing

Table 13.4: Connection and Disconnection Messages

Response	Meaning
206 PSWD	password accepted—the client is now "logged in"
215 PPLE	who command recognized, a list of connected users follows

Table 13.5: Responses To Successful Client Commands

Response	Meaning
300 MSG	another user has used the **msg** command to send a message to you—message follows
301 LOCN	updated location of a connected user within the server's world

Table 13.6: Asynchronous Responses—Not In Response To The Client

Response	Meaning
804 USER	client is not "logged in"
806 BADU	the specified user (for example, specified in a **msg** command) is not "logged in"
807 PWNV	the supplied username and password combination is not correct

Table 13.7: Responses To Unsuccessful Client Commands

```
import java.io.*;

public class ServerProtocol1 extends Thread
{

    public static final int LISTENING_PORT = 5000;
    int port;
    ServerSocket svsock;

    // start a server listening on the appropriate port
    // (the default or the one specified on the command
    // line)
    public static void main( String args[])
    {
        int port = LISTENING_PORT;

        if ( args.length == 1 ) {
```

```
        try {
            port = Integer.parseInt( args[0] );
        } catch ( NumberFormatException e ) {
            port = LISTENING_PORT;
        }
    }

    new ServerProtocol1( port );
}

// create a server socket and start the thread
// which listens for a client connecting
public ServerProtocol1( int port )
{
    this.port = port;
    try{
        svsock = new ServerSocket( port );
    } catch ( IOException e ) {
        System.err.println( "Can't create server" +
                            " socket:" + e );
        System.exit( 1 );
    }

    this.start();
}

// the thread start-up code: wait for a client to
// connect, then service that client
public void run()
{
    int localPort = svsock.getLocalPort();
    System.out.println( "Listening on port " +
                        localPort + "." );
    try {
        while( true ) {
            Socket client = svsock.accept();
            ClientTalk ct = new ClientTalk( client );
        }
    } catch ( IOException e ) {
```

```
                    System.err.println( "Error whilst accepting" +
                                        " connections: " + e   );
                    System.exit( 1 );
                }
            }
        }

class ClientTalk extends Thread
{

    static final int numCommands = 6;
    static final String protocolIn[] =
            { "user ",
              "pass ",
              "who ",
              "msg ",
              "loc ",
              "quit " };

    Socket client;
    DataInputStream in;
    PrintStream out;

    // get the input and output streams associated
    // with the connecting client, then start the
    // thread which will service that client
    public ClientTalk( Socket c )
    {
        client = c;

        try {
            in = new DataInputStream( client.getInputStream() );
            out = new PrintStream( client.getOutputStream() );
        } catch ( IOException e ) {
            System.err.println( "Can't open client streams: " +
                                                e );
            try {
                client.close();
            } catch ( IOException e2 ) {
```

```
                System.err.println( "Can't close client: " + e2 );
        }
        return;
    }

    this.start();
}

// return 'true' if the first word of the input line
// is one of the acceptable commands.  Return 'false'
// otherwise
boolean checkToken( String inLine )
{
    for ( int i = 0; i < numCommands; ++i ) {
        if ( inLine.startsWith( protocolIn[ i ] ) ) {
            return true;
        }
    }
    return false;
}

// thread start-up code for the thread which will service
// the client.  Read the input from the client, process
// that input, loop
public void run()
{
    String clientName = client.getInetAddress().getHostName();

    out.println( "200 HELLO " + clientName );

    boolean waitingForHellToFreezeOver = true;

    try {
        do {
            String lineIn = in.readLine();
            if ( checkToken( lineIn ) ) {
                if ( lineIn.equalsIgnoreCase( "quit" ) ) {
                    out.println( "500 BYE " + clientName );
                    waitingForHellToFreezeOver = false;
```

```
                } else {
                    out.println( "999 thanks for that command" );
                }
            } else {
                out.println( "299 ECHO " + lineIn );
            }
        } while ( waitingForHellToFreezeOver );
    } catch ( IOException e ) {
        System.out.println( "Caught an IOException: " + e );
    }

    try {
        in.close();
        out.close();
        client.close();
    } catch ( IOException e ) {
        System.err.println( "Can't close client: " + e );
    }
    }
}
```

Halt, Who Goes There?

Introduction

There are many cultures and societies around the world that believe that knowledge of a person's name (or of a demon's name, angel's name, spirit's name, etc.) gives power over that person (or demon, or angel, ...). Care is taken to protect a person's name from his or her enemies. Indeed, in some societies a person will publicly use a pseudonym and their real name will be known only to their immediate family.

This belief can be made into fact in the virtual world, as we shall see below...

Part of the negotiation when a client connects to the server can be to determine who the client-user is. This can have many uses, and how strictly the system checks the identity of the connecting user is constrained to some degree by the use that is made of the identity.

For example, when connecting to an archaeological reconstruction of Skara Brae, the server might not have the least interest in knowing who is connected.

But if Skara Brae is a popular meeting place for a group of virtual friends, it would be nice if the server knew who each client-user was so that a particular representation of each user can be used, allowing me to recognize my friends and my friends to recognize me. Much better than my having to talk to every connected client-user and asking: "Hello! Are you Katrina?" Or worse:

"Hello! Are you Katrina?"
"Yes."
"Have you seen Mike about?"
"I don't know anyone called Mike! You must have the wrong Katrina!"

And if you can walk into the Skara Brae virtual visitors' centre, you certainly don't want someone else buying postcards and Historic Scotland membership using *your* electronic cash because the server hasn't checked carefully enough before giving someone access to your account.

Basic authentication can be done quite simply by having the client give the server a username and password. More security can be provided by checking that the client is connecting from a particular domain or machine, and perhaps by performing all the negotiations over an encrypted link using Secure Sockets Layer (SSL) or some similar facility. How much security is appropriate depends largely on the purpose of the server: if you are providing a walk-through display of the archaeological discoveries in a prehistoric village then you mightn't care who your visitors are; if you are staging a multi-user role-playing game in the village then you might want to know who is connecting so that you can prevent someone connecting twice and improving their standing in the game by cheating, but a simple scheme would probably be more than adequate; if you are holding a virtual auction where the state treasures are being sold off to the highest bidder then you probably want a very solid authentication scheme—so that you know that only bidders with a good credit rating are allowed to bid, so that the bidders know that someone else isn't throwing away their cash, and so that you have some legal back-up when the purchaser has a change of heart and says: "No! That wasn't me bidding. It must have been an impostor!"

Be safe. Be secure. If it is important that you really know who is talking to your server then use a solid authentication scheme.[9]

This becomes somewhat more complicated if you want usernames and passwords to be recognized over multiple servers.

Authentication

In an isolated system, where the server is not interested in how client-users identify themselves to other servers, the server can keep a password file with a table of usernames and the (encrypted) passwords associated with those usernames. The client, during the initial negotiation, provides a username and password; the server compares these against entries in its password file and either lets the client continue with the connection if the username and password match its copy, or terminates the session if they don't.

Where users need to be recognized between a limited set of servers, one server can be designated as the "security master", and all username/password pairs are sent to the security master for authentication before determining whether to continue with or terminate a session.

This has the disadvantage that none of the servers will be able to allow authenticated connections if the security master is unavailable. However, its simplicity may make it attractive in many situations.

A more complicated, but more flexible, scheme allows all servers to perform their own authentication. Whenever a new username/password pair is set on one server, that server transmits the details to all other servers that wish to recognize the same users. This is not sufficient of itself, though—it is quite possible for two users, each of whom likes to go by the name of "superhero", to simultaneously connect to two different servers and set up new usernames with different passwords. Some servers will recognize when one "superhero" connects and refuse to authenticate the second, other servers will recognize when the second "superhero" connects but refuse to authenticate the first.

This problem can be solved by several methods, including:

---

[9]Oh...and don't smoke in bed. It's very dangerous! Poor authentication could bring you financial ruin, but it is good to keep things in perspective.

1. Democracy[10]—amongst a co-operating group of servers, when a new username and password are added to a server (which we will call the *originating server*), that server transmits details of the user and password to all the other servers in the co-operating group. Whenever a server is given username and password details from another server for a username that it *does not* recognize, it adds those details to its own password file along with a marker that these details have yet to be confirmed. It then sends an acknowledgement of the username to the originating server. Whenever a server is given username and password details from another server for a username that it *does* recognize (i.e., another user has already claimed this username), it again adds those details to its own password file along with a marker that these details have yet to be confirmed. However, this time it sends a non-acknowledgement of the username to the originating server. When an originating server receives acknowledgements from more than half of the servers in the co-operating group, it sends a confirmation that its details are the valid ones to all the servers in the group who can then flag that server's details as confirmed and delete all conflicting details for that user. When an originating server receives non-acknowledgements from more than half of the servers in the co-operating group, it sends a confirmation that its details are invalid to all the servers in the group who can then delete the invalid details from their password files.[11] To illustrate this, consider a small closed network consisting of six co-operating servers, named '1' to '6'—as shown in Figure 13.1. Client 'A' connects to server '1' and proceeds to add a username of "superhero" with a password of "fred". At the same time, client 'B' connects to server '5' and proceeds to add a username of "superhero" with a password of "albert". Server '1' tentatively stores "superhero/fred" in its password file and sends an acknowledgement to itself for this pair (as indicated by a black circle in the diagram). It also sends a copy of this username/password to all the other servers. Server '5' tentatively stores "superhero/albert" in its password file and sends an acknowledgement to itself for this pair (as indicated by a pale circle). It also sends a copy of this user-

---

[10]This method will only work when there are a known number of servers in a co-operating group. This will not work in an open-ended group where new servers can be added and existing servers removed without notice

[11]This step, where a server sends a confirmation that its details are invalid, is not strictly needed, but it allows for faster dissemination of correct data throughout the network and so is a Good Thing.

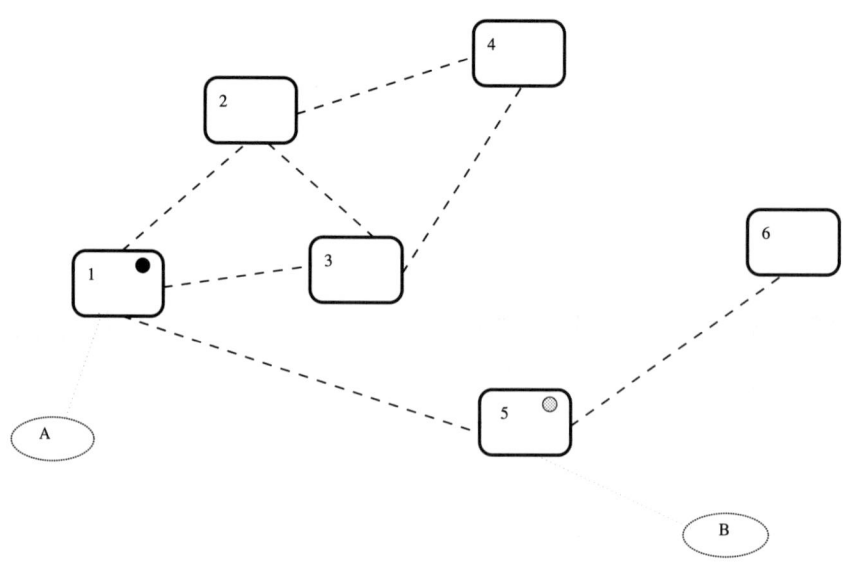

Figure 13.1: Small Network With Two Clients Simultaneously Setting The Same Username

name/password pair to all the other servers.

Servers '2' and '3' now send an acknowledgement of "superhero/fred" to server '1', and server '5' (which has already acknowledged "superhero/albert") sends a non-acknowledgement of the details of "superhero/fred" to server '1', as illustrated in Figure 13.2. Meanwhile, server '1' (which has already acknowledged "superhero/fred") sends a non-acknowledgement of "superhero/albert" to server '5', whilst server '6' sends an acknowledgement of "superhero/albert" to server '5'. At this stage, server '1' has received three acknowledgements and one non-acknowledgement, whereas server '5' has received two acknowledgements and one non-acknowledgement. Neither server yet believes that it has either won or lost.

The details propagate further across the network, as shown in Figure 13.3. Server '4' sends an acknowledgement of "superhero/fred" to server '1', and server '6' sends a non-acknowledgement of "superhero/fred" to server '1'. Servers '2' and '3' send non-acknowledgements of

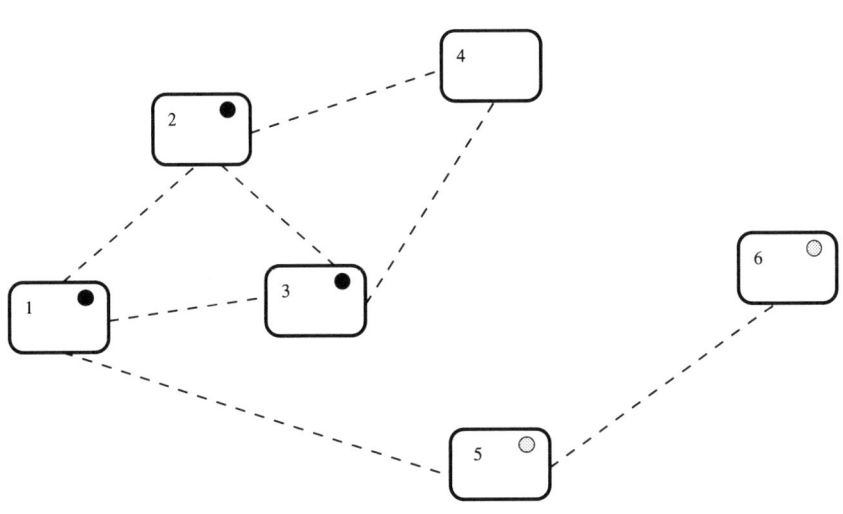

Figure 13.2: Rival Usernames Compete

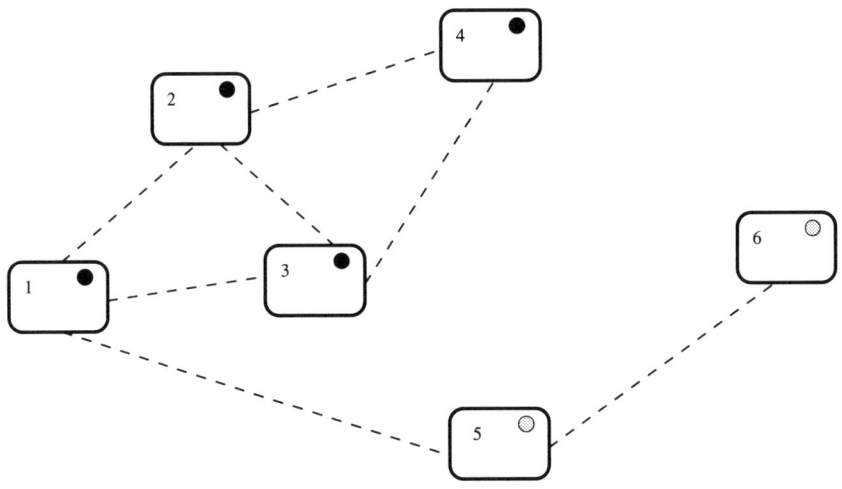

Figure 13.3: One Username Wins

"superhero/albert" to server '5'. At this stage, server '1' has received four acknowledgements (more than half!) and two non-acknowledgements, so it sends a confirmation message to all servers. Server '5' has now received two acknowledgements and four non-acknowledgements (more than half!) so it will send messages accepting defeat to all servers.

2. Republicanism—this is much like democracy above, except that a small group of servers are selected to make decisions on behalf of all the co-operating servers. This has several advantages: there is no limit to the number of servers which can co-operate in this way (if there is a fixed number of servers, say seven, adjudicating on username/password conflicts then so long as more than half of those seven servers are available at any one time they can make decisions without knowing how many servers they are making decisions for); as fewer machines are involved, decisions can be made much more rapidly.

If you are setting up a number of servers on a slow or unreliable network, or if the collection of servers which recognize each other reaches beyond the bounds of a network that you have control of—such as if a group of networks are co-operating to provide a distributed service—then the authentication schemes that have just been described do have potential drawbacks.

For example, if our friend "superhero" connects to a server in sub-network W in Figure 13.4 and if the links to sub-networks X, Y and Z are slow or unreliable then it might be quite a while before the server is confident that it is OK to accept our friend's commands knowing that they won't conflict with anyone else who is claiming to be "superhero". What is more, on the vast majority of occasions on the vast majority of servers there will not be two different people trying to connect within a few seconds of each other and trying to use the same username. So whilst our caution is necessary, it is perhaps a little overdone. A possibility is to take a more optimistic approach to clients who connect to servers and make the assumption that if the local server authenticates them then the entire network is *probably* going to accept them.

This can be likened to the *optimistic concurrency control* that is often used when files have to be shared amongst multiple machines on a network.

Until the new client is properly validated—perhaps using one of the methods discussed above—it is necessary to keep a note of all operations that

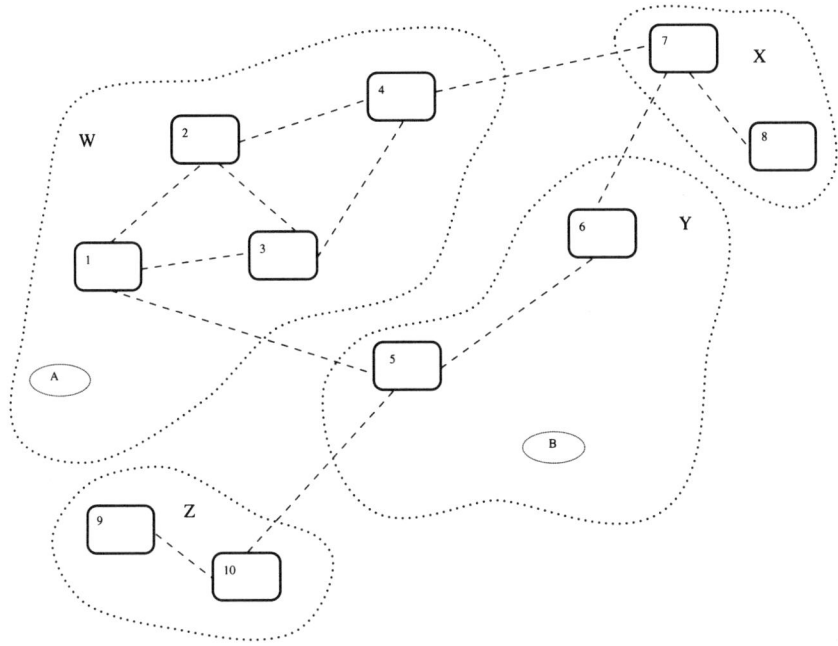

Figure 13.4: Network With Slow Links

they perform so that they can be undone in the rare case that the network refuses to authenticate the client. Any operations which would not be possible to undo cannot be permitted until the network provides the authentication.

Once a connected client is authenticated, the server needs to store an assortment of details about the client, and can optionally store other potentially useful information, in internal tables. These details include:

- the username of the client-user;

- the current round-trip time of packets from the server to the client and back again (for servers which behave in a friendly way towards clients which are connected by slow links, in ways which are explained below);

- the level to which the client has been authenticated (i.e. whether they have only been authenticated by the local server or whether they have been authenticated by the network).

The server also presents the client with useful information (which may vary depending on just what kind of world the server is presenting) and this would generally consist of the following:

- The server's current timestamp, for synchronizing events and for arbitrating between clients who think that they are performing operations that only one client can perform at any time, but more than one client thinks it is successfully doing it—for example, if there is one cup standing on a table and two client-users are standing near that table and both try to pick up the cup at the same time then only one can succeed. The timestamp provides a means for determining who succeeds. (More about this later.)

- A list of all the currently connected users (and pseudousers).

- Details of the static world model.

- Details of all the mobile objects within the world.

- Details of any mobile objects that are currently executing some behaviour.

- Messages that are being sent from one connected user to another (or from a pseudouser to a connected real user).

Structures For The Server To Hold Client Information

For every client which connects to a world server, there is a basic set of data which the server will hold. This basic information includes the following:

- The client's username.

- Relevant details about the client's host (such as IP address, hostname).

- Where the user is currently positioned in the world. (If the server doesn't know where the user is standing it cannot inform other clients about where that user is. The result is that no one will be able to see anyone as no one's machine will know where anyone else is. There are other significant reasons for the server to know where all the clients are, such as collision detection: tour guides in Skara Brae should walk *around* visitors, not *through* them!)

- Which direction the user is currently facing. (If you turn on the spot then your location doesn't change. However, if the server knows that you are turning then it can tell all the other clients that you are turning. They will then know whether you are facing them or not.)

There are a number of other details which a server should generally hold, but these could depend to a degree on what sort of world is stored on that server. For example, in the case of a simple server where all connected users appear identical to all other users there is no need to hold information about what an individual user looks like. In the more general case, users like to have their own particular appearance. Clearly this is information which the server needs to retain, at least whilst that user is connected. Very often, that information should be retained *between* connections. If I connect to a server and spend time modelling myself as a shaven-headed man with pierced nose and ear, I don't expect to connect to that server again a week later and look like anything other than a shaven-headed man with pierced nose and ear.

Many servers may allow different classes of user to connect, or a connected user may be in one of several states. For example, many servers may allow *administrator* users to perform operations, or enter areas of the world, that are forbidden to "normal" users. To give a concrete example, the Skara Brae village may be open to all users. However, if a puzzling new archaeological discovery were to be made at Skara Brae and if that discovery were open to controversial interpretation ("Oh look—the neolithic occupants of northern Scotland performed ritual human sacrifice!" "Nonsense; that's a tight necklace, not a garrotte.") then the owners of the Skara Brae might allow recognized archaeological researchers access to a representation of the new find, whilst Jo Public continues to happily watch the rather cute stone-carver going about his business none the wiser to the great debate. To give another example, a multi-user game might allow players to rise through a number of levels of experience depending on what quests they have successfully completed so far; these levels might give such players access to different areas of the world—both to protect inexperienced players from festering hordes of baddies that would devour them as soon as render a specular highlight, and to provide new challenges to keep the interest of more advanced players. Once again, this is information that should usually be retained for a player between visits to the world. Players who spend hours playing a game to attain a high level of competence are not going to return to the game too often if they find they are always reduced to the level of bumbling buffoon whenever they disconnect.

So there is less essential, but still important, data that a server might hold for each connection, including:

- the user's avatar definition;

- the user's e-mail address;

- the user's privileges;

- the user's current state/status;

In our Java code, all this could be held in an object. As we discussed above, depending on the server and its purpose, there could be an array[12] of users that have ever connected to this client and an array of users who are currently connected to this client.

```java
public class ClientDetails {

        // essential information
        String username;
        InetAddress host;
        Position avatarLocn;    // a class containing an
                                // (x, y, z) coordinate
        Vector avatarFacing;

        // server-specific information
        String email;
        URL avatarDefn;
        Priv priviledges;       // a class containing a set of
                                // varied values
        Status status;

}
```

---

[12]Of course, this could be an array, or a list, or a hash, or any of a host of structures.

Client Limits And Burying The Dead

Introduction

Take a while hopping around people's pages on the World Wide Web, and one of the things that you may notice (other than just how much crud and nonsense the average person clutters up the Internet with!) is that many pages have a counter showing how many times that page has been looked at. How relevant to the content of the page is this counter? In many cases—I would venture that it is in the majority of cases—none whatsoever. I, too, have a counter on my own pages. Of course, I have a very good and noble reason for putting a counter on my page: it's because... um... well... never mind! I know that I have a marvellous reason, but it escapes me just at the moment. Funny how that happens. But for all those people whose counters are not serving any great purpose: why is the counter there? One reason is that it is human nature to want to be seen,[13] and the counter lets them know how often they have been seen and tells everyone else how popular they are. Have you ever artificially enhanced your hit-count? What, *never?*

Returning to our virtual reality server: if you are going to the effort to creating a virtual world and then make that virtual world available on the Internet—or even on a private network—you probably will want people to make use of it. You will probably want as many people to make use of it as possible, and so any ways of improving the efficiency of the server to be able to service more clients will be a good thing. Writing better, faster, more memory-efficient and network-efficient code is the obvious route to take here. And a very worthwhile route. But there are other efficiency concerns as well.

Idle Users

In order to prevent a server from running infuriatingly slowly (a great way to dissuade visitors to your world from ever returning) it is usual to set a limit to the number of clients that can connect to the server. Obviously the value of this limit will depend on an assortment of things, including the speed of the machine on which the server is running, the bandwidth available for talking to the network, what other tasks (if any) the server machine has to

---

[13]Of course, this is a desire to be seen and *admired*. Most personal Web pages are probably not actually admired, but the owner of the counter can always be relied upon to have a suitably well-developed imagination when it comes to other people's opinion of their handiwork.

perform, the nature of the world that is being modelled, etc. In the simple case, once the maximum number of connected clients has been reached no more clients will be able to connect until one of the existing clients decides to leave. It only takes a small number of failures to connect to dissuade a potential visitor from ever trying to connect to your server again.

Anyone who has played a multi-user dungeon game will no doubt be aware that there can be a large number of "players" who are idle; that is, there are characters who are logged in to the game (and so taking up one of the precious client "slots") and who are taking no active part in the game (perhaps because they've gone away to get a cup of coffee, or because their network connection has "died" but left them logged in). There are schemes which can both reduce the deleterious effect of these idle clients and all but eliminate the inability to connect to the server even when all the client slots are filled with active clients. Whether these schemes are appropriate for a given server depends on the nature of the server and on the server-owner's personal preferences.

Floating Users

There are two kinds of people: those who divide the world into two kinds of people, and those who don't.

That's a joke. This isn't:

There are two kinds of server: those which divide the world into two kinds of client, and those which don't.

The two kinds of client are: those which are connected to the server; and those which aren't. Obvious, isn't it? But it need not be true and it can improve matters if we make it not true. Let's now make the issue a bit fuzzier and divide the world into several kinds of client: those which are strongly connected to the server; those which are loosely connected to the server; and those which might want to connect to the server.

What does this do for us? Well, if the server considers any client which is loosely connected to the server to be expendable, the problem of a client not being able to connect to a busy server is gone for good. Consider a server which can handle a maximum of 128 simultaneously connected clients. We can divide these 128 potential connections into, say, 16 loose connections and 112 strong connections. Whenever 112 or fewer clients are connected (case A in Figure 13.5), all connections are considered to be strong connections.

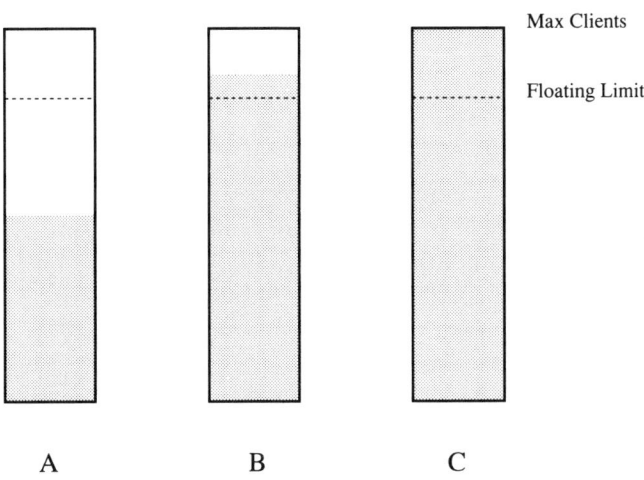

Figure 13.5: Floating Users

If client number 113 connects, its connection is a loose connection and that client is a *floating user* (case B in Figure 13.5). For the moment this distinction has *absolutely no effect* on how the server behaves towards the client, nor on what services the client can request. Should one of the 112 strongly connected clients disconnect, then our floating user is promoted to having a strong connection and is no longer floating. When client number 128 has connected, the server has its full complement of strong and loose connections (case C in Figure 13.5) and can handle no more connections from clients. However, if another client attempts to connect to the server then that new client is *not* rejected. Instead, one of the floating users is disconnected and the new client takes that loose connection to become a new floating user.

This becomes a really useful technique when the server keeps a note of the activity of all the connected clients. Any strongly connected client whose connection has been quiet for more than a fixed period—say, five minutes—can be considered idle and is relegated to being a loosely connected floating user. If there is a floating user whose client is not idle, then that loose connection can be promoted to a strong connection and can take the place of the demoted idle user. In this way, clients that are actually making use of the server can stay connected, clients that are actively trying to connect to the server can always connect, and clients who are just wasting the server's resources can be left to just fall away.

Of course, there has to be a fly in the ointment, doesn't there? What, I hear you ask, about the case where our example server has 128 active clients and another client connects? In doing so it will displace one of the "useful" clients. Surely that isn't fair? That is a question to which there is no simple answer: it is very unfair to the client who is lost, but very fair to the new client who connects. So long as any client receives a warning when it becomes a floating user (either when it connects as a floating user because there are no free slots for strong connections, or when it is demoted from a strong connection to a loose connection) that it may loose its connection at any time, it *may* be an appropriate way to manage the server. Remember, there are no *right* answers to this kind of problem: only possible solutions which may or may not be optimal for your application.

Demanding The World, And Getting It

Once connected, the client can request that the server provides it with a description of the world. This could be an explicit request from the client, or the simple act of connecting could be taken as an implicit request for details of the world to be transmitted.

The latter has the advantage of simplicity. In the very simplest case, a client connects to a server and the server sends all the world description (for example, an entire VRML world definition file) details to the client which then displays the contents of the world on the client-user's screen. But this does have disadvantages.

Consider the case where a world definition contains information about hundreds of locations scattered across a landscape. Each of these locations may contain thousands of objects. For example, one of the locations may be the village of Skara Brae containing models of houses, textures for the various types of stone used in the buildings, details of pseudousers who wander around the village or sit in houses working stone, audio clips for various aspects of village life, and so on. And yet the village may be behind you, beyond a range of mountains, behind a forest and over a stretch of sea—well out of sight and well out of earshot. None of the details of what is in Skara Brae, and many of the other locations throughout this world, are going to make any difference to what the client-user will see.

If the details of the world which need to be downloaded can be reduced, the parts of the world which can be seen will appear that much more quickly, less network bandwidth will be wasted (or there will be an increase in the number of clients which can be serviced using the available bandwidth) and the more popular your world (or game, or shop, or exhibit, ...) will be.

Techniques For Pruning The World Tree

In general, when a client connects to a server and obtains the current world definition only a small part of the world will actually be visible to the client. That is, the part of the world which is directly in front of the direction that the client is facing. In Figure 13.6 we look at a simple world from two different

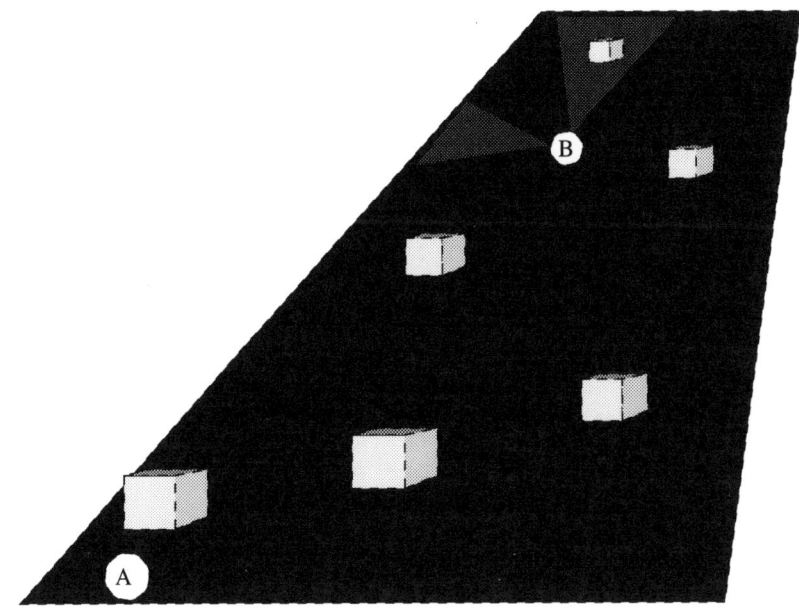

Figure 13.6: What You See Depends On Where You Are

clients' points of view. Client A, if looking away from us, can see pretty much the whole of the world and so needs to be supplied with all the world information in order to render an accurate scene. Client B, on the other hand, can only see one of the objects in the world if looking away from us. If client B were to be looking to the left, *none* of the world would be visible. It is not necessary for client B to receive all the world data before it can render an accurate scene. Indeed, it will be able to render the world more quickly if the server is selective about which parts of the world model it transmits to the client first. Clearly, it would be most efficient if the one object that is visible to client B is the object that is transmitted first. Objects that are not visible can be sent whenever the server and the client have got the time (or the network has the free bandwidth) to make the exchange.

Looks Really *Are* Everything

As mentioned earlier, how an avatar for a particular client-user appears to other client-users can be very important. Similarly, it may be important that the appearance of the avatar is consistent across a group of servers.

Avatar details can be distributed amongst a co-operating group of servers at the same time as confirmed username/password details when using a democratic or republican authentication system as described above. When large amounts of avatar information must be held, it may be better to keep the avatar details on just one server (or a small number of servers, to allow for times when some servers are out of action or otherwise unreachable) and distribute only the location(s) of the avatar details amongst all the co-operating servers.

Rather than hold the avatar details explicitly on the server, the server could simply hold the URL of an avatar definition (perhaps defined using VRML) which is held somewhere on the network—perhaps on the client's machine—and which can be modified by the avatar-owner independently of any servers which might actually make use of the avatar.

World-Shaking Events

When dealing with a world containing only static objects, a server can deliver the world description to a client and then forget that the client even exists—

the client has all the information that it needs to display the world and to allow the client-user to walk around it.

A slightly more complex world, with moving objects which behave in completely predictable ways, can be treated in much the same way. Water shooting out of a fountain will always describe the same arc through space before landing in the fountain base.[14]

But whenever an object's behaviour is triggered by an external event, this simple view of life is just not good enough.

Consider a vandal in our Skara Brae reconstruction: he goes into house 7, picks up all the stones in sight, carries them outside and throws them into the sea. At this point what should happen is: the stone-carver stops working his stones (as he has no stones left to work with), the stone-chipping sounds stop, and anyone walking into house 7 after this point sees no stones lying around.

Consider what this involves in terms of client–server interactions:

- the server tells the vandal's client where everything in the world is, including the stones in house 7;

- the client displays all the objects in the world (if they are in view) including the stones in house 7;

- the vandal picks up the stones—that is, the client tells the server that the location of the stones has changed;

- the vandal walks out of the house—the client again informs the server of the new location of the stones;

- the vandal throws the stones into the sea—once again the client updates the server.

Is that good enough? Not even close! Consider the vandal's friend who has followed the vandal into house 7—the server needs to tell him what is changing in the world so that he can see the vandal pick up the stones, carry them

---

[14]Obviously this is not true in the real world. In artificial worlds, objects can be much better behaved. Indeed, it is almost possible for a politician to keep a promise in an artificial world. Almost!

outside, and throw them in the sea. In fact, every user who is connected to the server needs to be told about the updated locations of the objects in case they walk in to house 7. As does every client who subsequently connects to that server.

And there is more! The server also needs to tell every client the location of the vandal whenever he moves so that his avatar appears at the right place on all the client screens.

In short, the location of every object that moves (or *any* change in *any* attribute of *any* object within the world) must be propagated to every client connected to the system. This, of course, includes all the client-users connected to the server. Whenever a user moves that user's avatar moves, and so the location of the avatar must be sent to all client-users.

In a similar way, once a new client connects to the server, and all the details of the static world have been sent to the client, all the locations of the mobile objects (and the attribute states of the variable-attribute objects) must be sent to the client so that it can correctly display the current state of the world.

This can be a scary amount of information to be throwing around a network! Look at our vandal again: he's carried the stones out of house 7 and along to the edge of the sea, and he's thrown them into... hang on! How do we know that it is the sea? It's not because it's blue: that could be a prairie on the planet Zogg where the soil is heavily contaminated by copper salts, giving it a distinct blue hue. Nor is it because there are waves on the surface: that could be just a ploughed field on the planet Zogg. No... we know it is the sea because it is blue, it has waves on it, and *the waves are rolling onto the beach.* Lots of waves. Thousands of them, going out towards the horizon as far as the eye can see (or as far as the client's screen resolution can distinguish between separate waves). And they continue down the coast for miles. If the change to each bit of the sea was transmitted to all the clients as it changed, there would be no bandwidth left to do anything other than watch a small bit of sea wobble up and down.

Which brings us back to objects which move predictably!

The rhythmic motion of the waves can be modelled. And the position of the waves can be defined at time 0. So the model will tell you what the position of the waves will be 103.4 seconds later. If all clients know what the model is, and all clients have synchronized times (which is the purpose of sending the timestamp to the client when the user is authenticated) then all the clients can manage the motion of the waves without needing any update from the server.

The server can also model the motion of the waves, so a piece of wood thrown into the sea can bob up and down on top of the waves by the server telling all the clients the position of just the piece of wood. The position of the waves will automatically be correct.

You Really Want To Know This...

As we have seen, there are lots of things that the server needs to tell to a connected client, or which a client will find useful, for example:

- a definition of the objects in the world;

- who is currently connected to the server;

- an object in the world has moved (for example, a tourist picks up a carved rock to examine it);

- a behaviour has been triggered (for example, a stone-carver has started chipping away at a piece of rock, and so the client needs to play "chipping" sounds as defined by that behaviour);

- a one-off event has occurred (for example, another visitor to this world who is within hearing distance has just banged two rocks together; therefore the client needs to make a "chipping" noise);

- another user is sending a message to you;

- streaming data is arriving (for example, in this world some randomly generated music may always play, or there may be a wall on which a movie image is playing).

These different types of information are likely to be of different priorities. For example, if you are playing a multi-user game in the village of Skara Brae and one of the other players runs at you whilst wielding a large and pointed stick, then you might be a bit peeved if the *moving object* information (i.e.

an image of a person and a big pointed stick moving towards you) is delayed for 15 seconds whilst a queue of tootly music is emptied and sent over the network to your client. By that time your character in the game will be dead and the big pointed stick will need wiping down. In this world, you want the streaming music data, which is constantly being sent from the server to the clients, to be "interruptible" in some sense by more important data such as the movement of objects and people.

Of course, the priority of certain types of data will vary from world to world and from server to server. In the "How To Play Cello" Masterclass World, the streaming music data may be of *much* more importance than keeping the movements of everyone's bow-hands up to date. There are no hard-and-fast rules about what is important data—don't believe anyone who claims otherwise. But there are general rules and principles which can be applied once you have settled on your priorities.

Perhaps the best way to control data of varying priorities is also one of the simplest. (Simplicity, of course, is often a good indicator!) Generally, a server and a client will talk to each other over a connection made up of a single socket pair (that is: one socket at the client, one socket at the server). There is nothing that says that only one socket pair may be used. Instead, have one socket pair for each priority of data (or each type of data, if you prefer). Depending on your world, a sensible set of sockets may be as follows:

- Top-priority data (such as information about triggered events, signals to synchronize all clients with the server, perhaps information giving details about users who have now connected to that world).

- Message data (user "Fred" sends you the message: "Meet me in the stone-carver's house in two minutes").

- High-priority data stream (perhaps containing details of objects which are moving in a non-predictable manner—this can include the avatars of other clients who are connected to the same world). This need *not* contain information about, say, moving staircases. A moving staircase moves in a predictable way and is best modelled by a behaviour script which "knows" that objects on the staircase move at a particular speed and follow a particular path. Each client should be able to perform the necessary calculations to determine the appearance of the moving staircase at any particular moment. Passing this information over the network would generally be a complete waste of bandwidth.

- Low-priority data stream (perhaps containing non-essential sounds to be played, non-essential texture maps, etc.).

The great majority of the data that is to go out from the server to the client is directed at a particular client, rather than being sent to all the clients. Or, to be more accurate, whilst much of the data will eventually be sent to all the clients that are connected to the server at any time, at any one moment the data that is needed by any client will be needed by only that client at that time. For example, when any client connects to the server it will need to be sent the details of the current world definition. This information should most certainly not be sent to all the clients at that time. But there is some data that should be broadcast to all clients, such as information about new clients connecting to the world, synchronization signals, event signals, etc. So each client will need its own output queue for each data stream, and appropriate methods will need to be available to add data to any of those queues for a particular client and to add data to any of those queues for all clients.

Let's add some extensions to our server which implements this, with a table of connected clients and methods to send data to each of those clients as needed.

```java
// Basic multi-threaded server
// Handles a simple protocol which allows messaging
//   and has multiple data streams

import java.lang.System;
import java.net.*;
import java.io.*;

public class ServerStreams1 extends Thread
{

    // constant values for ports that the server will use
    public static final int LISTENING_PORT = 5000;
    public static final int MAIN_PORT = LISTENING_PORT;
    public static final int MSG_PORT_OFFSET = 1;
    public static final int HI_DATA_PORT_OFFSET = 2;
```

```
public static final int LO_DATA_PORT_OFFSET = 3;

// the limit to the number of clients that this server will
// accept.  Should be tuned depending on the capability of
// the machine that the server will be running on, the
// nature of the world that is being modelled, and the
// bandwidth of the network connection.
public static final int MAX_CLIENTS = 128;

Hashtable clientList = new Hashtable( MAX_CLIENTS );

int port;
ServerSocket svsock;

// start a server listening on the appropriate port
// (the default or the one specified on the command
// line)
public static void main( String args[])
{
    int port = LISTENING_PORT;

    if ( args.length == 1 ) {
        try {
            port = Integer.parseInt( args[0] );
        } catch ( NumberFormatException e ) {
            port = MAIN_PORT;
        }
    }

    new ServerStreams1( port );
    new ServerStreams1( port + MSG_PORT_OFFSET );
    new ServerStreams1( port + HI_DATA_PORT_OFFSET );
    new ServerStreams1( port + LO_DATA_PORT_OFFSET );
}

// create a server socket and start the thread
// which listens for a client connecting
public ServerStreams1( int port )
{
```

```
        this.port = port;
        try{
            svsock = new ServerSocket( port );
        } catch ( IOException e ) {
            System.err.println( "Can't create server" +
                                " socket:" + e +
                                "\nPort is " + port );
            System.exit( 1 );
        }

        this.start();
    }

    // the thread start-up code: wait for a client to
    // connect, then service that client
    public void run()
    {
        int localPort = svsock.getLocalPort();
        System.out.println( "Listening on port " +
                            localPort + "." );
        try {
            while( true ) {
                Socket client = svsock.accept();
                ClientTalk ct = new ClientTalk( client );
            }
        } catch ( IOException e ) {
            System.err.println( "Error whilst accepting" +
                                " connections: " + e  );
            System.exit( 1 );
        }
    }
}

class ClientTalk extends Thread
{

    static final int numCommands = 6;
    static final String protocolIn[] =
        { "user ",
```

```
                    "pass ",
                    "who ",
                    "msg ",
                    "loc ",
                    "quit " };

Socket client;
DataInputStream in;
PrintStream out;

// get the input and output streams associated
// with the connecting client, then start the
// thread which will service that client
public ClientTalk( Socket c )
{
    client = c;

    try {
        in = new DataInputStream( client.getInputStream() );
        out = new PrintStream( client.getOutputStream() );
    } catch ( IOException e ) {
        System.err.println( "Can't open client streams: " +
                                    e );
        try {
            client.close();
        } catch ( IOException e2 ) {
            System.err.println( "Can't close client: " + e2 );
        }
        return;
    }

    this.start();
}

// return 'true' if the first word of the input line
// is one of the acceptable commands.  Return 'false'
// otherwise
boolean checkToken( String inLine )
{
```

```
        for ( int i = 0; i < numCommands; ++i ) {
            if ( inLine.startsWith( protocolIn[ i ] ) ) {
                return true;
            }
        }
        return false;
    }


    // thread start-up code for the thread which will service
    // the client.  Read the input from the client, process
    // that input, loop
    public void run()
    {
        String clientName = client.getInetAddress().getHostName();

        out.println( "200 HELLO " + clientName );

        boolean waitingForHellToFreezeOver = true;

        try {
            do {
                String lineIn = in.readLine();
                if ( checkToken( lineIn ) ) {
                    if ( lineIn.equalsIgnoreCase( "quit" ) ) {
                        out.println( "500 BYE " + clientName );
                        waitingForHellToFreezeOver = false;
                    } else {
                        out.println( "999 thanks for that command" );
                    }
                } else {
                    out.println( "299 ECHO " + lineIn );
                }
            } while ( waitingForHellToFreezeOver );
        } catch ( IOException e ) {
            System.out.println( "Caught an IOException: " + e );
        }

        try {
            in.close();
```

```
        out.close();
        client.close();
    } catch ( IOException e ) {
        System.err.println( "Can't close client: " + e );
    }
  }
}
```

See Me, Hear Me

Networks, of course, are used for many serious and worthy purposes. The Internet sprang from the need to provide communications within and between military and governmental computers and computer networks, and later between academic institutions. The World Wide Web developed from a need to communicate information among physicists. And yet there is a very significant amount of usage of the Internet dedicated to IRC (Internet Relay Chat), which is a way of providing a world-wide conference call where you have to type rather than speak, there are big delays in transmission, and people are rude and demonstrate their abilities to cause havoc by taking over chat "channels" and removing "legitimate" users of the system. Given so many disadvantages to the system, why do so many people want to make use of it? Whatever the psychology behind it (and that is something that we *will* leave to the psychologists!) people like to use the Internet to chat. So if you are providing a virtual reality server, verbal communication between clients should be considered at least reasonably important. Maybe of very high importance.

Of course, there are plenty of "serious" reasons for messaging between clients (and for messaging between clients and pseudousers, but more about these *non-persons* in a moment). If a party of archaeologists (or wannabe archaeologists) are exploring the virtual ruins of Skara Brae there is little point in their being there all together if they cannot communicate about the things that they can see. Not to mention pretty mundane stuff like the administrator of a server being able to tell all the clients that are currently connected that the machine is going to have to be switched off in half an hour.

Don't leave inter-client messaging as an afterthought. It is simple to implement and a vital resource.

Non-persons

OK, so we have our world with its village of Skara Brae set up as an archae-ological site. There are stone-built houses to walk around, there are stone tools to pick up and examine, and there are notice boards which give detailed information about what can be seen. And there are visitors who have come to look at the site with whom you can interact. This is not wildly dissimilar to the real-life version of Skara Brae at the moment. The real Skara Brae has a custodian who can answer questions and prevent visitors from scribbling graffiti on the village remains. The same can be done in our artificial world—the virtual custodian could have a username and password and behave much as any other visitor. But most of the time that the custodian is there, they will not have anything to do. Additionally, it would be unreasonably expensive to have a custodian present for 24 hours a day (you do want your virtual world to be available 24 hours a day, don't you?). Surely we can do something better?

Of course we can. Welcome to the wonderful world of *pseudousers*—non-existent beings who can inhabit virtual worlds and appear to all intents and purposes like any other visitor to the world. Of course, you might well notice their artificial nature when you actually interact with them.[15]

The principle is very, very simple (although, as usual, the practice of making a worthwhile, intelligent pseudouser who adds worth to your world is much harder as it requires your imagination and invention to create a personality)—your server needs to know about what pseudousers are required by the system; VRML doesn't have a concept of pseudousers so you will want to either hard-code the details into your server (which, I hope you don't need telling, is usually a bad idea) or store the details in a separate file. All the server needs to do is to create a separate thread for each pseudouser and add an entry to the connection table for that pseudouser with a flag to indicate that they are not a regular user. Then whenever something happens in the world which that pseudouser needs to know about the same details that would be sent to an ordinary user are sent to the pseudouser, but the information is sent internally (either by a local socket in exactly the same way as to a real user, or via some different but perhaps more convenient or faster means of

---

[15]You might not! I've certainly met plenty of *real* people who have a pretty artificial nature as well.

inter-process/inter-thread communication). The pseudouser thread then requires a small parser to handle the incoming information and a bit of trivial intelligence to handle the outgoing information (or a lot of non-trivial intelligence if you want a *really* useful pseudouser!). Very often this intelligence will be there to handle message from users in a very simple way:

Real User Shopper: "I bought this yesterday and it doesn't work. What are you going to do about it?"

Pseudouser Assistant: "I'm sorry, sir/madam...all our intelligent assistants are busy just now. I shall inform them that you are waiting and one of them will get back to you as soon as possible."

Real User Shopper: "That's no good. Help me now. Oh, and you smell!"

Pseudouser Assistant: "I'm sorry, sir/madam...all our intelligent assistants are busy just now. I shall inform them that you are waiting and one of them will get back to you as soon as possible."

A pseudocode implementation of this could be as simple as:

```
read pseudouser details
for each pseudouser
    create_thread for pseudouser
    add details to connection table
endfor
    .
    .
    .

method send_message( user, sender, message )
    if user is psuedouser
        send_message_to_pseudouser( user, sender, message )
    else
        send_message_to_real_user( user, sender, message )
    endif
endmethod
    .
    .
    .

pseudouser_thread
```

```
    if there is an incoming message
        if sender is a real user
            send_message_to_real_user( sender, my_name,
                                      "I'm sorry..." )
        else
            send_message_to_pseudouser( sender, my_name,
                                      "I'm sorry..." )
        endif
    endif
end
```

It really is as simple as that to create pseudousers. Making them do something useful is another trick. But you might create them as automated tour guides, or points of access to a database, or as game masters and score-keepers. If you want a *really* smart pseudouser then you really need to find yourself a good introduction to artificial intelligence, but a few simple pseudousers can provide a useful function to a world. They can also make a new and sparsely populated world look that little bit more attractive to early visitors to your site... after all, there's no reason why a pseudouser should identify itself as such a being to other users of the world!

Chapter 14

Space: The Final Frontier

The difference between utility and utility plus beauty is the difference between telephone wires and the spider's web.

EDWIN WAY TEALE
"September 18"
Circle of the Seasons (1953)

Introduction

In this chapter we will look at worlds which cannot fit onto a single server machine—either because they are too big, or because there are so many objects within them that a single server would be overloaded if it tried to keep track of them all (particularly if a significant number of those objects had behaviours associated with them, or if they were otherwise mobile), or if parts of these worlds were very detailed. Here, a world can be handled by splitting it into somewhat separate chunks which can be administered by separate servers with an appropriate means of communicating information relating to the overall picture of the world to each other.

We will also look at the opposite case, where there are several worlds running on separate servers, but which have a common theme. The administrators of these worlds may feel that the common theme is strong enough that they can actually be considered as sub-worlds of a larger world. In fact, this coming together of worlds results in a situation similar to the outcome of the above subdividing of worlds.

When a world has been split over several machines in this way, one aspect that could easily be overlooked is the idea that the visitor to the world—the client browser—shouldn't need to know beforehand which of the several machines it needs to connect to in order to see a particular part of the world. Indeed, it would be unusual to expect the browser to ever care whether it is connecting to a distributed server or a monolithic server.

A brief word on the terminology that we will use in this chapter: when several machines are co-operating to provide a distributed service, it may not be clear whether the word "server" is referring to an individual machine which is providing part of the distributed-server system, or whether it is referring to the system as a whole. We will use the word *server* to mean the distributed-server system as a whole; individual parts of the *server* (which could be individual machines, or which could be subgroups of machines acting in concert to provide a particular service) will be referred to as *sub-servers*. If *sub-server* is being used to refer to a subgroup of machines, then the units within that group will be referred to as *sub-sub-servers*. So unless we make it clear that we mean otherwise, *server* is a group of co-operating machines and *sub-server* is one of the machines which is co-operating with other sub-servers.

Subdividing The World

The Mainland island of Orkney contains many sites of archaeological interest. As well as the neolithic village of Skara Brae there are: the Iron Age and Viking settlements at Gurness; mediaeval buildings in the capital, Kirkwall; assorted chambered cairns around the island; and the stone circles of Brodgar and Stenness.[1] Given a suitable machine, these could all be modelled quite happily on a single server. However, if your server was particularly limited, of if you were expecting significant numbers of visitors to the world, or if you were going to provide plenty of pseudousers at several of the sites to act as tour guides, or "actors" demonstrating how people may have lived and behaved in and around the sites, or "pretend visitors" to make it look like

---

[1]This doesn't even begin to be an exhaustive list. If you are interested in things ancient, and not just things virtual, then the Orkney Islands should be high on your list of places to visit.

your sites are really popular if you are trying to pull visitors in in the first place, then you might consider improving the performance of the server and the world by splitting the world up into several logical sections and placing them each on different sub-servers. If these different worlds could then be seamlessly linked (or even provide some kind of "reasonably seamless" links between them) a visitor should be able to enter the world at Skara Brae, travel to Gurness, cut across the island via Brodgar and Stenness and arrive at the magnificent chambered cairn of Maes Howe—in making this journey the visitor could actually cross from one world into another several times, and be talking to several different sub-servers, without ever knowing it.

This can be likened to the hyperlinks in HTML pages on the World Wide Web. Links take you from one page to another and you need not necessarily be aware that one page is on one Web server and the next page is on a server on the other side of the Earth.

In the case of a virtual world, the "hyperlinks" could be geographical margins, and when you cross from one side of a line to another you are—following the WWW analogy—surfing from one page to the next.

Mind The Gap

This is all very basic, but it doesn't take too much effort to pull up problems that would arise from this flexibility. The Ring of Brodgar and the Stones of Stenness are not very far away from each other. Certainly you would expect to see the Ring of Brodgar if you stood in the centre of the Stones of Stenness and looked north-west. If the models for the two stone circles were held on different sub-servers, what could you expect to see?

This is probably best considered (at least at the most basic level) in terms of what you could see if these were simply Web pages. What you see is the contents of the page that is held on the local server, plus a *link* to the page that is held on another server. What you absolutely do not see is the contents of both pages at once. Following this analogy, if you were standing in the midst of the Stones of Stenness and looked towards the "link" that connects the Stones of Stenness to the Ring of Brodgar you should not expect to see the distant stones, but just the link.

Is this acceptable? The obvious (and understandable) answer is: *No!* But maybe there are ways to make it more acceptable. If you were to put all your links against physical barriers then the effects would not be so noticeable...except for an inability to see through open doorways and windows. Where there is no physical barrier (as is the case between Brodgar and Stenness) then the link could be hidden in a convenient bank of mist which prevents you from being able to see across sub-server boundaries.

This may all sound a little contrived, but should not be rejected out of hand as it is a very simple way of provided distributed worlds and in very many cases the "unrealism" will simply go unnoticed.

I Can See For Miles

As has been said, in many cases the "unrealism" of hiding the join where two worlds (or two parts of the same world) meet is not something that should be worried about. Which, of course, cannot be the whole story—if there are "only" many cases where it does not matter then there must be at least some cases where it *does* matter.

For example, whilst northern Britain is not renowned for its tropical weather it is most certainly *not* always foggy on the main island of Orkney. Indeed, I have never been in the area when it was not possible to see all the way from the Stones of Stenness to the Ring of Brodgar. If you need a better degree of realism, then the mist must go!

Unlimited Bandwidth

Given unlimited bandwidth (which may well effectively be the case in a situation where all the components of the world are held on sub-servers on a local network, for example, if the components of the world are not *too* large) then it is quite feasible for *all* of the sub-servers to send the information for all of their models to the client. Unfortunately in the real world this becomes unreasonable in a very short time and networks and machines will soon start straining at the seams.

The trick here is to find ways to reduce the amount of wasted information— by which we mean information that the client will not be able to make use of, such as details of objects which are out of sight—either by calculating carefully what can be seen, or by hiding as much as possible. Hiding objects might sound like a very artificial thing to do, but it is simply a matter of putting sub-server boundaries in sensible places. But for maximum speed and ease of programming... yes, you might like to be a bit artificial about it.

For example, if your world has walls then why not put the sub-server boundaries along the walls? If you can't see through the wall, you don't need to worry about what can be seen in the other sub-server. It does no harm to think in similar terms to Web page design, where you would probably put related documents on the one machine and less related documents on another machine, rather than randomly scatter them about.

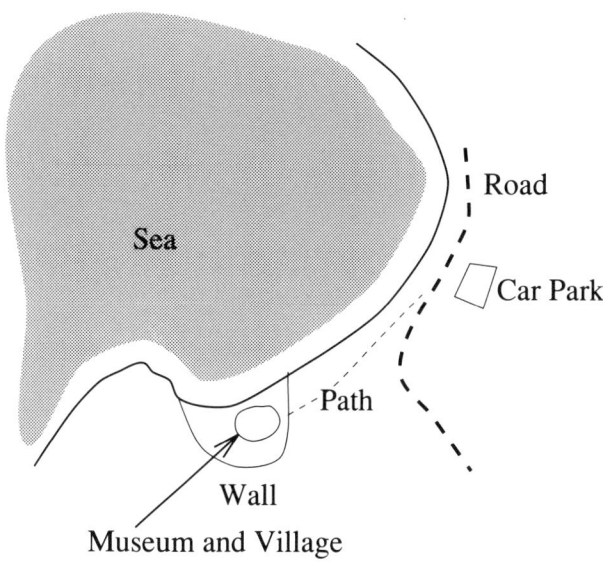

Figure 14.1: The Area Around Skara Brae

But if you have a wall, you probably have a doorway. And here you really do need to see from one sub-server to the next. Yet there are still good ways to avoid tricky and slow computations to find what can be seen from one sub-server to another, and it is still possible to avoid those computations entirely.

Consider present-day Skara Brae. The village and museum lie on the coast, around them are a wall, some fields, more walls, the road, more walls and the car park, as in Figure 14.1.

Given the amount of detail within the village and the museum and contrast-
ing that with the relatively few interesting features in the immediate area,
it might make sense to split this world, with one sub-server handling everything within the wall surrounding the village and another sub-server handling
everything outside the wall. The only difficulty, then, is in the vicinity of
the wall. This difficulty can be side-stepped by splitting the world in a less
obvious way. Consider Figure 14.2.

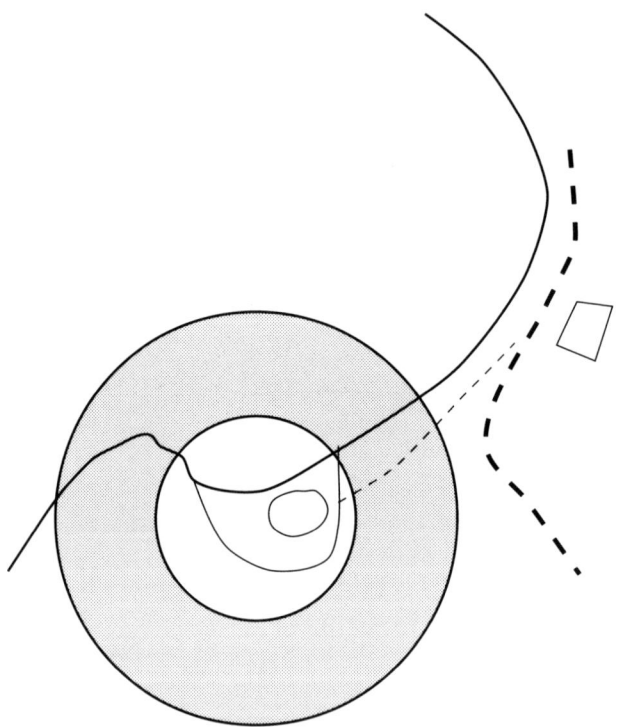

Figure 14.2: The Area Around Skara Brae With Overlapping Sub-Servers

Here, everything within the *outer* circle is held on one sub-server and everything outside the *inner* circle is held on another sub-server. As a result,
there is quite a significant area (shaded in Figure 14.2) which is held on *both*
sub-servers. Couple this with a light fog where the shaded area is (a fog that
is just thick enough to obscure the view for more than half the width of the

overlap area) and it will be possible to walk from the car park to the museum, with a shift from one sub-server to the other when you cross the mid-point of the overlapping area, and not have to reach an obvious junction beyond which you cannot see. The light fog prevents you from seeing from one server to the other, but the overlap means that the fog can be light enough to always be able to see some way into the distance.

Enclosed spaces are still more effective as you could have groups of rooms, or levels of the building, held on seperate sub-servers and keep entire corridors or connecting rooms on both servers. No need for the fog and no need for the visitor to ever be aware of having crossed from one sub-server to another.

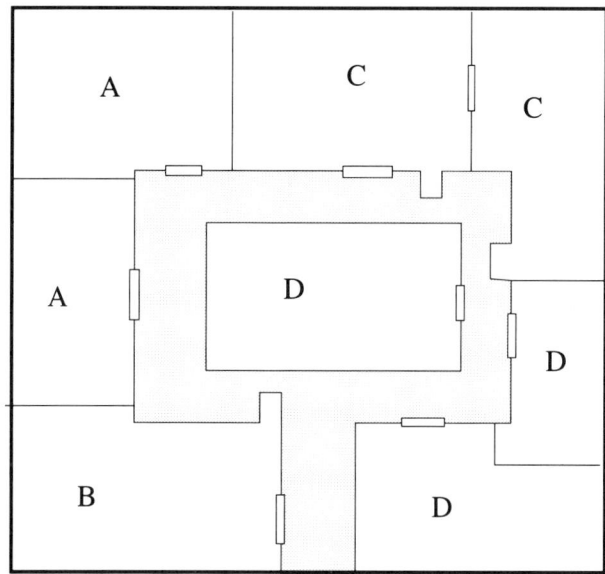

Figure 14.3: Enclosed Areas Can Be Easily Managed With Overlapping Sub-Servers

Figure 14.3 shows a good example of this. Rooms with the same letter must be.held on the same sub-server as line of sight allows a person to see into more than one of those rooms from certain points. Rooms with different letters can be safely held on separate sub-servers as there is no point in the world where it is possible to see into, say, an A room and a B room at the same time. The shaded area can be seen from rooms with all labels and must be shared by

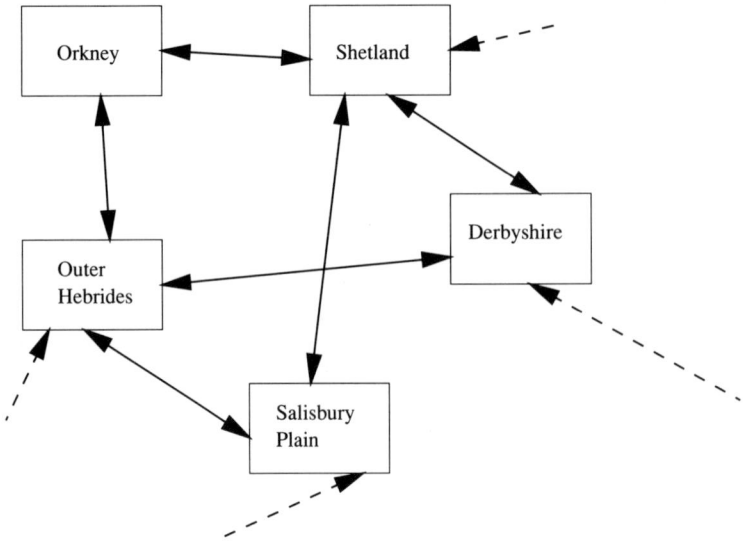

Figure 14.4: Distributed Server: Different Archaeological Sites On Different Machines

all the sub-servers.

Communicating Between Sub-Servers

Before we look at how we can create a distributed virtual reality server it is necessary to understand some of the problems and pitfalls that surround any kind of general distributed server. These can be divided into two pretty broad areas:

- synchronization—making sure that all the sub-servers that hold the data for the world agree on what the world "looks like" at any one time;

- security—making sure that only authorised clients can interact with the servers in authorised ways (and, indeed, making sure that only authorised sub-servers can interact with the other sub-servers in authorised ways).

There are, of course, many other factors which are going to affect how the distributed server is built, including:

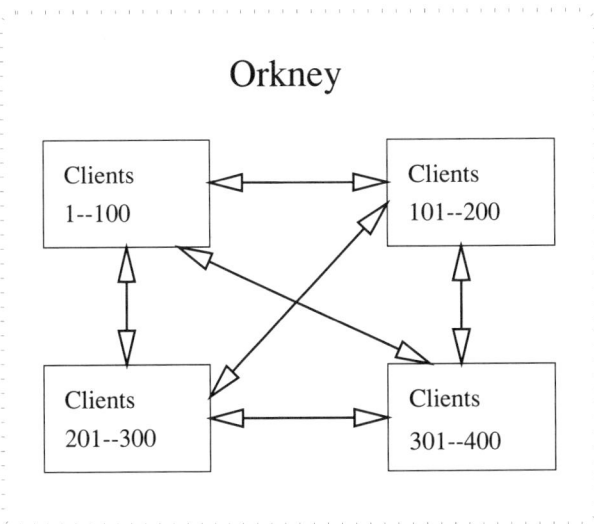

Figure 14.5: Distributed Server: Copies Of The Same Model On Different Machines

- *Why* the server is being distributed—if the world model is so big that different sub-servers must hold different parts of the world model then the various individual sub-server machines must know where other parts of the world model are held (or at least know how to find this information out). For example, if your server held a model of all the archaeological sites in the British Isles it might make sense to put all the Orkney sites on one machine, all the Outer Hebrides sites on another machine, all the Salisbury Plain sites on a third machine, etc., as illustrated in Figure 14.4.

On the other hand, if the number of clients is expected to be large but the world model is relatively small then the best solution may well be to hold the complete model on each individual sub-server machine. For example, if the server is to hold a model of all the Orkney sites and you expect there to be many visitors to Orkney you may have several machines which can cope with, say, 100 visitors each, as in Figure 14.5.

Here the problem is more one of keeping all the sub-servers aware of the

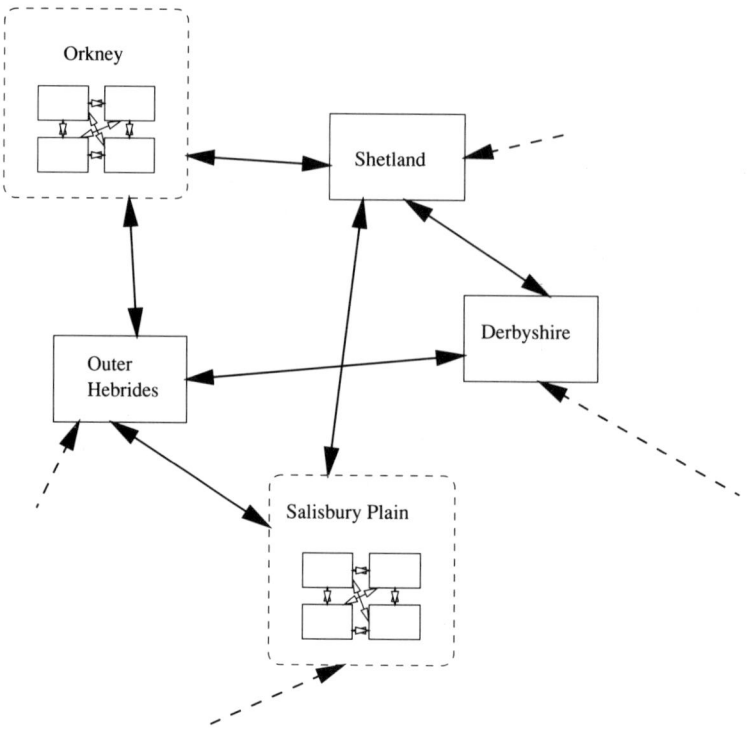

Figure 14.6: Distributed Server: Different Archaeological Sites On Different Machines, Some Sites On Multiple Machines

current state of the world—if one of the visitors grabs the stones out of the hands of our stone-carver then everyone should hear the tapping of stones cease, not just those visitors who are connected to the same sub-server as the visiting thief. Obviously there is also a more complex case that is a combination of these—you may have a large world model and expect areas of the world to have large numbers of visitors. These might be best considered as a tree of sub-servers and sub-sub-servers, as in Figure 14.6.

- The speed of the internal network.

- The speed of the external network (if you are serving non-local clients; for example, over the Internet).

Synchronization

If an object within the world model is held on more than one machine at a time then it is important, as we stated earlier, that the data contained within this object remains consistant over all those machines; otherwise one client's view of the world could be different from another client's. For static objects this is trivially easy. The object will never change. For objects which have a behaviour attached to them but which cannot be influenced by any external forces—for example, a museum/visitor centre at Skara Brae may have a Historic Scotland flag flying above it on a flag-pole; this could be inaccessible to any visitors and modelled simply so as to "flap in the wind" in a way determined by the current time—the only synchronization required is one which keeps the *current time* synchronized on all the sub-servers. When the object moves on one sub-server, it will move on all the sub-servers at the same time. No extra communication between the sub-servers is necessary to make this happen. *Time synchronization* is dealt with seperately, below.

Life becomes more interesting when the world model contains objects which *can* be influenced by external forces. For example, consider a box lying on the ground. This can be picked up by any visitor to the world. Once the box has been picked up, it is not available to be picked up by any other visitor until it has been set down. Additionally, the box is no longer where it used to be—so every client connecting to the world must be informed of where the box currently is.

An easy mistake here is to have a scheme where the sub-server on which the box is picked up simply informs all the other sub-servers within the system that the box has been picked up and where it currently is. Of course, it isn't too hard to spot the race condition here. Two different clients connected to two different sub-servers could attempt to pick up the box at almost the same time. If the time between these two events is less than the time it takes to inform all sub-servers within the system of an action, then it is possible to have valid but contradictory information being held in the system. Take a look at Figure 14.7. Client A tells sub-server 1 that it is picking up the box. At almost the same moment, client B tells sub-server 5 that *it* is picking up the box. Both sub-server 1 and sub-server 5 are ignorant about any other client performing any action on the box, and they both believe that the box is available to be picked up, so they allow the operation to go ahead and start to inform the other machines within the server that the box has been picked up.

At this point, the world as seen from different sub-servers within the system can be very different!

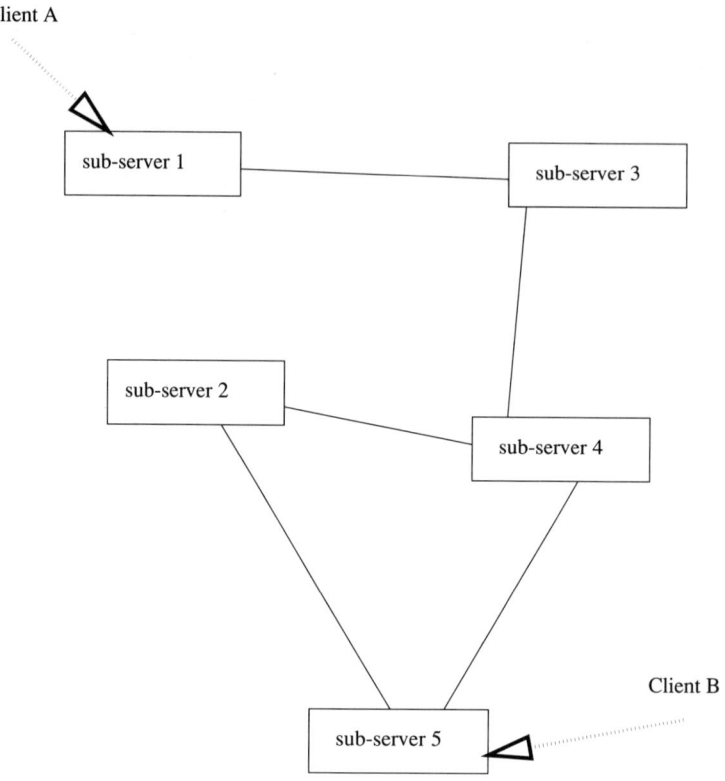

Figure 14.7: Naïve Synchronization

A simple solution is to have one of the sub-servers nominated as a *synchronization master*, and no sub-server will manipulate an object until given explicit permission by the synchronization master. If, for example, sub-server 2 in Figure 14.7 has been nominated as the synchronization master for the server then the following sequence of events could occur:

1.
   - Client A tells sub-server 1 that it wants to pick up the box.
   - Client B tells sub-server 5 that it wants to pick up the box.

2.
- Sub-server 1 tells sub-server 3 that client A wants to pick up the box.
- Sub-server 5 tells sub-server 2 that client B wants to pick up the box.

3.
- Sub-server 3 tells sub-server 4 that client A wants to pick up the box.
- Sub-server 2 notes that client B is picking up the box and informs sub-server 5 that it has done so.

4.
- Sub-server 4 tells sub-server 2 that client A wants to pick up the box.
- Sub-server 5 informs client B that the synchronization master has given permission to proceed with picking up the box.

5.
- Sub-server 2 tells sub-server 4 that permission has been denied, as it has a note that another client is manipulating the box.
- Client B broadcasts information about what it is doing with the box.

This continues until client A learns that it cannot manipulate the box and all the sub-servers have been informed of what client B has done with the box.

When (and if) client B sets down the box it must inform the synchronization master that the box is once again available to be manipulated, so that the synchronization master can update its records.

The synchronization master could be a machine which is otherwise no different from the other sub-servers in the system (as suggested in Figure 14.7), or it could be a machine which is dedicated to managing the synchronization of clients manipulating objects. In the latter case, the synchronization master need not know about all objects in the system beforehand—it only needs to keep track of those objects which are currently *locked*. If a client were to request a lock on an object for which the synchronization master does not have a record, then the synchronization master can be sure that no other client has requested a lock on that object and so can safely register the requested lock.

In the example above, none of the machines *except* for the synchronization master itself actually knows who the synchronization master is. This allows for the widest flexibility, so the server can continue to operate if one synchronization master were to take over from another, but for the vast majority of cases that is more complex than is needed. The usual thing would be to have a nominated synchronization master to which all the sub-servers would communicate their requests directly.

This is enough synchronization to allow us to build the basics of a distributed server, but there are a few mundane things that we need to worry about. For one thing, each sub-server needs to know which other sub-servers it should connect to and which is the synchronization master. There are many ways to do this and which is most appropriate depends on the server that you are trying to build. One possibility, which we will use for the example here, is to have an agreed synchronization master which has fairly wide control over the entire server; in particular, it will tell any sub-servers connecting to it which other sub-servers they should connect to. It will also expect those sub-servers which have connected to it to continue listening as it may choose to update that list as time goes on. That will allow for a reasonably flexible ability to reorganise the server *on the fly*. For example, when the first connection is made by a sub-server to the synchronization master there will be no other sub-servers for that first sub-server to connect to. When a second sub-server connects to the synchronization master, the second sub-server can be told to talk to the first sub-server, and the first sub-server can be updated with the details of the second sub-server and told to connect.

The synchronization master can also tell the sub-servers which is to open a passive socket and which is to actively connect to the other sub-server. An alternative to this, if you want to remove some control from the sub-server, would be to have some scheme whereby each of the sub-servers can decide if it is going to open a `java.net.ServerSocket` to provide the passive end to the connection, or a `java.net.Socket` to provide the active end of the connection. These could be "fast but unfair", perhaps a rule such as *the sub-server with the highest value IP address provides the passive socket*; or "slow but fair", perhaps a rule such as *both ends open a passive socket as well as actively connect to the other end. Each sends a random number down the active socket. If one is higher than the other, close the link down which the highest number went. Otherwise repeat.* Use whatever scheme is appropriate for your application.

Further, if one of the sub-servers disconnects from the system the synchroniza-

Command	Action
location *data*	specifies the new location of an object (specified by *data* within the world model
quit	close the connection

Table 14.1: Sub-Server to Sub-Server

Command	Action
lock *data*	request a lock on an object (specified by *data*) so that this sub-server can manipulate that object
unlock *data*	release the lock on an object (specified by *data*) so that it is now free to be manipulated by other sub-servers
quit	close the connection

Table 14.2: Sub-Server to Synchronization Master

tion master can tell all the other connected sub-servers that that sub-server is no longer available and so help keep all the connections clean.

We also need a simple protocol for the sub-servers to communicate with each other and for the sub-servers to communicate with the synchronization master. The protocol that we will use here (see Tables 14.1–14.3) assumes that each of the sub-servers trusts the others, so there are no security or authentication concerns, and is aimed at providing clarity rather than efficiency. Each command in the protocol consists of a single keyword, optionally followed by a line of data, and is terminated at the first end-of-line.

The code that implements this protocol is as follows:

```
// Basic multi-threaded distributed server
// Handles a simple protocol which allows messaging
//   and has multiple data streams
```

Command	Action
grant *data*	confirm a successful lock has been granted on an object (specified by *data*) so that this sub-server has requested via lock
deny *data*	report that the requested lock on an object (specified by *data*), requested by this sub-server via lock, has been denied because a lock is already held by another sub-server
accept *data*	provide a passive socket for a sub-server (specified by *data*)
connect *data*	make an active connection to a sub-server (specified by *data*)
disconnect *data*	disconnect from a sub-server (specified by *data*)
quit	close the connection

Table 14.3: Synchronization Master to Sub-Server

```
import java.lang.System;
import java.net.*;
import java.io.*;

public class DistServer1 extends ServerStreams1 {

  // constant values for ports that the server will use
  public static final int SERVER_PORT_OFFSET = 4;

  // maximum number of sub-servers in the distributed server
  public static final int MAX_SERVERS = 128;

  Hashtable serverList = new Hashtable( MAX_SERVERS );

  int port;
  ServerSocket svsock;
```

```
// start a server listening on the appropriate port
// (the default or the one specified on the command
// line)
public static void main( String args[]) {
  int port = LISTENING_PORT;

  if ( args.length == 1 ) {
    try {
      port = Integer.parseInt( args[0] );
    } catch ( NumberFormatException e ) {
      port = MAIN_PORT;
    }
  }

  new ServerStreams1( port );
  new ServerStreams1( port + MSG_PORT_OFFSET );
  new ServerStreams1( port + HI_DATA_PORT_OFFSET );
  new ServerStreams1( port + LO_DATA_PORT_OFFSET );
}

// create a server socket and start the thread
// which listens for a client connecting
public ServerStreams1( int port ) {
  this.port = port;
  try{
    svsock = new ServerSocket( port );
  } catch ( IOException e ) {
    System.err.println( "Can't create server" +
                        " socket:" + e +
                        "\nPort is " + port );
    System.exit( 1 );
  }

  this.start();
}

// the thread start-up code: wait for a client to
// connect, then service that client
public void run() {
```

```
      int localPort = svsock.getLocalPort();
      System.out.println( "Listening on port " +
                          localPort + "." );
      try {
        while( true ) {
          Socket client = svsock.accept();
          ClientTalk ct = new ClientTalk( client );
        }
      } catch ( IOException e ) {
        System.err.println( "Error whilst accepting" +
                          " connections: " + e  );
        System.exit( 1 );
      }
    }
}

class ClientTalk extends Thread {

    static final int numCommands = 6;
    static final String protocolIn[] =
          { "user ",
            "pass ",
            "who ",
            "msg ",
            "loc ",
            "quit " };

    Socket client;
    DataInputStream in;
    PrintStream out;

    // get the input and output streams associated
    // with the connecting client, then start the
    // thread which will service that client
    public ClientTalk( Socket c ) {
      client = c;

      try {
        in = new DataInputStream( client.getInputStream() );
```

```
      out = new PrintStream( client.getOutputStream() );
  } catch ( IOException e ) {
    System.err.println( "Can't open client streams: " +
                        e );
    try {
      client.close();
    } catch ( IOException e2 ) {
      System.err.println( "Can't close client: " + e2 );
    }
    return;
  }

  this.start();
}

// return 'true' if the first word of the input line
// is one of the acceptable commands.  Return 'false'
// otherwise
boolean checkToken( String inLine ) {
  for ( int i = 0; i < numCommands; ++i ) {
    if ( inLine.startsWith( protocolIn[ i ] ) ) {
      return true;
    }
  }
  return false;
}

// thread start-up code for the thread which will service
// the client.  Read the input from the client, process
// that input, loop
public void run() {
  String clientName = client.getInetAddress().getHostName();

  out.println( "200 HELLO " + clientName );

  boolean waitingForHellToFreezeOver = true;

  try {
    do {
```

```
        String lineIn = in.readLine();
        if ( checkToken( lineIn ) ) {
          if ( lineIn.equalsIgnoreCase( "quit" ) ) {
            out.println( "500 BYE " + clientName );
            waitingForHellToFreezeOver = false;
          } else {
            out.println( "999 thanks for that command" );
          }
        } else {
          out.println( "299 ECHO " + lineIn );
        }
      } while ( waitingForHellToFreezeOver );
    } catch ( IOException e ) {
      System.out.println( "Caught an IOException: " + e );
    }

    try {
      in.close();
      out.close();
      client.close();
    } catch ( IOException e ) {
      System.err.println( "Can't close client: " + e );
    }
  }
}
```

Improving Efficiency

This simple scheme provides us with a safe way of manipulating objects within a distributed system, but it is not terribly efficient. There is a lot of message-passing before the whole system knows that an object has been moved:

- I want to move object A (message from the client to the synchronization master);

- it is OK/not OK to move object A (message from the synchronization master to the client);

- I have moved object A to position (x,y,z) (message from the client to all the sub-servers);

- I no longer want to move object A (message from the client to the synchronization master).

Very often this might not be a problem—on a high-speed local network with plenty of available bandwidth, this simple scheme might be fine. Over a wide area network with significant lag between machines it might be worth finding a more efficient mechanism.

It is worth bearing in mind that this synchronization scheme is there to prevent conflicting operations being performed by different clients (such as two visitors to a world attempting to perform different manipulations on an object at the same time) and that this is likely to be a pretty rare occurrance. So a way to improve the performance would be for clients to assume that their requests for a lock from the synchronization master are going to succeed until they are told otherwise, rather than wait for the confirmation before proceeding.

So a client could send a request to the synchronization master *and* broadcast what it is intending to do to the object to all the sub-servers. When the synchronization master receives the request it can broadcast the success or failure of the request to all the sub-servers. The sub-servers can then recognise the *pending* manipulation as an *actual* manipulation (if the request was successful), or they can discard the pending manipulation (if the request was unsuccessful). If the request was successful then the sub-server to which the client is directly connected can note that it now has a lock on that object and any further manipulations that the client wished to perform can be broadcast as actual manipulations rather than pending manipulations.

As a slight variation on this—and to bring everything down to a more homogeneous level—the sub-server could simply broadcast its pending operation and when the synchronization master receives a pending operation it interprets it as a request for a lock. As with the previous example, this provides for much greater flexibility as none of the sub-servers needs to know (or care) which machine is the actual synchronization master; but it is still a level of flexibility which is not required and would add further unnecessary complexity to most server implementations.

Time Synchronization

We have already recognised that the various sub-servers that make up our server need to agree on what the current time is, not least so that any time-dependent behaviours are acting in the same way on all the sub-servers and—most importantly—on all the clients. However, it is worth stressing that it is not important that the sub-servers know the *right* time, just that they agree on what the time is.

There are some very solid and clever (and usually pretty complex) methods for getting extremely high accuracy for time over several networked machines, not least of these being the Network Time Protocol, as described by D.L. Mills in `RFC 1305`. But there is no need to add complexity in order to provide more accuracy than will be needed, so we will use a fairly simple (but quite good enough) scheme.

First, though, let's consider why there is a need for any complexity at all. Surely all that we need to do is nominate one machine to be the master time-keeper and all the other sub-servers can take their time settings from this. Well, yes, that's really all that we need to do. But there is one problem. The master time-keeper will be telling us what the current time is, but that time will be out of date by the time it gets across the network to us. So we need to know by how much it is out of date. This just takes a little effort, as can be demonstrated by the following (real) output from the `ping` command:

```
eco:~$ ping kafka
PING kafka (192.168.1.2): 56 data bytes
64 bytes from 192.168.1.2: icmp_seq=0 ttl=251 time=1770.8 ms
64 bytes from 192.168.1.2: icmp_seq=1 ttl=251 time=1574.9 ms
64 bytes from 192.168.1.2: icmp_seq=2 ttl=251 time=1624.8 ms
64 bytes from 192.168.1.2: icmp_seq=3 ttl=251 time=954.5 ms
64 bytes from 192.168.1.2: icmp_seq=4 ttl=251 time=364.8 ms
64 bytes from 192.168.1.2: icmp_seq=5 ttl=251 time=215.4 ms
64 bytes from 192.168.1.2: icmp_seq=6 ttl=251 time=175.0 ms
64 bytes from 192.168.1.2: icmp_seq=7 ttl=251 time=1635.6 ms
64 bytes from 192.168.1.2: icmp_seq=8 ttl=251 time=1148.6 ms
64 bytes from 192.168.1.2: icmp_seq=9 ttl=251 time=1400.2 ms
^C
```

Over the 10-second period that we ran `ping`, the time taken to send a packet of data from `eco` to `kafka` and back again varied from just under 0.2 seconds to almost 1.8 seconds. Anyone who has accessed busy sites on the Internet at busy periods will know only too well that the time taken to transmit data from one machine to another can vary by *much* larger amounts than that.

But so long as we are happy to be *reasonably* acurate and don't have to be *very* acurate we can keep a track of what the delay is between each of the sub-servers and the master time-keeper and allow for that delay. Of course, computer clocks don't tend to drift very much as a rule. There is little point in having your sub-servers synchronize with the master time-keeper every few seconds. Synchronizing times when a sub-server connects up with the other sub-servers in a system is a must. After that you may not want to synchronize more often than once every few hours or even every few days. However, that is true only if you have confidence in the synchronization. If you have reason to think that the calculation of the delay between the sub-server and the synchronization master is suspect then you will probably want to synchronize again pretty soon until you are happy that the two machines are in agreement.

So how do we calculate the delay and how do we decide if it is reliable? A quick calculation of the delay is simple. Get the round-trip time for a small number—say, five—packets of data and take the average. And reliability? Again, there is a simple way to get a good enough idea of that. Calculate the percentage difference between the actual round-trip time for each packet. If the sum of all the percentage differences is outside a certain range—say $\pm 10\%$—or if any one of the percentage differences is outside a certain range—again perhaps $\pm 10\%$—then the synchronization could be considered suspect and should be retried at regular intervals. Set the sub-server time to any values which appears to be more reliable, and keep trying until a good value is obtained.

Unfortunately, Java only provides network classes that can send data packets using UDP or TCP but the data packets that are needed to calculate the round-trip time need to use ICMP data packets. A solution to this is to generate these packets using a program such as `ping` and having a C program which gathers the round-trip times and communicates the data to our Java server using a higher-level TCP socket. Now it might seem that adding this extra socket to the loop is going to add a further delay to the calculation, but not so. The round-trip time is calculated within the C program—any delay in the transfer of that data to the server doesn't have any bearing on the time taken to communicate between two machines.

A simple C program which uses `ping` is shown below:

```
/*********************
**
** pinger.c
**
**   a program to calculate the round-trip time
**   between the local machine and a remote
**   machine.  Requests for a calculation are
**   taken on a specified socket---the name
**   of the remote machine is taken in and
**   the round-trip time in milliseconds (or an
**   error indication) is sent out.  Then the socket
**   is closed.
**
*/

#include <stdio.h>
#include <netinet/in.h>
#include <sys/types.h>
#include <sys/socket.h>

/* the port that other programs can use to
** request round-trip time calculations
*/
#define  REQUEST_PORT  5010

#define  MAX_SOCK_RQSTS 5
#define  MAXLINE 256

int main( void )
{

   int rqst_socket;

   if ( -1 == ( rqst_socket = open_listening_socket() ) )
```

```
  {
    return -1;
  }

  for( ;; )
  {
    if ( -1 == ( process_rqst( rqst_socket ) ) )
    {
      return -1;
    }
  }
}

int open_listening_socket( void )
{

  int rqst_socket;

  int set_opt = 1;
  struct sockaddr_in req_port_addr;
  struct hostent *srvhost_ptr;

  req_port_addr.sin_family = AF_INET;
  req_port_addr.sin_addr.s_addr = htonl( INADDR_ANY );
  req_port_addr.sin_port = htons( REQUEST_PORT );

  if ( -1 == ( rqst_socket = socket(
               AF_INET, SOCK_STREAM, IPPROTO_TCP ) ) )
  {
    perror( "socket" );
    return -1;
  }
  if ( -1 == setsockopt( rqst_socket, SOL_SOCKET,
               SO_REUSEADDR, (char*)&set_opt,
               sizeof( set_opt ) ) )
  {
    perror( "setsockopt" );
    return -1;
  }
```

```
  if ( -1 == bind( rqst_socket, (struct sockaddr*)
             &req_port_addr, sizeof( req_port_addr ) ) )
  {
    perror( "bind" );
    return -1;
  }
  if ( -1 == listen( rqst_socket, MAX_SOCK_RQSTS ) )
  {
    perror( "listen" );
    return -1;
  }

  return rqst_socket;
}


int process_rqst( int rqst_socket )
{

  int rtt;

  int accepted_socket;
  char hostname[256];
  char reply[256];
  struct sockaddr_in soc_addr;

  int sock_size = sizeof( soc_addr );

  /* wait for a request */
  if ( -1 == ( accepted_socket = accept( rqst_socket,
                 (struct sockaddr*)&soc_addr,
                 &sock_size ) ) )
  {
    perror( "accept" );
    return -1;
  }

  if ( -1 == read( accepted_socket, hostname,
             sizeof( hostname ) ) )
```

```
  {
    perror( "read" );
    return -1;
  }

  rtt = ping_host( hostname );
  if ( -1 == rtt )
  {
    strcpy( reply, "!Error\n" );
  }
  else
  {
    sprintf( reply, "%d\n", rtt );
  }
  write( accepted_socket, reply, strlen( reply ) );

  close( accepted_socket );
  return 0;
}

int ping_host( char* hostname )
{
  FILE* ping_data;
  char cmd[256];
  char pline[MAXLINE];
  int rtt = 0;
  char* timeptr;
  const char* timeline = "64 bytes from";
  const char* timeeql  = "time=";

  while ( hostname[strlen(hostname)-1] < ' '
        && hostname[strlen(hostname)-1] > 0 )
  {
    hostname[strlen(hostname)-1] = 0;
  }
  sprintf( cmd, "/bin/ping -c 1 %s", hostname );

  if ( NULL == ( ping_data =
                        popen( cmd, "r" ) ) )
```

```
  {
    perror( "popen" );
    return -1;
  }

  while( NULL !=
        fgets( pline, MAXLINE, ping_data ) )
  {
    if ( !strncmp( pline, timeline, sizeof(timeline) ) )
    {
      timeptr = strstr( pline, timeeql )
                    + strlen( timeeql );
      break;
    }
  }

  rtt = strtol( timeptr, NULL, 10 );

  return rtt;

}
```

This program waits for a TCP connection to port 5010. It expects a valid hostname to be sent down the socket and it will send the round-trip time in milliseconds back up the socket and the socket is then closed.

This can be easily used by a Java program, as demonstrated by the following program:

```
// Class that uses the pinger daemon to obtain
// round-trip time details for a given host
//

import java.lang.System;
import java.net.*;
import java.io.*;

public class Pinger {
```

```java
public static final int PINGER_PORT = 5010;
static String pingerhost = "localhost";

public static void main( String[] args )
{
  Socket s = null;
  String rtt;

  try {
    s = new Socket( pingerhost, PINGER_PORT );

    DataInputStream dataIn = new DataInputStream(
           s.getInputStream() );

    PrintStream dataOut = new PrintStream(
           s.getOutputStream() );

    // ask for the RTT for host
    dataOut.println( args[0] );
    // read the RTT
    rtt = dataIn.readLine();

    System.out.println( "RTT to " + args[0] +
                              " is " + rtt );

  } catch( IOException e ) {
    System.err.println( e );
  } finally {
    if ( s != null ) try {
      s.close();
    } catch( IOException e2 ) {
      System.err.println( e2 );
    }
  }
}
}
```

Note that the example Java program expects the C program to be running on the same machine (as it connects to `localhost`), and expects the name of the host for which the round-trip time is to be calculated to be given as a command-line parameter.

Summary

We have looked at some of the fundamental problems that underly synchronizing multiple sub-servers making up a distributed server. The problems, whilst complex, are by no means insurmountable.

Appendix A

The VRML Specification

The CD-ROM that acompanies this book contains the complete current Virtual Reality Modelling Language (VRML) specification. The specification is also available on the World Wide Web from

```
http://www.vrml.org/Specifications/VRML97/index.html
```

The effort to produce the VRML specification was headed by Gavin Bell, Rikk Carey and Chris Marrin, and we thank them for their permission to include the document with this book.

Index

accessing field information, 213

active sounds, *see* sounds, active sounds

`addRoute()`, 229

`addValue()`, 215

aims of virtual reality, *see* virtual reality, aims

`Anchor`, 45, 47, 49, 187

animation, 116, 172, 173, 177, 197, 229

anti-clockwise ordering, 74

`Appearance`, 59

Application Layer, 276

arbitrary polygons, 72

ARPANET, 268

array pre-allocation, 215

ASCII, 156

atmospheric effects, 123

audio complexity, *see* sound, audio complexity

authentication, 308–310, 315
  democracy, 311
  on slow or unreliable networks, 314
  republicanism, 314

authentication of clients, 292

authorization, 296

`autoOffset` field, 163

avatars, 159, 188, 194, 230, 292, 294, 324

AWT, 222

back-face culling, 61, 74

bandwidth, 291

BASE64 encoding, 198

behaviour, 197

behaviour model, 150

`Billboard`, 49, 187
  `axisOfRotation`, 50

blending, 125

Blinn, Jim, 1

boosting performance, 52

bounding box, 52, 54, 188–190, 192

bounding box culling, 51

bounding box optimization, 80

bounding spheres, 191

`Box`, 44, 54, 60

brochs, 232

Brodgar, Ring of, 232, 233, 340–342

carving
  stone, 138, 145, 147

chambered cairns, 340, 341

changing the shape of a `Sphere`, 68

Childe, Professor Gordon, 232

Clarke, David, 232

classes of client, 317

client promotion and demotion, 322

client protocol, 296, 301
collideTime event, 194
Collision, 50, 187, 188, 193, 194
collision detection, 50, 186–188, 190, 191, 193
ColorInterpolator, 172, 174
colour, 107–112, 116, 117, 153, 155, 157, 172
   emissive, 109
   specular, 109
colour blending, 111, 174
colour pulsing, 174
colour shifting, 172
colouring, 110, 111
   diffuse, 109
   solid, 108
Cone, 62
   bottomRadius, 62
   height, 62
co-ordinate systems, 10–14, 30
CoordinateInterpolator, 172, 175, 177
createVrmlFromString(), 226, 229
createVrmlFromURL(), 226
cumulative transformations, 43
currentThread() method, 246
custom fields, 201, 204
custom node definition, 197
cyberspatial design, 41
cycleTime event, 171, 204
Cylicone, 65
Cylinder, 54, 64
   height, 64
   radius, 64
   side, 64
CylinderSensor, 159, 162–164, 166, 170

DARPA, 268

datagrams, 270
death, thread, 243
Deering, Steve, 288
defining custom fields, 204
deformation, 175
deleteRoute(), 229
depth cueing, 123
descending mist effect, 185
design of cyberspace, 41
directOutput, 201
disabling Script nodes, 169
distributed authentication, 310
distributed servers, 292
DOS, 247
dragging, 163
Dutch cheese, 95

earth-houses, 232
ElevationGrid, 81, 201
encryption, 309
enterTime event, 169, 170
event, 150
   collideTime, 194
   cycleTime, 171, 204
   enterTime, 169, 170
   exitTime, 169, 170
   fraction_changed, 171, 175
   hitNormal_changed, 161
   hitPoint_changed, 161
   hitTextureCoord_changed, 161
   isActive, 160, 170
   isOver, 160, 161
   orientation_changed, 168
   position_changed, 168
   removeChildren, 229
   set_fraction, 172
   time, 172
   touchTime, 160, 162
   value_changed, 172, 179, 183

eventIn, 152
eventIn field, 150
eventOut, 152
eventOut field, 150
events, 216
eventsProcessed(), 208
examiner viewer, 164
exception
    IllegalArgumentException, 254
exitTime event, 169, 170
exposedField, 152
EXTERNPROTO, 101
Extrusion, 83
    beginCap, 97
    crossSection, 83
    endCap, 97
    orientation, 93
    scale, 86
    spine, 84

field, 152
flag effect, 217
floating users, 320
Fog, 173, 185
fog, 123
    exponential, 123
    linear, 123
    natural, 123
FontStyle, 97
fraction_changed event, 171, 175
Frame, 222
frame rate, 230
free-form shapes, 83

garbage collector, Java, 246
geometry nodes, 59
get1Value(), 215
getBlue(), 215
getCurrentFrameRate(), 230

getCurrentSpeed(), 230
getEventIn(), 211
getEventOut(), 211
getField, 210
getGreen(), 215
getName(), 216, 230
getPriority() method, 254
getRed(), 215
getSize(), 215
getTimeStamp(), 216
getValue(), 213, 216
getVersion(), 230
getWorldURL(), 230
GIS, 83
gloom, 123
Gouraud, Henri, 35
Grooks, 129
Group, 44, 51, 187
grouping nodes, 42, 44
Gurness, 340, 341

Hall, Christopher, 41
handedness, 13, 14
headlight, 118
heads-up display, 50
Hein, Piet, 129
Heraclitus, 149
hitNormal_changed event, 161
hitPoint_changed event, 161
hitTextureCoord_changed event,
    161
Holmes, Sherlock, 123
host addressing under TCP/IP, 278
HTML, 341
HUD, 50
hyperlinks, 341, 342

ICMP, 273
idle clients, 319, 321

IllegalArgumentException exception, 254
IllegalMonitorStateException exception, 258, 259
IndexedFaceSet, 54, 70, 72, 74, 175, 177
  ccw, 77
  creaseAngle, 77
  solid, 74
IndexedLineSet, 54, 72, 77
  ccw, 77
  convex, 77
  creaseAngle, 77
initialize(), 206, 211
Inline, 54, 55, 58
inlining objects, 54
inserting nodes into the scene graph, 226
insertValue(), 215
interactivity, 150, 197
interfacing Java and VRML, 222
internal scripting, 200
Internet, 144
Internet Layer, 270
interpolator key, 173
interpolator keyValue, 173
interpolators, 172, 173
InterruptedException exception, 258, 259
intersection of ProximitySensors, 168
Iron Age, 340
IS, 203
isActive event, 160, 170
isOver event, 160, 161

Java, 197
  addRoute(), 229
  addValue(), 215

AWT, 222
class
  Object, 258
  Thread, 242, 243, 246
  ThreadGroup, 262
createVrmlFromString(), 226, 229
createVrmlFromURL(), 226
deleteRoute(), 229
Event, 216
eventsProcessed(), 208
exception
  IllegalMonitorStateException, 258, 259
  InterruptedException, 258, 259
Frame, 222
garbage collector, 246
get1Value, 215
getBlue(), 215
getCurrentFrameRate(), 230
getCurrentSpeed(), 230
getEventIn(), 211
getField(), 210
getGreen(), 215
getName(), 216, 230
getRed(), 215
getSize(), 215
getTimeStamp(), 216
getValue(), 213, 216
getVersion(), 230
getWorldURL(), 230
initialize(), 206, 211
insertValue(), 215
interface
  Runnable, 243, 246
loadURL(), 229
method
  currentThread(), 246

join(), 246
main(), 241
notify(), 256, 259–261
run(), 241–243, 250
sleep(), 246
start(), 242
stop(), 246
Thread.getPriority(), 254
Thread.setPriority(), 252, 253
wait(), 256, 258–261
modifier
  synchronized, 256
monitors, 257, 258
multi-threading, 239
processEvent(), 206, 215, 216
processEvents(), 207
read-only classes, 213
replaceWorld(), 229
set1Value(), 215
setDescription(), 229
setValue(), 214
shutdown(), 206
String, 216
vrml.* hierarchy, 205
vrml.Browser, 226, 230
vrml.Event, 207, 215, 216
vrml.field.*, 213
vrml.field.ConstSFFloat, 213
vrml.field.SFFloat, 210, 213
vrml.node.Script, 206, 208
Java datatypes, 213
Java Scripting API, 205
Java Scripting Interface, 228
JavaScript, 197
JavaScript execution tree, 200
join() method, 246

Kirkwall, 340

landscape modelling, 82
level of detail, 55
lighting, 107, 109, 117–119, 123
  ambient intensity, 109
  highlights, 109
  sunrise, 118
  sunset, 118
link death, 295
links between worlds, *see* hyperlinks
Liquid Reality, 65, 230
loadURL(), 229
LOD, 55, 77
loose connections, 320
Lovecraft, H.P., 123

Maes Howe, 232, 233, 341
main() method, 241
MAX_PRIORITY, 252, 253
MBone, 286
megalith, 118
megaphone, 134, 136
mesh deformation, 175
meshes, 16, 37
messaging, 293
MFColor, 157
MFFloat, 157
MFInt32, 157
MFNode, 157
MFRotation, 157
MFString, 158
MFVec2f, 158
MFVec3f, 158, 172
Microsoft Windows, 247
MIDI, 146
MIN_PRIORITY, 252, 253
mobile lighting, 180
monitors, 257, 258
morphing, 173

movies, 115, 116
   MPEG-1, 116
MS-DOS, 247
multicasting, 285
multiple processors, 247
multi-threading, 239, 295, 298
multi-user, 169
mustEvaluate, 201

NavigationInfo, 230
neolithic pot, 91
nested transformations, 45
net death, 295
Network Access Layer, 270
networks
   limitations, 144
Neutral File Format, 41
NFF, 41
nightfall, 127
nightfall effect, 185
NORMAL_PRIORITY, 252, 253
NormalInterpolator, 173, 177
notify() method, 256, 258–261

Object class, 258
Object Oriented Geometry Language,
   41
OOGL, 41
opacity, 117, 154
Open Inventor, 41
optimistic concurrency control, 314
optimization of primitives, 69
orientation_changed event, 168
OrientationInterpolator, 150, 173,
   179, 180, 183
Orkney, 231, 340, 342
OSI Network Reference Model, 269

panoramic lens, 123
peering, 266

per vertex colouring, 108, 110, 111
perceived realism, 71
performance boosts, 78
Persistence of Vision, 41
Picts, 232
PlaneSensor, 159, 160, 166, 167
plug-in modules, 294
Poe, Edgar Allen, 123
point, 10
point cloud, 16, 97
point-to-point, 266
PointLight, 180
PointSet, 97
polygons, 17
   definition of, 17
   representation of, 17
   vertex ordering in, 17
position_changed event, 168
PositionInterpolator, 173, 183
POSIX threads, 254
potter's wheel, 45
POV, 41
priority, thread, 252
processEvent(), 206, 215, 216
processEvents(), 207
PROTO, 98, 201
prototypes, 98
ProximitySensor, 159, 167, 169,
   170
pruning, 323
pseudousers, 294, 316, 340

querying the browser, 230

Rabelais, François, 59
RAM usage, 80
reacting to stimuli, 150
read-only classes, 213
realism, 149

reference point, 11
removeChildren event, 229
rendering, 43
reparenting objects, 52
replaceWorld(), 229
Ring of Brodgar, *see* Brodgar, Ring of
rippling effects, 202
root node, 43
rotary quern, 69
rotation, 44, 156, 157, 164, 173, 179
ROUTE, 150, 160, 173, 179
routing tables, 284
run() method, 241–243, 250
Runnable interface, 241, 243, 246

ScalarInterpolator, 173, 185
scale, 44
scatter graphs, 97
scene description languages, 41
  Neutral File Format, 41
  NFF, 41
  Object Oriented Geometry Language, 41
  OOGL, 41
  Open Inventor, 41
  Persistence of Vision, 41
  POV, 41
  Virtual Reality Modelling Language, 42
  VRML, 42
scene graph, 42
scene graph optimization, 51
scene management, 51
scene structure, 42
scheduling
  threads, 246, 247
scheduling threads, 252, 256

Script, 197, 198, 201
  accessing field information, 213
  directOutput, 198, 201
  fields and events, 209
  inlined Java bytecode, 198
  Java, 198
  JavaScript, 199
  mustEvaluate, 198, 201
  url, 198
  VRMLScript, 200
scripting problems, 205
Secure Sockets Layer, 309
security, 295
security master, 310
sense in Virtual Reality, *see* VRML, sound
sensors, 159
server
  distributed, 339–342, 346
server protocol, 293
Servers, 291
servers, 235
set1Value(), 215
set_fraction event, 172
setDescription(), 229
setPriority() method, 252, 253
setValue(), 214
SFBool, 153
SFColor, 153, 157, 172
SFFloat, 153, 157, 173, 185
SFImage, 154, 155
SFInt32, 153, 157
SFNode, 153, 157
SFRotation, 156, 157, 168
SFString, 156, 158
SFTime, 156, 169, 171, 194
SFVec2f, 156, 158
SFVec3f, 156, 158
Shape, 57, 59

`appearance`, 59
`geometry`, 59
shear, 44
shininess, 109
`shutdown()`, 206
Skara Brae, 55, 88, 99, 127, 130,
    138, 139, 145, 147, 149, 170,
    186, 232, 233, 294, 309, 316,
    317, 322, 340, 341
`sleep()` method, 246
smooth motion, 173, 183
smooth shading, 16, 37
solidity, 186
sound
    active sounds, 147
    audio complexity, 146
    audio formats, 146
    circular, *see* sound, undirected
    compression, 146
    corridor effect, 139
    directed, 131, 135, 136, 145,
        147
    elliptical, *see* sound, directed
    hidden-surface removal, 137
    incidental, 146
    limited computing power, 145
    limited network bandwidth, 146
    MIDI, 146
    propagation, 138, 139, 141, 143
    realism, 136, 137, 139, 143, 144
    shape, 143
    synchronization, 139
    three-dimensional, 129
    transmission through solids, 137
    undirected, 131, 133–135, 138,
        145, 147
    volume, 137
    VRML, 129
    wave format, 146

    wire-frame, 136
sound in VRML, *see* VRML, sound
sounds
    active sounds, 145
spatial sensor, 167
`Sphere`, 68
    `radius`, 68
`SphereSensor`, 159, 164
splitting a world, *see* world, split-
    ting
`SpotLight`, 173
SSL, 309
Starbuck's pebbles, 17
`start()` method, 242
Stenness, Stones of, 232, 233, 340–
    342
stone-carving, *see* carving, stone
stone circles, 340, 341
Stones of Stenness, *see* Stenness,
    Stones of
`stop()` method, 246
strong connections, 320
subnetting, 280
surfaces of revolution, 94
synchronization, 240, 316
`synchronized` modifier, 256
synchronizing threads, 254, 257, 258

tapering, 86
TCP, 275
TCP/IP, 265, 268–271, 275, 276
Teale, Edwin Way, 339
teleporter, 122
temporal sensor, 159
tent building, 18
terrain modelling, 82
tessellation, 70
`Text`, 97
texture, 108

texture mapping, 16, 36–39, 49, 112, 115, 116, 203
Thread class, 241–243, 246, 250
thread death, 246
thread identifier, 246
thread scheduling, 246, 247
threads, 239
    POSIX, 254
    scheduling, 252, 256
    synchronization, 254
    synchronizing, 257, 258
time datatype, 156
time event, 172
TimeSensor, 150, 159, 170, 175, 183, 204, 229
timestamp, 160, 207
timestamping, 316
touch sensors, 159
TouchSensor, 159–161
TouchSensor events, 160
touchTime event, 160, 162
tours, 122
tracking, 168, 169
tradeoff between download time/frame rate, 69
Transform, 43, 44, 51, 68, 179, 183, 187
translation, 44, 166, 183
transparency, 110, 117, 154, 155
Transport Layer, 274
triangulation, 18
trilithon, 99
tuning the framework, 42
twist, 44
twisting, 86, 93

UDP, 274
undirected sound, *see* sound, undirected

universal character set, 156
UNIX, 247
UTF-8, 156

value_changed event, 172, 179, 183
vector
    three-dimensional, 156
    two-dimensional, 156
vertex, 10, 16, 30
vertex ordering in polygons, *see* polygons, vertex ordering in
vertex sharing, 78
video, 115, 116
    MPEG-1, 116
viewpoint, 47, 122
viewpoint jumping, 48
Viking, 340
virtual reality
    aims, 129
VisibilitySensor, 159, 169
VRML
    ambientIntensity, 109
    Anchor, 45, 47, 49, 187
    Appearance, 59, 108
    AudioClip, 132
    Background, 107, 127
        skyColor, 127
    Billboard, 49, 187
        axisOfRotation, 50
    Box, 44, 54, 60, 108, 150
    Collision, 50, 149, 187, 188, 193, 194
    ColorInterpolator, 172, 174
    Cone, 62, 108
        bottomRadius, 62
        height, 62
    CoordinateInterpolator, 172, 175, 177
    Cylinder, 54, 64

height, 64
radius, 64
side, 64
CylinderSensor, 159, 162–164, 166, 170
diffuseColor, 109
DirectedSound, 135
DirectionalLight, 118, 119
earlier drafts, 135
ElevationGrid, 81, 108, 111, 112, 201
emissiveColor, 109
EXTERNPROTO, 101
Extrusion, 83
  beginCap, 97
  crossSection, 83
  endCap, 97
  orientation, 93
  scale, 86
  spine, 84
Fog, 107, 123, 125, 127, 173, 185
  fogColor, 127
  fogType, 127
  visibilityLimit, 127
  visibilityRange, 127
FontStyle, 97
geometry, 59
getEventOut(), 211
Group, 44, 51, 187
ImageTexture, 108, 112, 115
  repeatS, 114, 115
  repeatT, 114, 115
IndexedFaceSet, 54, 70, 72, 77, 108, 110, 112, 114, 175, 177
  ccw, 74
  creaseAngle, 75
  solid, 74

IndexedLineSet, 54, 72, 77
  ccw, 77
  convex, 77
  creaseAngle, 77
Inline, 54, 55, 58
Interpolator, 149
IS, 203
LOD, 55, 77
Material, 108, 109
  shininess, 109, 110
  specularColor, 109, 110
  TextureTransform, 115
  transparency, 110
MFColor, 157
MFFloat, 157
MFInt32, 157
MFNode, 157
MFRotation, 157
MFString, 158
MFVec2f, 158
MFVec3f, 158, 172
MovieTexture, 108, 115, 116
  loop, 115
  speed, 115
NavigationInfo, 107, 127, 230
NormalInterpolator, 173, 177
OrientationInterpolator, 150, 173, 179, 180, 183
PixelTexture, 108, 116
PlaneSensor, 159, 160, 166, 167
PointLight, 118, 119, 180
PointSet, 97
PointSound, 131
PointSound implementation, 132
PositionInterpolator, 173, 183
PROTO, 98, 201

ProximitySensor, 159, 167, 168, 169

root node, 43

ROUTE, 150, 151, 160, 174, 194

ScalarInterpolator, 173, 185

Script, 112, 197, 198, 201
  directOutput, 198, 201
  fields and events, 209
  inlined Java bytecode, 198
  Java, 198
  JavaScript, 199
  mustEvaluate, 198, 201
  url, 198
  VRMLScript, 200

Sensor, 149

SFBool, 153

SFColor, 153, 157, 172

SFFloat, 153, 157, 173, 185

SFImage, 116, 117, 154, 155

SFInt32, 153, 157

SFNode, 153, 157

SFRotation, 156, 157, 168

SFString, 156, 158

SFTime, 156, 169, 171, 194

SFVec2f, 156, 158

SFVec3f, 156, 158

Shape, 57, 59
  appearance, 59
  geometry, 59

Sound, 129, 131, 135
  intensity, 134
  limitations, 136
  location, 134
  maxBack, 135, 139, 143, 145
  maxFront, 135, 139, 145
  maxRange, 134, 139, 145
  minBack, 135, 139
  minFront, 135
  minRange, 134, 138, 139

volume, 137, 139

sound, 129, 131

Sphere, 68
  radius, 68

SphereSensor, 159, 164

SpotLight, 118, 119, 173
  beamWidth, 122
  cutOffAngle, 122
  direction, 122
  location, 122
  radius, 122

Text, 97

TextureTransform, 108

TimeSensor, 150, 159, 170, 175, 183, 204, 229

TouchSensor, 150, 159–161
  eventIn, 150
  eventOut, 150

Transform, 43, 44, 51, 68, 151, 179, 183, 187

Viewpoint, 107, 122, 123
  fieldOfView, 123
  jump, 122
  orientation, 122
  position, 122

VisibilitySensor, 159, 169

vrml.node.Script, 210

VRML 1.0, 149

VRML character set, 156

VRML datatypes, 152, 214

VRML graphics primitives, 60

vrml.Browser, 226, 230

vrml.Event, 207, 215, 216

vrml.field.*, 213

vrml.field.ConstSFFloat, 213

vrml.field.SFFloat, 210, 213

vrml.node.Script, 206, 208, 210

VRML1.0, 42

VRML2.0, 42

VRMLScript, 197

`wait()` method, 256, 258–261
wave effect, 83, 201
wave format sound, 146
wave generation, 202
wayward children, 52
Web in three dimensions, 9
wide-angle lens, 123
Windows, 247
Windows 95, 247
Windows NT, 247
wire-frame rendering, 77
world
    distributed, 339
    splitting, 339
    subdividing, 340
world definition, 322
World Wide Web, 319, 341
WWW, 341

`yield()` method, 250

Licensing Agreement

This book comes with a CD software package. By opening this package, you are agreed to be bound by the following: